Hospitality Insurance and Risk Management

HOSPITALITY INSURANCE AND RISK MANAGEMENT

Kartik Lamba

CENTRUM PRESS
NEW DELHI-110002 (INDIA)

CENTRUM PRESS

H.O.: 4360/4, Ansari Road, Daryaganj,
New Delhi-110002 (India)
Tel: 23278000, 23261597, 23255577, 23286875

B.O.: No. 1015, Ist Main Road, BSK IIIrd Stage,
IIIrd Phase, IIIrd Block, Bengaluru-560085 (INDIA)
Tel: 080-41723429

Email: centrumpress@gmail.com
Visit us at: www.centrumpress.com

Hospitality Insurance and Risk Management

First Edition, 2013

ISBN 978-93-81460-11-5

PRINTED IN INDIA

Printed at Balaji Offset, Delhi.

Contents

	Preface	*(vii)*
1.	Risk Management Strategies for the Hospitality Industry	1
2.	Operational Risk Management	67
3.	Enterprise Risk Management	127
4.	Hotel Lifecycle and Risk Components	162
5.	Steps of Crisis Communications	206
	Bibliography	245
	Index	247

Preface

Ongoing changes to legislation and from authorities relating to licensed premise operations means that hotel owners and operators are required to take a detailed approach to protecting their staff, their business and themselves. A major part of this process is a tailored insurance program and a risk management strategy developed with broker. Insurance hassles keeping you up at night? Now that's one less thing for you to worry about because we've done the hard work on finding the right insurance cover for you. Our insurance brings together the policies most commonly sought by motels to offer you a comprehensive solution that's easy to understand.

Companies have developed a range of insurance solutions specific to the needs of your industry while providing you with the flexibility to tailor coverage if you have specific needs. To provide a quote we only need your postcode, turnover, and replacement value of your assets—it's that simple. Bed and breakfast insurance provides a comprehensive policy that allows bed and breakfast business owners to concentrate on what they do best - providing their guests with a memorable stay. Cover can be arranged for home and business contents, business activities, theft and malicious damage by guests, and theft of guest's cash and property resulting from forcible entry.

Hospitality businesses are exposed to ever changing legal, financial, strategic, and hazard risks. All risks, regardless of the type, must be effectively managed to protect both the assets of the business and the health and safety of their guests and their employees. Risk management ensures that an organization identifies and understands the risks to which it is exposed. Risk management also guarantees that the organization creates and implements an effective plan to prevent losses or reduce the impact if a loss occurs. A risk management plan includes strategies and techniques for recognizing and confronting these threats. Risk management provides a clear and structured approach to identifying risks. Having a clear understanding of all risks allows an organization to measure and prioritize them and take the appropriate actions to reduce losses. Insurance is a valuable risk-financing tool. Few organizations have the reserves or funds necessary to take on the risk themselves and pay the total costs following a loss. Purchasing insurance, however, is not risk management. A thorough and thoughtful risk management plan is the commitment to prevent harm. Risk management also addresses many risks that are not insurable, including brand integrity, potential loss of tax-exempt status for volunteer groups, public goodwill and continuing donor support.

This book places this subject in its most modern context as the foundation of this subject It is an authoritative resource of the subject that will benefit researchers, students, and teachers alike.

—*Author*

1

Risk Management Strategies for the Hospitality Industry

Does your organization integrate the management of risk and opportunity? Have you evaluated non-traditional risk exposures? These are critically important questions as today's increasingly complex business environment exposes hospitality companies to numerous risks.

We have witnessed many new types of risks being faced by hospitality companies and other related businesses. During the winter and spring months, both commercial and residential energy consumers throughout the nation have been exposed to soaring energy costs. For businesses and communities in California, this cost increase is further complicated by mandatory power blackouts ordered by government officials. For hotel companies, these energy issues affect every point of guest service from check-in at the front desk to ascent in an elevator, from the utilization of meeting space to food and beverage operations and safety. Hotel owners and managers should continuously reevaluate their energy risk management strategies including alternative sources, disaster recovery plans, financing, and hedging strategies.

During the last several years, hospitality companies—like many other industries—have increased the utilization of outsourcing arrangements for items such as procurement services, network and other data host sites, and food and beverage. Hotel owners and managers need to measure and monitor the risk to their organizations should these business partners not be in a position to honour their contractual obligations. A well-publicized example of a recent business failure of a service organization within the hospitality industry is h-Supply, a provider of e-procurement services. Another case occurred with Eziaz, which provided broadband telecommunication services. Eziaz, formerly known as SiteLine, Inc., went out of business in April, leaving some customers with service interruptions.

Clearly, leaders in the hospitality industry face the challenges mentioned above as well as a variety of new challenges in their drive to enhance value. Globalization, e-business, system privacy and security concerns (especially in light of increased Internet bookings), new organizational partnerships, and the increasing speed of business activity are rapidly changing and expanding the risks hospitality organizations face.

One significant result is that risk management should now extend well beyond traditional financial and insurable hazards to encompass a wide variety of strategic, operational, reputation, regulatory, and information risks.

For example, developing a privacy strategy should be at the top of every chief executive's risk agenda. The four major benefits are:

- It is one way for a company to separate itself from the competition;
- A privacy strategy can mitigate risk, be it brand, reputation, customer trust, litigation, or compliance;
- It will help ensure that the privacy processes and practices are cost-effective; and
- A privacy strategy is desirable, if for no other reason than to protect a company's own intellectual capital and customer lists.

Most important, a successful, well-executed strategy can bring about increased customer comfort and, ultimately, higher revenue.

It is our experience that successful organizations take calculated risks to achieve their objectives. They weigh opportunities against threats and act decisively. In other words, risk management can become a strategic competitive advantage to help hospitality organizations shift their focus from crisis response and compliance to evaluating risks in business strategies proactively.

Some critical success factors that should be included in a risk management program include:

- The need to create a risk-aware culture throughout the organization;
- Establish risk management objectives that are measurable and establish accountability;
- Establish an infrastructure for risk management;
- Empower business areas/departments to be responsible for managing risk in accordance with the organization's risk management approach—reward risk optimization initiatives;
- Communicate commitment to risk optimization by the board and its committees;
- Communicate and train management and staff in risk identification and avoidance techniques; and
- Continually identify and fill gaps in the risk management process.

Hotel guests demand high-quality goods and services at competitive prices, while investors expect outstanding performance and growth from their stocks. This puts heavy pressure on hotel owners, boards, and management, who can no longer rely on old, established strategies and practices.

They need to do a better job of taking and managing risks both at the property level and at the enterprise level. At KPMG, we believe that risk management is so important that we have invested in a structured technology-enabled approach to risk optimization.

It is our belief that risks can only be managed and optimized if they are identified. Today's business environment demands it.

Hope for Hospitality

In general, the hospitality business is experiencing an upswing—modest as it may be. "Occupancy percentage, room rates and payroll exposures have stabilized and, in most cases, there is limited but steady growth," says Joseph Dolce, CPCU, executive vice president of National Accounts for Venture Insurance Programs. Venture's hospitality focus is largely on golf destination resorts and hospitality management companies with multiple-location hotels, resorts and restaurants.

Dusty Rowland, president and CEO of Mainstay Insurance Group, which recently launched a new hotel and resort insurance program, is seeing similar growth. "The industry is slowly improving in most segments," he says, "with upscale and luxury showing the strongest growth."

Improvements taking place in the hospitality market are allowing hotels to pursue new initiatives to drive business, Rowland adds. "Travelers are seeking out new experiences and are more aware of hotels' environmental impacts," he notes. Some hotel owners have achieved LEED and Energy Star status to reduce their environmental impact while improving their image and attracting new guests, he adds. "In addition, the non-profit Association of Green Property Owners and Managers has identified a connection between quality of risk and going green," Rowland notes. "The organization offers an entry-level green building platform where owners can reduce insurance costs, along with utility costs, and boost guest satisfaction."

Restaurants are also seeing a rebound. "Most of our clients are reporting higher revenues as policies renew," explains Heidi Strommen, president of ProHost USA. "This follows a 24-month period of steady exposure decrease. That's good for our customers and for us."

In the midst of the turnaround, Michael Maher, marketing vice president at RCA Insurance, draws a correlation between the business—restaurants in particular—and the hospitality insurance arena. "In the restaurant business, the mantra has been 'Location, Location, Location,'" he explains. "During this endless soft market, in our restaurant and tavern segment, the insurance business can be best described as 'Competition, Competition, Competition.'"

Protecting Businesses

In the midst of such competition, agents and brokers can help clients and prospects adequately cover their risks—at generally good prices. "In the restaurant/tavern segment, many insureds fail to take advantage of additional coverages, such as umbrellas, property enhancement endorsements and mechanical breakdown,"

Maher says. "Also, they often carry insufficient liquor liability limits and they don't really understand business income coverage."

For instance, he adds, "They are surprised when business interruption claim recoveries are less than anticipated, because loss is 'net' and not the gross income they thought they'd recover."

Strommen says cyber liability is another area of under-protection. "A lot of restaurants—and probably too many agents—think that if you're not actually selling a product on the Internet, you don't really have a cyber liability exposure," she says. "That's not true."

The issue hit home in her own community. "Our local paper ran an article about cyber crime," she says, "and an example they used was a restaurant just outside the Twin Cities where a hacker infiltrated the restaurant's customer database and sold credit and debit card information. The owner had to notify those who were affected—to the tune of $20,000."

This coverage is normally excluded under standard GL forms, she notes. "Unless somebody actively addresses it, the restaurant won't be covered. Fortunately, there is an education process going on both with agents and with restaurants as to the actual exposures."

Another area where restaurants have skimped on coverage is umbrellas. "They're opting out or reducing limits," Strommen explains. "They've looked at their bottom line and, where they felt coverage was expendable, they cut it."

In the resorts and hospitality management arena, business income and extra expense are especially important, notes Dolce. "Any business interruption can have a long-term impact on bookings for weddings, banquets, tournaments, conferences and trade shows," he explains. "While property can be repaired/replaced relatively quickly, loss of income due to cancellations can extend for years. This must be factored into BI/EE limits."

Dolce cites as an example a private country club loss. "It took a year and half of extensive renovation and reconstruction before the facility was completed," he recalls. "But the business income extended well beyond the completion date, due to the lack of advance bookings. The unlimited extended period of indemnity offered to this club was crucial in letting it retain potential lost income."

For restaurants, Strommen says agents and brokers should address industry-specific coverages. "For instance, make sure they have coverage for contamination and spoilage," she says. "If you buy a generic package policy, you may not have those. Especially when changing from one carrier to another, make sure you compare policies and endorsements. They're not all created equal." And, she adds, document when clients turn down recommended coverages or go against suggested limits.

Rowland, who has been insuring hotels, resorts and casinos since the late 1990s, has seen more than his fair share of corner cutting. Areas that concern him include those listed in the box located on page 102.

Delivering Value

Agents and brokers should build partnerships with experienced providers and rely on their expertise. "A good provider will help educate their good partners and teach them the important coverages needed in each segment," says Rowland.

Maher encourages agents and brokers in his marketplace to learn all they can about the business. "This is a specialized segment," he says, "and brokers need to provide expert service to their client."

Learning can involve taking part in local, regional and national hospitality trade shows or conferences, Dolce points out. "Ask a hospitality client for a list of conferences and trade shows that hospitality senior managers, CFOs or controllers attend," he says. "You may not know all of the insurance issues facing the industry, but you will get a much better understanding of the issues facing your client."

Participation in loss control surveys and claim review meetings can also drive learning. "Use information learned to become an expert," Dolce notes. "Walking through a hotel, resort or restaurant with a qualified safety engineer or sitting through a claim review meeting on hospitality-specific claims are fast, efficient and worthwhile training tools."

Strommen encourages agents to click their way to knowledge. "I can't emphasize enough how many resources are on the Internet," she says. "And I'm surprised at how little they are used. In addition to restaurant industry Web sites, a lot of carrier Web sites have good information, whether or not you use that carrier."

In working with clients, Rowland suggests using a market-specific BI worksheet and keeping a reference checklist of important coverages. Maher agrees. "Offer and explain available additional coverages," he says, "and make certain clients insure to value on their property."

Add value by focusing on risk management and loss control. "Encourage clients to self-inspect their businesses every day for obvious hazards, both inside and out," Maher says. "Teach employees to watch for and immediately report hazards."

Strommen adds, "Make sure clients treat loss control representatives as partners in their program. It should not be an antagonistic relationship. The key is to really participate in the inspection process, and not put it off to a low-level manager."

Dolce stresses accountability. "Require on-site property management to be fiscally responsible and accountable for its loss experience," he says. "Base it on factors on-site management can control and measure—not just frequency and severity of losses."

He also encourages use of early/modified return-to-work programs for injured employees. "This may seem counterintuitive," he explains, "but the positive impact can be both short-and long-term. The overall loss experience is affected and, more important, the positive message sent to other employees is invaluable."

Maher's closing advice is simple: "The restaurant segment has many markets available to agents and brokers when the market is soft, but if and when there is a firming, many of the players that drifted into this segment will leave. An agent or broker focused on this segment would be wise to have markets that have demonstrated that they are also specialists, and will remain viable partners no matter how the markets ebb and flow." It's valid counsel for the entire hospitality insurance arena.

Areas of Concern for Hotels

Dusty Rowland, president and CEO of Mainstay Insurance Group, lists the following cautions for hotels and related risks.

- Proper insurance to value (ITV). The market sometimes offers blanket and agreed amount limits, which can help buyers overcome an instance where the insured has purchased too little building coverage.

- Employee dishonesty limits. Hotel owners think they'll never use this, and then learn their controller has been siphoning off small amounts of money for years, and the total loss is substantial.
- Guest discrimination coverage. Hotels might buy employment practices coverage and not the guest coverage. Some specialty programs provide the coverage in the GL form.
- Property in your care, custody or control. This is a "must have" for all hotels. Agents can offer this in the GL form or buy it as a legal liability (innkeepers) coverage on the crime policy.
- Health care professionals as insureds. Resorts with spas have this exposure and need this coverage.
- Valet parking services. Most full service upscale and luxury hotels and resorts offer valet parking services and need to be sure they are covered properly.
- Ordinance and law. This is key property coverage with the ever-changing building codes. Buyers either buy too little or go without to help control cost. That's not a good decision.
- Green building coverage. The three key coverages are:
  * Green certified coverage. For a loss to a green certified building, coverage available from AGPOM will apply to rebuilding and additional expenses driven by regaining green certification.
  * Green upgrade coverage. This coverage pays the extra expense when a non-certified building opts to go green after a loss. Added costs might result from use of Energy Star equipment; eco-friendly lighting, paint and carpet; or water-efficient plumbing fixtures.
  * Green commissioning expense. This coverage provides for a commissioning engineer to inspect a newly built or repaired system after a covered loss to confirm operation at peak performance and expected efficiency.

- Business income limits. Most insurance buyers don't take time to complete a BI worksheet—a valuable tool to determine proper exposure levels. The tool forces buyers and agents to address all aspects of a potential loss and its business impact.
- Abuse and molestation coverage. Depending on hotel amenities, this can be an important coverage that is overlooked. If there is an exposure, most underwriters will try to exclude it or increase the premium. Either way, agents and clients need to address the exposure.
- Pollution exclusions givebacks. Hotels and resorts should never buy a stripped-down GL form with an absolute pollution exclusion. Specialty programs will give back hostile fire and exposures to swimming pool pollution from the pool chemicals. Resorts with golf courses need coverage for pesticide and herbicide applications, since an absolute pollution exclusion might cause a gap in coverage.

Hospitality Insurance at a Glance

Thanks to the Soccer World Cup, the hospitality industry is booming. As the industry grows in South Africa, more hospitality-type business owners rely on their establishments as a primary or sole source of income or as a supplement to an inadequate retirement fund.

As the SMEs (smaller to medium-sized enterprises) account for more than half of South Africa's economic output, it is understandable that a variety of short-term insurance products are available to this sector. Typically, these insurance products are divided into two categories: standard commercial insurance and specialised insurance. The standard commercial policy is aimed at the majority of business's insurance requirements, whereas the specialised niche products address the specific needs of risks in any given sector. As is the case with specialised hospitality-type products specifically aimed at the BnB, Guesthouse, self-catering and Lodge-type risks, which, if required, also caters for the business being run from private homes to accommodate tourists and business individuals who do not want or need hotel accommodation.

Many owners still fail to understand the implication of incorrect or no insurance; this could possibly be one of the main reasons why the industry lags behind in global standard regarding insurance protection. Another contributing factor could be intermediaries lacking the necessary skills to underwrite these risks correctly and not providing clients with comprehensive insurance solutions.

Intermediaries still seem to place the majority of these risks on a standard commercial policy which offers limited cover. Even though most businesses will find a standard commercial insurance policy sufficient for their insurance requirements, a hospitality-type risk would, nine times out of 10, find that a commercial policy lacks certain criteria to meet their insurance requirements.

One of the most important requirements for a hospitality establishment owner is Liability cover, which provides peace of mind in the event of a claim or law suit being laid against the owner or business should something happen to a guest during his/her stay. Insurers generally limit liability and legal costs in a standard commercial policy, where a specialised product caters for larger amounts and wider cover.

Loss of revenue and theft usually also have limited cover with a number of clauses such as theft needs to be accompanied with "forcible and violent entry". A hospitality establishment owner cannot comply with some of these conditions as they have no control over guests' behaviour such as when they come and go and sometimes leave doors unlocked or even open.

Hospitality risks usually require bilking (where guests leave without paying) and accidental damage cover (caused by guests to the contents) normally excluded in a standard commercial policy.

Hospitality insurance products provide cover for a range of losses such as fire, flood, theft, liability and a variety of other events. As some of these risks are part of residential homes, some policies have extended cover to include these homes in the same fashion as traditional short-term household insurance. The insurance industry offers a variety of insurance solutions where a single policy caters for both the business and personal insurance needs of owners of these types of establishments.

Insurance intermediaries specialising in the hospitality sector usually work closely with key individuals from the industry, which also enables them to understand the main activity – selling of accommodation, food and beverages, as this is the key factor in providing insurance solutions and expertise to meet industry requirements. These intermediaries recognise and appreciate the exposure (Asset, Financial, People, Risk) these businesses are faced with and can offer customised cover to all sectors of the Hospitality insurance market.

It is therefore recommended that the Guesthouse, BnB, Lodge, self-catering and Restaurant owner find an intermediary, specialising in the Hospitality insurance sector, as he/she understands the industry and how it needs to be protected. Trustco has launched such a Guesthouse product, Guest-inn-Sure, to its intermediary base for the sale to Guesthouse owners and the like.

Role of Information Security Risk Management in the BFSI Sector

The introduction of One Time Passwords (OTP) for Interactive Voice Response (IVR) transactions is an added layer of security for people who lose their debit or credit cards as well as for those who are careless while performing transactions through the phone. This is the latest development by the RBI focusing on how to counter the process and security risks created by people with malicious intent.

The BFSI segment is facing a big challenge in terms of securing sensitive information, especially when dealing with customers. This is a result of the increasing number of products and services offered and the sector's high dependence on technology.

Banks and other financial institutions are providing facilities such as 'Anywhere Banking', encouraging the use of ATMs, Net Banking, mobile banking, Real Time Gross Settlement System (RTGS) and various payment methods including the Electronic Clearing Systems (ECS), National Electronic Funds Transfer (NEFT) System, online trading, online purchase of mutual funds and e-insurance etc. All of these facilities have transformed the way that banking is done and customers have a wide array of options to choose from.

However, in recent times, these services provided by financial institutions have also been accompanied by ever increasing security threats such as identity theft, phishing attacks, social engineering attacks and fraud that directly affect customers. These are more dangerous as against the technical threats such as Web site hijacking, server attacks, browser-based attacks, denial of service attacks etc.

Security frameworks are becoming vital for ensuring the safe transmission of information using technology. In earlier days, transactions were subject to checks such as the verification of signatures to ensure the genuineness and authenticity of an individual. In the current scenario, where technology is being used, these authenticity procedures are vulnerable and have become fragile over a period of time. For this reason, it has become important for financial institutions to put their Security Risk management framework in place in order to ensure that the customer's information is secure and that the opportunity for such threats and for fraudulent acts are minimized.

Earlier, organizations were focusing on their network, perimeter security and IT processes by installing firewalls, IDS, IPS, implementing DMZs, anti phishing systems, strengthening processes such as access control, log monitoring, entitlement reviews etc. Nowadays, however, financial institutions have become more aggressive and have started adopting a newer way of identifying threats.

The focus has shifted towards business processes and data flowing in and out of these processes. In this manner, they are able to track the end-to-end flow of information through a process and arrest the point at which sensitive information leaves the organization in an insecure manner or where there is any possibility of information leakage and an opportunity for misuse or fraud.

Many financial institutions have adopted a risk management process which includes the following areas that serve as the framework:

- Process mapping: Mapping of business processes and the end-to-end information flow and identification of the touch points where information leaves the organization.
- Information Asset Classification: Inventorying the information assets flowing through the process

- Information Security Risk Assessment: Process to identify threats, vulnerabilities and assessing their severity, probabilities of occurrence and impact
- Information Security Risk Treatment: A plan to mitigate risks arising out of Risk Assessment
- Controls Implementation: Acquiring and implementing the required tools and products. Assignment of responsibilities to staff with time lines and ensuring that they have the required knowledge, skill and understood their responsibilities.
- Control Effectiveness Monitoring: The use of various audit methodologies to gain assurance that the implemented controls are operating effectively by verifying evidence and documentation.

Risk Management has played a vital role in devising a strategy while dealing with customers and their sensitive information. Financial institutions have implemented controls such as the use of encryption for online transactions, One transaction per entry of PIN at ATMs, OTP for IVR transactions, the use of multiple security questions, the use of objects and quotes, password protected statements through e-mail and so on.

Some institutions have gone a step forward and have been focusing on the awareness of customers and vendors, who handle almost the same amount of their critical information.

Need for a Dedicated Risk Management Team

Though this framework is designed by many financial institutions it is difficult to sustain as this needs a lot of effort and time. A risk management team would play an important role in the continuous improvement of business processes and in creating a proactive method of identifying threats including a fraud prevention detection system and an effective management reporting system.

As a result of an effective risk management process, financial institutions are formulating appropriate incident response plans to detect, manage, contain and minimize such problems.

Lastly, it is imperative that financial institutions maintain an ongoing information security risk management program that effectively gathers data regarding new and emerging threats, analyzes the probability and impact associated with the known threats and vulnerabilities to its assets and prioritizes the risks and designs an effective risk mitigation plan.

Insurance

Insurance is a risk management technique primarily used to hedge against the risk of a contingent, uncertain loss that may be suffered by those individuals or entities who have an insurable interest in scarce resources, by transferring the possibility of this loss from one interested person, persons, or entity to another. The scarce resources referred to here fall into three divisions: human resources, financial resources, and capital, or tangible resources. In the context of insurance, scarce resources are also known as "exposures," because they are "exposed" to perils, those things, or forces, which cause destruction or reduction, in the usefulness, or value, of an exposed resource.

Human resources are thus exposed to perils such as illness or death; financial resources to legal judgements that may result from negligent acts, and capital resources to physical perils such as fire, theft, windstorm, and vandalism, to name but a few. A hazard is the cause of a peril. It is that thing or condition which increases the likelihood of a peril. Thus perils and hazards are identified by the exposure that they threaten. For example a slippery roadway could be viewed as a financial hazard, capital hazard, or human hazard by automobile owners, and rightly so, since this condition increases the likelihood of an automobile accident that might result in an unfavorable legal judgement, automobile damage, and bodily injury.

In the context of commercial trade, insurance is further defined as the equitable transfer of the risk of a loss, from one entity to another, in exchange for consideration, payment, in the form of a risk premium. The insurance premium develops at an actuarily-determined rate. This rate is a factor used to determine the amount of premium to charge for a certain limit, and type, of insurance on the scarce resource. The premium can further be viewed as a guaranteed, known, relatively small financial loss to the insured, paid to the insurer, in exchange for the insurer's promise to compensate (indemnify) the insured in the case of a loss to the insured resource(s). The insured receives a contract, called the insurance policy, which details the conditions and circumstances under which the insured will be indemnified.

Principles

Insurance involves pooling funds from *many* insured entities (known as exposures) to pay for the losses that some may incur. The insured entities are therefore protected from risk for a fee, with the fee being dependent upon the frequency and severity of the event occurring. In order to be insurable, the risk insured against must meet certain characteristics in order to be an insurable risk. Insurance is a commercial enterprise and a major part of the financial services industry, but individual entities can also self-insure through saving money for possible future losses.

Insurability

Risk which can be insured by private companies typically share seven common characteristics:

1. *Large number of similar exposure units:* Since insurance operates through pooling resources, the majority of insurance policies are provided for individual members of large classes, allowing insurers to benefit from the law of large numbers in which predicted losses are similar to the actual losses. Exceptions include Lloyd's of London, which is famous for insuring the life or health of actors, sports figures and other famous individuals. However, all exposures will have particular differences, which may lead to different premium rates.
2. *Definite loss:* The loss takes place at a known time, in a known place, and from a known cause. The classic example is death of an insured person on a life insurance policy. Fire, automobile accidents, and worker injuries may all easily meet this criterion. Other types of losses may only be definite in theory. Occupational disease, for instance, may involve prolonged exposure to injurious conditions where no specific time, place or cause is identifiable. Ideally, the time, place and cause of a loss should be clear enough that a reasonable person, with sufficient information, could objectively verify all three elements.

3. *Accidental loss:* The event that constitutes the trigger of a claim should be fortuitous, or at least outside the control of the beneficiary of the insurance. The loss should be pure, in the sense that it results from an event for which there is only the opportunity for cost. Events that contain speculative elements, such as ordinary business risks or even purchasing a lottery ticket, are generally not considered insurable.
4. *Large loss:* The size of the loss must be meaningful from the perspective of the insured. Insurance premiums need to cover both the expected cost of losses, plus the cost of issuing and administering the policy, adjusting losses, and supplying the capital needed to reasonably assure that the insurer will be able to pay claims. For small losses these latter costs may be several times the size of the expected cost of losses. There is hardly any point in paying such costs unless the protection offered has real value to a buyer.
5. *Affordable premium:* If the likelihood of an insured event is so high, or the cost of the event so large, that the resulting premium is large relative to the amount of protection offered, it is not likely that the insurance will be purchased, even if on offer. Further, as the accounting profession formally recognizes in financial accounting standards, the premium cannot be so large that there is not a reasonable chance of a significant loss to the insurer. If there is no such chance of loss, the transaction may have the form of insurance, but not the substance.
6. *Calculable loss:* There are two elements that must be at least estimable, if not formally calculable: the probability of loss, and the attendant cost. Probability of loss is generally an empirical exercise, while cost has more to do with the ability of a reasonable person in possession of a copy of the insurance policy and a proof of loss associated with a claim presented under that policy to make a reasonably definite and objective evaluation of the amount of the loss recoverable as a result of the claim.

7. *Limited risk of catastrophically large losses:* Insurable losses are ideally independent and non-catastrophic, meaning that the losses do not happen all at once and individual losses are not severe enough to bankrupt the insurer; insurers may prefer to limit their exposure to a loss from a single event to some small portion of their capital base. Capital constrains insurers' ability to sell earthquake insurance as well as wind insurance in hurricane zones. In the U.S., flood risk is insured by the federal government. In commercial fire insurance it is possible to find single properties whose total exposed value is well in excess of any individual insurer's capital constraint. Such properties are generally shared among several insurers, or are insured by a single insurer who syndicates the risk into the reinsurance market.

Legal

When a company insures an individual entity, there are basic legal requirements. Several commonly cited legal principles of insurance include:

1. Indemnity–the insurance company indemnifies, or compensates, the insured in the case of certain losses only up to the insured's interest.
2. Insurable interest–the insured typically must directly suffer from the loss. Insurable interest must exist whether property insurance or insurance on a person is involved. The concept requires that the insured have a "stake" in the loss or damage to the life or property insured. What that "stake" is will be determined by the kind of insurance involved and the nature of the property ownership or relationship between the persons.
3. Utmost good faith – the insured and the insurer are bound by a good faith bond of honesty and fairness. Material facts must be disclosed.
4. Contribution–insurers which have similar obligations to the insured contribute in the indemnification, according to some method.

5. Subrogation–the insurance company acquires legal rights to pursue recoveries on behalf of the insured; for example, the insurer may sue those liable for insured's loss.
6. Causa proxima, or proximate cause–the cause of loss (the peril) must be covered under the insuring agreement of the policy, and the dominant cause must not be excluded
7. Principle of loss minimization-In case of any loss or casualty, the asset owner must attempt to keep the loss to a minimum, as if the asset was not insured.

Indemnification

To "indemnify" means to make whole again, or to be reinstated to the position that one was in, to the extent possible, prior to the happening of a specified event or peril. Accordingly, life insurance is generally not considered to be indemnity insurance, but rather "contingent" insurance (i.e., a claim arises on the occurrence of a specified event). There are generally two types of insurance contracts that seek to indemnify an insured:

1. an "indemnity" policy, and
2. a "pay on behalf" or "on behalf of" policy.

The difference is significant on paper, but rarely material in practice.

An "indemnity" policy will never pay claims until the insured has paid out of pocket to some third party; for example, a visitor to your home slips on a floor that you left wet and sues you for $10,000 and wins. Under an "indemnity" policy the homeowner would have to come up with the $10,000 to pay for the visitor's fall and then would be "indemnified" by the insurance carrier for the out of pocket costs (the $10,000).

Under the same situation, a "pay on behalf" policy, the insurance carrier would pay the claim and the insured (the homeowner in the above example) would not be out of pocket for anything. Most modern liability insurance is written on the basis of "pay on behalf" language.

An entity seeking to transfer risk (an individual, corporation, or association of any type, etc.) becomes the 'insured' party once risk is assumed by an 'insurer', the insuring party, by means of a contract, called an insurance policy. Generally, an insurance contract includes, at a minimum, the following elements: identification of participating parties (the insurer, the insured, the beneficiaries), the premium, the period of coverage, the particular loss event covered, the amount of coverage (i.e., the amount to be paid to the insured or beneficiary in the event of a loss), and exclusions (events not covered). An insured is thus said to be "indemnified" against the loss covered in the policy.

When insured parties experience a loss for a specified peril, the coverage entitles the policyholder to make a claim against the insurer for the covered amount of loss as specified by the policy. The fee paid by the insured to the insurer for assuming the risk is called the premium. Insurance premiums from many insureds are used to fund accounts reserved for later payment of claims — in theory for a relatively few claimants — and for overhead costs. So long as an insurer maintains adequate funds set aside for anticipated losses (called reserves), the remaining margin is an insurer's profit.

Effects

Insurance can have various effects on society through the way that it changes who bears the cost of losses and damage. On one hand it can increase fraud, on the other it can help societies and individuals prepare for catastrophes and mitigate the effects of catastrophes on both households and societies.

Insurance can influence the probability of losses through moral hazard, insurance fraud, and preventive steps by the insurance company. Insurance scholars have typically used morale hazard to refer to the increased loss due to unintentional carelessness and moral hazard to refer to increased risk due to intentional carelessness or indifference. Insurers attempt to address carelessness through inspections, policy provisions requiring certain types of maintenance, and possible discounts for loss mitigation efforts.

While in theory insurers could encourage investment in loss reduction, some commentators have argued that in practice insurers had historically not aggressively pursued loss control measures-particularly to prevent disaster losses such as hurricanes-because of concerns over rate reductions and legal battles. However, since about 1996 insurers began to take a more active role in loss mitigation, such as through building codes.

Insurers' Business Model

Underwriting and Investing

The business model is to collect more in premium and investment income than is paid out in losses, and to also offer a competitive price which consumers will accept. Profit can be reduced to a simple equation: Profit = earned premium + investment income-incurred loss-underwriting expenses.

Insurers make money in two ways:

1. Through underwriting, the process by which insurers select the risks to insure and decide how much in premiums to charge for accepting those risks;
2. By investing the premiums they collect from insured parties.

The most complicated aspect of the insurance business is the actuarial science of ratemaking (price-setting) of policies, which uses statistics and probability to approximate the rate of future claims based on a given risk. After producing rates, the insurer will use discretion to reject or accept risks through the underwriting process.

At the most basic level, initial ratemaking involves looking at the frequency and severity of insured perils and the expected average payout resulting from these perils. Thereafter an insurance company will collect historical loss data, bring the loss data to present value, and comparing these prior losses to the premium collected in order to assess rate adequacy. Loss ratios and expense loads are also used. Rating for different risk characteristics involves at the most basic level comparing the losses with "loss relativities"- a policy with twice as money policies would therefore be charged twice as much. However, more complex multivariate analyses through generalized linear modelling are sometimes used when multiple characteristics are involved and a univariate analysis could produce confounded results. Other statistical methods may be used in assessing the probability of future losses.

Upon termination of a given policy, the amount of premium collected and the investment gains thereon, minus the amount paid out in claims, is the insurer's underwriting profit on that policy.

Underwriting performance is measured by something called the "combined ratio" which is the ratio of expenses/losses to premiums. A combined ratio of less than 100 percent indicates an underwriting profit, while anything over 100 indicates an underwriting loss. A company with a combined ratio over 100% may nevertheless remain profitable due to investment earnings.

Insurance companies earn investment profits on "float". Float, or available reserve, is the amount of money on hand at any given moment that an insurer has collected in insurance premiums but has not paid out in claims. Insurers start investing insurance premiums as soon as they are collected and continue to earn interest or other income on them until claims are paid out. The Association of British Insurers (gathering 400 insurance companies and 94% of UK insurance services) has almost 20% of the investments in the London Stock Exchange.

In the United States, the underwriting loss of property and casualty insurance companies was $142.3 billion in the five years ending 2003. But overall profit for the same period was $68.4 billion, as the result of float. Some insurance industry insiders, most notably Hank Greenberg, do not believe that it is forever possible to sustain a profit from float without an underwriting profit as well, but this opinion is not universally held.

Naturally, the float method is difficult to carry out in an economically depressed period. Bear markets do cause insurers to shift away from investments and to toughen up their underwriting standards, so a poor economy generally means high insurance premiums. This tendency to swing between profitable and unprofitable periods over time is commonly known as the underwriting, or insurance, cycle.

Claims

Claims and loss handling is the materialized utility of insurance; it is the actual "product" paid for. Claims may be filed by insureds directly with the insurer or through brokers or agents.

The insurer may require that the claim be filed on its own proprietary forms, or may accept claims on a standard industry form, such as those produced by ACORD.

Insurance company claims departments employ a large number of claims adjusters supported by a staff of records management and data entry clerks. Incoming claims are classified based on severity and are assigned to adjusters whose settlement authority varies with their knowledge and experience.

The adjuster undertakes an investigation of each claim, usually in close cooperation with the insured, determines if coverage is available under the terms of the insurance contract, and if so, the reasonable monetary value of the claim, and authorizes payment.

The policyholder may hire their own public adjuster to negotiate the settlement with the insurance company on their behalf. For policies that are complicated, where claims may be complex, the insured may take out a separate insurance policy add on, called loss recovery insurance, which covers the cost of a public adjuster in the case of a claim.

Adjusting liability insurance claims is particularly difficult because there is a third party involved, the plaintiff, who is under no contractual obligation to cooperate with the insurer and may in fact regard the insurer as a deep pocket.

The adjuster must obtain legal counsel for the insured (either inside "house" counsel or outside "panel" counsel), monitor litigation that may take years to complete, and appear in person or over the telephone with settlement authority at a mandatory settlement conference when requested by the judge.

If a claims adjuster suspects under-insurance, the condition of average may come into play to limit the insurance company's exposure.

In managing the claims handling function, insurers seek to balance the elements of customer satisfaction, administrative handling expenses, and claims overpayment leakages. As part of this balancing act, fraudulent insurance practices are a major business risk that must be managed and overcome. Disputes between insurers and insureds over the validity of claims or claims handling practices occasionally escalate into litigation.

Marketing

Insurers will often use insurance agents to initially market or underwrite their customers. Agents can be captive, meaning they write only for one company, or independent, meaning that they can issue policies from several companies. Commissions to agents represent a significant portion of an insurance cost and insurers such as State Farm that sell policies directly via mass marketing campaigns can offer lower prices. The existence and success of companies using insurance agents (with higher prices) is likely due to improved and personalized service.

History of Insurance

In some sense we can say that insurance appears simultaneously with the appearance of human society. We know of two types of economies in human societies: natural or non-monetary economies (using barter and trade with no centralized nor standardized set of financial instruments) and more modern monetary economies (with markets, currency, financial instruments and so on). The former is more primitive and the insurance in such economies entails agreements of mutual aid. If one family's house is destroyed the neighbours are committed to help rebuild. Granaries housed another primitive form of insurance to indemnify against famines. Often informal or formally intrinsic to local religious customs, this type of insurance has survived to the present day in some countries where modern money economy with its financial instruments is not widespread.

Turning to insurance in the modern sense (i.e., insurance in a modern money economy, in which insurance is part of the financial sphere), early methods of transferring or distributing risk were practised by Chinese and Babylonian traders as long ago as the 3rd and 2nd millennia BC, respectively. Chinese merchants travelling treacherous river rapids would redistribute their wares across many vessels to limit the loss due to any single vessel's capsizing. The Babylonians developed a system which was recorded in the famous Code of Hammurabi, c. 1750 BC, and practised by early Mediterranean sailing merchants. If a merchant received a loan to fund his shipment, he would pay the lender an additional sum in exchange for the lender's guarantee to cancel the loan should the shipment be stolen or lost at sea.

Achaemenian monarchs of Ancient Persia were the first to insure their people and made it official by registering the insuring process in governmental notary offices. The insurance tradition was performed each year in Norouz (beginning of the Iranian New Year); the heads of different ethnic groups as well as others willing to take part, presented gifts to the monarch. The most important gift was presented during a special ceremony. When a gift was worth more than 10,000 Derrik (Achaemenian gold coin) the issue was registered in a special office. This was advantageous to those who presented such special gifts. For others, the presents were fairly assessed by the confidants of the court. Then the assessment was registered in special offices.

The purpose of registering was that whenever the person who presented the gift registered by the court was in trouble, the monarch and the court would help him. Jahez, a historian and writer, writes in one of his books on ancient Iran: "[W]henever the owner of the present is in trouble or wants to construct a building, set up a feast, have his children married, etc. the one in charge of this in the court would check the registration. If the registered amount exceeded 10,000 Derrik, he or she would receive an amount of twice as much."

A thousand years later, the inhabitants of Rhodes invented the concept of the *general average*. Merchants whose goods were being shipped together would pay a proportionally divided premium which would be used to reimburse any merchant whose goods were deliberately jettisoned in order to lighten the ship and save it from total loss.

The Talmud deals with several aspects of insuring goods. Before insurance was established in the late 17th century, "friendly societies" existed in England, in which people donated amounts of money to a general sum that could be used for emergencies.

Separate insurance contracts (i.e., insurance policies not bundled with loans or other kinds of contracts) were invented in Genoa in the 14th century, as were insurance pools backed by pledges of landed estates. These new insurance contracts allowed insurance to be separated from investment, a separation of roles that first proved useful in marine insurance. Insurance became far more sophisticated in post-Renaissance Europe, and specialized varieties developed.

Some forms of insurance had developed in London by the early decades of the 17th century. For example, the will of the English colonist Robert Hayman mentions two "policies of insurance" taken out with the diocesan Chancellor of London, Arthur Duck. Of the value of £100 each, one relates to the safe arrival of Hayman's ship in Guyana and the other is in regard to "one hundred pounds assured by the said Doctor Arthur Ducke on my life".

Hayman's will was signed and sealed on 17 November 1628 but not proved until 1633. Toward the end of the seventeenth century, London's growing importance as a centre for trade increased demand for marine insurance. In the late 1680s, Edward Lloyd opened a coffee house that became a popular haunt of ship owners, merchants, and ships' captains, and thereby a reliable source of the latest shipping news. It became the meeting place for parties wishing to insure cargoes and ships, and those willing to underwrite such ventures. Today, Lloyd's of London remains the leading market (note that it is an insurance market rather than a company) for marine and other specialist types of insurance, but it operates rather differently than the more familiar kinds of insurance.

Insurance as we know it today can be traced to the Great Fire of London, which in 1666 devoured more than 13,000 houses. The devastating effects of the fire converted the development of insurance "from a matter of convenience into one of urgency, a change of opinion reflected in Sir Christopher Wren's inclusion of a site for 'the Insurance Office' in his new plan for London in 1667." A number of attempted fire insurance schemes came to nothing, but in 1681 Nicholas Barbon, and eleven associates, established England's first fire insurance company, the 'Insurance Office for Houses', at the back of the Royal Exchange. Initially, 5,000 homes were insured by Barbon's Insurance Office.

The first insurance company in the United States underwrote fire insurance and was formed in Charles Town (modern-day Charleston), South Carolina, in 1732. Benjamin Franklin helped to popularize and make standard the practice of insurance, particularly against fire in the form of perpetual insurance. In 1752, he founded the Philadelphia Contributionship for the

Insurance of Houses from Loss by Fire. Franklin's company was the first to make contributions toward fire prevention. Not only did his company warn against certain fire hazards, it refused to insure certain buildings where the risk of fire was too great, such as all wooden houses.

In the United States, regulation of the insurance industry is highly Balkanized, with primary responsibility assumed by individual state insurance departments. Whereas insurance markets have become centralized nationally and internationally, state insurance commissioners operate individually, though at times in concert through a national insurance commissioners' organization.

In recent years, some have called for a dual state and federal regulatory system (commonly referred to as the (OFC)) for insurance similar to that which oversees state banks and national banks.

Types of Insurance

Any risk that can be quantified can potentially be insured. Specific kinds of risk that may give rise to claims are known as perils. An insurance policy will set out in detail which perils are covered by the policy and which are not. Below are non-exhaustive lists of the many different types of insurance that exist. A single policy may cover risks in one or more of the categories set out below.

For example, vehicle insurance would typically cover both the property risk (theft or damage to the vehicle) and the liability risk (legal claims arising from an accident). A home insurance policy in the U.S. typically includes coverage for damage to the home and the owner's belongings, certain legal claims against the owner, and even a small amount of coverage for medical expenses of guests who are injured on the owner's property.

Business insurance can take a number of different forms, such as the various kinds of professional liability insurance, also called (PI), which are discussed below under that name; and the (BOP), which packages into one policy many of the kinds of coverage that a business owner needs, in a way analogous to how homeowners' insurance packages the coverages that a homeowner needs.

Auto Insurance

Auto insurance protects the policyholder against financial loss in the event of an incident involving a vehicle they own, such as in a traffic collision.

Coverage typically includes:

1. Property coverage, for damage to or theft of the car;
2. Liability coverage, for the legal responsibility to others for bodily injury or property damage;
3. Medical coverage, for the cost of treating injuries, rehabilitation and sometimes lost wages and funeral expenses.

Most countries, such as the United Kingdom, require drivers to buy some, but not all, of these coverages. When a car is used as collateral for a loan the lender usually requires specific coverage.

Home Insurance

Home insurance provides coverage for damage or destruction of the policyholder's home. In some geographical areas, the policy may exclude certain types of risks, such as flood or earthquake, that require additional coverage. Maintenance-related issues are typically the homeowner's responsibility. The policy may include inventory, or this can be bought as a separate policy, especially for people who rent housing. In some countries, insurers offer a package which may include liability and legal responsibility for injuries and property damage caused by members of the household, including pets.

Health Insurance

Health insurance policies cover the cost of medical treatments. Dental insurance, like medical insurance, protects policyholders for dental costs. In the U.S. and Canada, dental insurance is often part of an employer's benefits package, along with health insurance.

Accident, Sickness and Unemployment Insurance

- Disability insurance policies provide financial support in the event of the policyholder becoming unable to work because of disabling illness or injury. It provides monthly support to help pay such obligations as mortgage loans and credit cards. Short-term and long-term disability policies are available to individuals, but considering the expense, long-term policies are generally obtained only by those with at least six-figure incomes, such as doctors, lawyers, etc. Short-term disability insurance covers a person for a period typically up to six months, paying a stipend each month to cover medical bills and other necessities.

- Long-term disability insurance covers an individual's expenses for the long term, up until such time as they are considered permanently disabled and thereafter. Insurance companies will often try to encourage the person back into employment in preference to and before declaring them unable to work at all and therefore totally disabled.
- Disability overhead insurance allows business owners to cover the overhead expenses of their business while they are unable to work.
- Total permanent disability insurance provides benefits when a person is permanently disabled and can no longer work in their profession, often taken as an adjunct to life insurance.
- Workers' compensation insurance replaces all or part of a worker's wages lost and accompanying medical expenses incurred because of a job-related injury.

Casualty

Casualty insurance insures against accidents, not necessarily tied to any specific property. It is a broad spectrum of insurarce that a number of other types of insurance could be classified, such as auto, workers compensation, and some liability insurances.

- Crime insurance is a form of casualty insurance that covers the policyholder against losses arising from the criminal acts of third parties. For example, a company can obtain crime insurance to cover losses arising from theft or embezzlement.
- Political risk insurance is a form of casualty insurance that can be taken out by businesses with operations in countries

in which there is a risk that revolution or other political conditions could result in a loss.

Life

Life insurance provides a monetary benefit to a descendant's family or other designated beneficiary, and may specifically provide for income to an insured person's family, burial, funeral and other final expenses. Life insurance policies often allow the option of having the proceeds paid to the beneficiary either in a lump sum cash payment or an annuity.

Annuities provide a stream of payments and are generally classified as insurance because they are issued by insurance companies, are regulated as insurance, and require the same kinds of actuarial and investment management expertise that life insurance requires.

Annuities and pensions that pay a benefit for life are sometimes regarded as insurance against the possibility that a retiree will outlive his or her financial resources. In that sense, they are the complement of life insurance and, from an underwriting perspective, are the mirror image of life insurance.

Certain life insurance contracts accumulate cash values, which may be taken by the insured if the policy is surrendered or which may be borrowed against. Some policies, such as annuities and endowment policies, are financial instruments to accumulate or liquidate wealth when it is needed.

In many countries, such as the U.S. and the UK, the tax law provides that the interest on this cash value is not taxable under certain circumstances. This leads to widespread use of life insurance as a tax-efficient method of saving as well as protection in the event of early death.

In the U.S., the tax on interest income on life insurance policies and annuities is generally deferred. However, in some cases the benefit derived from tax deferral may be offset by a low return. This depends upon the insuring company, the type of policy and other variables (mortality, market return, etc.). Moreover, other income tax saving vehicles (e.g., IRAs, 401(k) plans, Roth IRAs) may be better alternatives for value accumulation.

Burial Insurance

Burial insurance is a very old type of life insurance which is paid out upon death to cover final expenses, such as the cost of a funeral. The Greeks and Romans introduced burial insurance circa 600 AD when they organized guilds called "benevolent societies" which cared for the surviving families and paid funeral expenses of members upon death. Guilds in the Middle Ages served a similar purpose, as did friendly societies during Victorian times.

Property

Property insurance provides protection against risks to property, such as fire, theft or weather damage. This may include specialized forms of insurance such as fire insurance, flood insurance, earthquake insurance, home insurance, inland marine insurance or boiler insurance. The term *property insurance* may, like casualty insurance, be used as a broad category of various subtypes of insurance, some of which are listed below:

- Aviation insurance protects aircraft hulls and spares, and associated liability risks, such as passenger and third-party liability. Airports may also appear under this subcategory, including air traffic control and refuelling operations for international airports through to smaller domestic exposures.
- Boiler insurance (also known as boiler and machinery insurance, or equipment breakdown insurance) insures against accidental physical damage to boilers, equipment or machinery.
- Builder's risk insurance insures against the risk of physical loss or damage to property during construction. Builder's risk insurance is typically written on an "all risk" basis covering damage arising from any cause (including the negligence of the insured) not otherwise expressly excluded. Builder's risk insurance is coverage that protects a person's or organization's insurable interest in materials, fixtures and/or equipment being used in the construction or renovation of a building or structure should those items sustain physical loss or damage from an insured peril.

- Crop insurance may be purchased by farmers to reduce or manage various risks associated with growing crops. Such risks include crop loss or damage caused by weather, hail, drought, frost damage, insects, or disease.
- Earthquake insurance is a form of property insurance that pays the policyholder in the event of an earthquake that causes damage to the property. Most ordinary home insurance policies do not cover earthquake damage. Earthquake insurance policies generally feature a high deductible. Rates depend on location and hence the likelihood of an earthquake, as well as the construction of the home.
- Fidelity bond is a form of casualty insurance that covers policyholders for losses incurred as a result of fraudulent acts by specified individuals. It usually insures a business for losses caused by the dishonest acts of its employees.
- Flood insurance protects against property loss due to flooding. Many insurers in the U.S. do not provide flood insurance in some parts of the country. In response to this, the federal government created the National Flood Insurance Program which serves as the insurer of last resort.
- Home insurance, also commonly called hazard insurance, or homeowners insurance (often abbreviated in the real estate industry as HOI), is the type of property insurance that covers private homes, as outlined above.
- Landlord insurance covers residential and commercial properties which are rented to others. Most homeowners' insurance covers only owner-occupied homes.
- Marine insurance and marine cargo insurance cover the loss or damage of vessels at sea or on inland waterways, and of cargo in transit, regardless of the method of transit. When the owner of the cargo and the carrier are separate corporations, marine cargo insurance typically compensates the owner of cargo for losses sustained from fire, shipwreck, etc., but excludes losses that can be recovered from the carrier or the carrier's insurance. Many

marine insurance underwriters will include "time element" coverage in such policies, which extends the indemnity to cover loss of profit and other business expenses attributable to the delay caused by a covered loss.

- Supplemental natural disaster insurance covers specified expenses after a natural disaster renders the policyholder's home uninhabitable. Periodic payments are made directly to the insured until the home is rebuilt or a specified time period has elapsed.
- Surety bond insurance is a three-party insurance guaranteeing the performance of the principal.
- Terrorism insurance provides protection against any loss or damage caused by terrorist activities. In the U.S. in the wake of 9/11, the Terrorism Risk Insurance Act 2002 (TRIA) set up a federal Program providing a transparent system of shared public and private compensation for insured losses resulting from acts of terrorism. The program was extended until the end of 2014 by the Terrorism Risk Insurance Program Reauthorization Act 2007 (TRIPRA).
- Volcano insurance is a specialized insurance protecting against damage arising specifically from volcanic eruptions.
- Windstorm insurance is an insurance covering the damage that can be caused by wind events such as hurricanes.

Liability

Liability insurance is a very broad superset that covers legal claims against the insured. Many types of insurance include an aspect of liability coverage. For example, a homeowner's insurance policy will normally include liability coverage which protects the insured in the event of a claim brought by someone who slips and falls on the property; automobile insurance also includes an aspect of liability insurance that indemnifies against the harm that a crashing car can cause to others' lives, health, or property. The protection offered by a liability insurance policy is twofold: a legal defence in the event of a lawsuit commenced against the policyholder and indemnification (payment on behalf of the insured) with respect to a settlement or court verdict. Liability policies typically cover only the negligence of the insured, and will not apply to results of wilful or intentional acts by the insured.

- Public liability insurance covers a business or organization against claims should its operations injure a member of the public or damage their property in some way.
- Directors and officers liability insurance (D&O) protects an organization (usually a corporation) from costs associated with litigation resulting from errors made by directors and officers for which they are liable.
- Environmental liability insurance protects the insured from bodily injury, property damage and cleanup costs as a result of the dispersal, release or escape of pollutants.
- Errors and omissions insurance is business liability insurance for professionals such as insurance agents, real estate agents and brokers, architects, third-party administrators (TPAs) and other business professionals.
- Prize indemnity insurance protects the insured from giving away a large prize at a specific event. Examples would include offering prizes to contestants who can make a half-court shot at a basketball game, or a hole-in-one at a golf tournament.
- Professional liability insurance, also called insurance (PI), protects insured professionals such as architectural corporations and medical practitioners against potential negligence claims made by their patients/clients. Professional liability insurance may take on different names depending on the profession. For example, professional liability insurance in reference to the medical profession may be called medical malpractice insurance.

Credit

Credit insurance repays some or all of a loan when certain circumstances arise to the borrower such as unemployment, disability, or death.

- Mortgage insurance insures the lender against default by the borrower. Mortgage insurance is a form of credit insurance, although the name "credit insurance" more often is used to refer to policies that cover other kinds of debt.

- Many credit cards offer payment protection plans which are a form of credit insurance.

Other Types

- All-risk insurance is an insurance that covers a wide-range of incidents and perils, except those noted in the policy. All-risk insurance is different from peril-specific insurance that cover losses from only those perils listed in the policy. In car insurance, all-risk policy includes also the damages caused by the own driver.
- Bloodstock insurance covers individual horses or a number of horses under common ownership. Coverage is typically for mortality as a result of accident, illness or disease but may extend to include infertility, in-transit loss, veterinary fees, and prospective foal.
- Business interruption insurance covers the loss of income, and the expenses incurred, after a covered peril interrupts normal business operations.
- Collateral protection insurance (CPI) insures property (primarily vehicles) held as collateral for loans made by lending institutions.
- Defence Base Act (DBA) insurance provides coverage for civilian workers hired by the government to perform contracts outside the U.S. and Canada. DBA is required for all U.S. citizens, U.S. residents, U.S. Green Card holders, and all employees or subcontractors hired on overseas government contracts. Depending on the country, foreign nationals must also be covered under DBA. This coverage typically includes expenses related to medical treatment and loss of wages, as well as disability and death benefits.
- Expatriate insurance provides individuals and organizations operating outside of their home country with protection for automobiles, property, health, liability and business pursuits.
- Kidnap and ransom insurance is designed to protect individuals and corporations operating in high-risk areas

around the world against the perils of kidnap, extortion, wrongful detention and hijacking.

- Legal expenses insurance covers policyholders for the potential costs of legal action against an institution or an individual. When something happens which triggers the need for legal action, it is known as "the event". There are two main types of legal expenses insurance: before the event insurance and after the event insurance.
- Locked funds insurance is a little-known hybrid insurance policy jointly issued by governments and banks. It is used to protect public funds from tamper by unauthorized parties. In special cases, a government may authorize its use in protecting semi-private funds which are liable to tamper. The terms of this type of insurance are usually very strict. Therefore it is used only in extreme cases where maximum security of funds is required.
- Livestock insurance is a specialist policy provided to, for example, commercial or hobby farms, aquariums, fish farms or any other animal holding. Cover is available for mortality or economic slaughter as a result of accident, illness or disease but can extend to include destruction by government order.
- Media liability insurance is designed to cover professionals that engage in film and television production and print, against risks such as defamation.
- Nuclear incident insurance covers damages resulting from an incident involving radioactive materials and is generally arranged at the national level.
- Pet insurance insures pets against accidents and illnesses; some companies cover routine/wellness care and burial, as well.
- Pollution insurance usually takes the form of first-party coverage for contamination of insured property either by external or on-site sources. Coverage is also afforded for liability to third parties arising from contamination of air, water, or land due to the sudden and accidental release of hazardous materials from the insured site. The policy

usually covers the costs of cleanup and may include coverage for releases from underground storage tanks. Intentional acts are specifically excluded.

- Purchase insurance is aimed at providing protection on the products people purchase. Purchase insurance can cover individual purchase protection, warranties, guarantees, care plans and even mobile phone insurance. Such insurance is normally very limited in the scope of problems that are covered by the policy.
- Title insurance provides a guarantee that title to real property is vested in the purchaser and/or mortgagee, free and clear of liens or encumbrances. It is usually issued in conjunction with a search of the public records performed at the time of a real estate transaction.
- Travel insurance is an insurance cover taken by those who travel abroad, which covers certain losses such as medical expenses, loss of personal belongings, travel delay, and personal liabilities.

Insurance Financing Vehicles

- Fraternal insurance is provided on a cooperative basis by fraternal benefit societies or other social organizations.
- No-fault insurance is a type of insurance policy (typically automobile insurance) where insureds are indemnified by their own insurer regardless of fault in the incident.
- Protected self-insurance is an alternative risk financing mechanism in which an organization retains the mathematically calculated cost of risk within the organization and transfers the catastrophic risk with specific and aggregate limits to an insurer so the maximum total cost of the program is known. A properly designed and underwritten Protected Self-Insurance Program reduces and stabilizes the cost of insurance and provides valuable risk management information.
- Retrospectively rated insurance is a method of establishing a premium on large commercial accounts. The final premium is based on the insured's actual loss experience during the policy term, sometimes subject to a minimum

and maximum premium, with the final premium determined by a formula. Under this plan, the current year's premium is based partially (or wholly) on the current year's losses, although the premium adjustments may take months or years beyond the current year's expiration date. The rating formula is guaranteed in the insurance contract. Formula: retrospective premium = converted loss + basic premium × tax multiplier. Numerous variations of this formula have been developed and are in use.

- Formal self insurance is the deliberate decision to pay for otherwise insurable losses out of one's own money. This can be done on a formal basis by establishing a separate fund into which funds are deposited on a periodic basis, or by simply forgoing the purchase of available insurance and paying out-of-pocket. Self insurance is usually used to pay for high-frequency, low-severity losses. Such losses, if covered by conventional insurance, mean having to pay a premium that includes loadings for the company's general expenses, cost of putting the policy on the books, acquisition expenses, premium taxes, and contingencies. While this is true for all insurance, for small, frequent losses the transaction costs may exceed the benefit of volatility reduction that insurance otherwise affords.
- Reinsurance is a type of insurance purchased by insurance companies or self-insured employers to protect against unexpected losses. Financial reinsurance is a form of reinsurance that is primarily used for capital management rather than to transfer insurance risk.
- Social insurance can be many things to many people in many countries. But a summary of its essence is that it is a collection of insurance coverages (including components of life insurance, disability income insurance, unemployment insurance, health insurance, and others), plus retirement savings, that requires participation by all citizens. By forcing everyone in society to be a policyholder and pay premiums, it ensures that everyone can become a claimant when or if he/she needs to. Along the way this inevitably becomes related to other concepts such as the

justice system and the welfare state. This is a large, complicated topic that engenders tremendous debate, which can be further studied in the following articles (and others):

- o National Insurance
- o Social safety net
- o Social security
- o Social Security debate (United States)
- o Social Security (United States)
- o Social welfare provision.

- Stop-loss insurance provides protection against catastrophic or unpredictable losses. It is purchased by organizations who do not want to assume 100% of the liability for losses arising from the plans. Under a stop-loss policy, the insurance company becomes liable for losses that exceed certain limits called deductibles.

Closed Community Self-insurance

Some communities prefer to create virtual insurance amongst themselves by other means than contractual risk transfer, which assigns explicit numerical values to risk. A number of religious groups, including the Amish and some Muslim groups, depend on support provided by their communities when disasters strike. The risk presented by any given person is assumed collectively by the community who all bear the cost of rebuilding lost property and supporting people whose needs are suddenly greater after a loss of some kind. In supportive communities where others can be trusted to follow community leaders, this tacit form of insurance can work. In this manner the community can even out the extreme differences in insurability that exist among its members. Some further justification is also provided by invoking the moral hazard of explicit insurance contracts.

In the United Kingdom, The Crown (which, for practical purposes, meant the civil service) did not insure property such as government buildings. If a government building was damaged, the cost of repair would be met from public funds because, in the long run, this was cheaper than paying insurance premiums. Since many UK government buildings have been sold to property companies, and rented back, this arrangement is now less common and may have disappeared altogether.

Insurance Companies

Insurance companies may be classified into two groups:

- Life insurance companies, which sell life insurance, annuities and pensions products.
- Non-life, general, or property/casualty insurance companies, which sell other types of insurance.

General insurance companies can be further divided into these sub categories.

- Standard lines
- Excess lines.

In most countries, life and non-life insurers are subject to different regulatory regimes and different tax and accounting rules. The main reason for the distinction between the two types of company is that life, annuity, and pension business is very long-term in nature—coverage for life assurance or a pension can cover risks over many decades. By contrast, non-life insurance cover usually covers a shorter period, such as one year.

In the United States, standard line insurance companies are "mainstream" insurers. These are the companies that typically insure autos, homes or businesses. They use pattern or "cookie-cutter" policies without variation from one person to the next. They usually have lower premiums than excess lines and can sell directly to individuals. They are regulated by state laws that can restrict the amount they can charge for insurance policies.

Excess line insurance companies (also known as Excess and Surplus) typically insure risks not covered by the standard lines market. They are broadly referred as being all insurance placed with non-admitted insurers. Non-admitted insurers are not licensed in the states where the risks are located.

These companies have more flexibility and can react faster than standard insurance companies because they are not required to file rates and forms as the "admitted" carriers do. However, they still have substantial regulatory requirements placed upon them. State laws generally require insurance placed with surplus line agents and brokers not to be available through standard licensed insurers.

Insurance companies are generally classified as either mutual or stock companies. Mutual companies are owned by the policyholders, while stockholders (who may or may not own policies) own stock insurance companies. Demutualization of mutual insurers to form stock companies, as well as the formation of a hybrid known as a mutual holding company, became common in some countries, such as the United States, in the late 20th century.

Other possible forms for an insurance company include reciprocals, in which policyholders reciprocate in sharing risks, and Lloyd's organizations.

Insurance companies are rated by various agencies such as A. M. Best. The ratings include the company's financial strength, which measures its ability to pay claims. It also rates financial instruments issued by the insurance company, such as bonds, notes, and securitization products.

Reinsurance companies are insurance companies that sell policies to other insurance companies, allowing them to reduce their risks and protect themselves from very large losses. The reinsurance market is dominated by a few very large companies, with huge reserves. A reinsurer may also be a direct writer of insurance risks as well.

Captive insurance companies may be defined as limited-purpose insurance companies established with the specific objective of financing risks emanating from their parent group or groups. This definition can sometimes be extended to include some of the risks of the parent company's customers. In short, it is an in-house self-insurance vehicle. Captives may take the form of a "pure" entity (which is a 100% subsidiary of the self-insured parent company); of a "mutual" captive (which insures the collective risks of members of an industry); and of an "association" captive (which self-insures individual risks of the members of a professional, commercial or industrial association). Captives represent commercial, economic and tax advantages to their sponsors because of the reductions in costs they help create and for the ease of insurance risk management and the flexibility for cash flows they generate. Additionally, they may provide coverage of risks which is neither available nor offered in the traditional insurance market at reasonable prices.

The types of risk that a captive can underwrite for their parents include property damage, public and product liability, , employee benefits, employers' liability, motor and medical aid expenses. The captive's exposure to such risks may be limited by the use of reinsurance.

Captives are becoming an increasingly important component of the risk management and risk financing strategy of their parent. This can be understood against the following background:

- heavy and increasing premium costs in almost every line of coverage;
- difficulties in insuring certain types of fortuitous risk;
- differential coverage standards in various parts of the world;
- rating structures which reflect market trends rather than individual loss experience;
- insufficient credit for deductibles and/or loss control efforts.

There are also companies known as 'insurance consultants'. Like a mortgage broker, these companies are paid a fee by the customer to shop around for the best insurance policy amongst many companies. Similar to an insurance consultant, an 'insurance broker' also shops around for the best insurance policy amongst many companies. However, with insurance brokers, the fee is usually paid in the form of commission from the insurer that is selected rather than directly from the client.

Neither insurance consultants nor insurance brokers are insurance companies and no risks are transferred to them in insurance transactions. Third party administrators are companies that perform underwriting and sometimes claims handling services for insurance companies. These companies often have special expertise that the insurance companies do not have.

The financial stability and strength of an insurance company should be a major consideration when buying an insurance contract. An insurance premium paid currently provides coverage for losses that might arise many years in the future. For that reason, the viability of the insurance carrier is very important. In recent years, a number of insurance companies have become insolvent, leaving their policyholders with no coverage (or coverage only from a government-backed insurance pool or other arrangement with less attractive payouts for losses). A number of independent rating agencies provide information and rate the financial viability of insurance companies.

Across the World

Global insurance premiums grew by 3.4% in 2008 to reach $4.3 trillion. For the first time in the past three decades, premium income declined in inflation-adjusted terms, with non-life premiums falling by 0.8% and life premiums falling by 3.5%. The insurance industry is exposed to the global economic downturn on the assets side by the decline in returns on investments and on the liabilities side by a rise in claims. So far the extent of losses on both sides has been limited although investment returns fell sharply following the bankruptcy of Lehman Brothers and bailout of AIG in September 2008. The financial crisis has shown that the insurance sector is sufficiently capitalised. The vast majority of insurance companies had enough capital to absorb losses and only a small number turned to government for support.

Advanced economies account for the bulk of global insurance. With premium income of $1,753bn, Europe was the most important region in 2008, followed by North America $1,346bn and Asia $933bn. The top four countries generated more than a half of premiums. The US and Japan alone accounted for 40% of world insurance, much higher than their 7% share of the global population. Emerging markets accounted for over 85% of the world's population but generated only around 10% of premiums. Their markets are however growing at a quicker pace.

Regulatory Differences

In the United States, insurance is regulated by the states under the McCarran-Ferguson Act, with "periodic proposals for federal intervention", and a nonprofit coalition of state insurance agencies called the National Association of Insurance Commissioners works to harmonize the country's different laws and regulations. The

National Conference of Insurance Legislators (NCOIL) also works to harmonize the different state laws.

In the European Union, the Third Non-Life Directive and the Third Life Directive, both passed in 1992 and effective 1994, created a single insurance market in Europe and allowed insurance companies to offer insurance anywhere in the EU (subject to permission from authority in the head office) and allowed insurance consumers to purchase insurance from any insurer in the EU.

The insurance industry in China was nationalized in 1949 and thereafter offered by only a single state-owned company, the People's Insurance Company of China, which was eventually suspended as demand declined in a communist environment. In 1978, market reforms led to an increase in the market and by 1995 a comprehensive Insurance Law of the People's Republic of China was passed, followed in 1998 by the formation of China Insurance Regulatory Commission (CIRC), which has broad regulatory authority over the insurance market of China.

In India, IRDA is insurance regulatory authority. As per the section 4 of IRDA Act' 1999, Insurance Regulatory and Development Authority (IRDA), which was constituted by an act of parliament. National Insurance Academy, Pune is apex insurance capacity builder institute promoted with support from Ministry of Finance and by LIC, Life & General Insurance compnies.

Controversies

Insurance Insulates Too Much

By creating a "security blanket" for its insureds, an insurance company may inadvertently find that its insureds may not be as risk-averse as they might otherwise be (since, by definition, the insured has transferred the risk to the insurer), a concept known as moral hazard. To reduce their own financial exposure, insurance companies have contractual clauses that mitigate their obligation to provide coverage if the insured engages in behavior that grossly magnifies their risk of loss or liability.

For example, life insurance companies may require higher premiums or deny coverage altogether to people who work in hazardous occupations or engage in dangerous sports. Liability insurance providers do not provide coverage for liability arising from intentional torts committed by or at the direction of the insured. Even if a provider were so irrational as to want to provide such coverage, it is against the public policy of most countries to allow such insurance to exist, and thus it is usually illegal.

Complexity of Insurance Policy Contracts

Insurance policies can be complex and some policyholders may not understand all the fees and coverages included in a policy. As a result, people may buy policies on unfavorable terms. In response to these issues, many countries have enacted detailed statutory and regulatory regimes governing every aspect of the insurance business, including minimum standards for policies and the ways in which they may be advertised and sold.

For example, most insurance policies in the English language today have been carefully drafted in plain English; the industry learned the hard way that many courts will not enforce policies against insureds when the judges themselves cannot understand what the policies are saying. Typically, courts construe ambiguities in insurance policies against the insurance company and in favour of coverage under the policy.

Many institutional insurance purchasers buy insurance through an insurance broker. While on the surface it appears the broker represents the buyer (not the insurance company), and typically counsels the buyer on appropriate coverage and policy limitations, it should be noted that in the vast majority of cases a broker's compensation comes in the form of a commission as a percentage of the insurance premium, creating a conflict of interest in that the broker's financial interest is tilted towards encouraging an insured to purchase more insurance than might be necessary at a higher price. A broker generally holds contracts with many insurers, thereby allowing the broker to "shop" the market for the best rates and coverage possible.

Insurance may also be purchased through an agent. Unlike a broker, who represents the policyholder, an agent represents the insurance company from whom the policyholder buys. Just as there is a potential conflict of interest with a broker, an agent has a different type of conflict. Because agents work directly for the insurance company, if there is a claim the agent may advise the client to the benefit of the insurance company. It should also be noted that agents generally can not offer as broad a range of selection compared to an insurance broker.

An independent insurance consultant advises insureds on a fee-for-service retainer, similar to an attorney, and thus offers completely independent advice, free of the financial conflict of interest of brokers and/or agents. However, such a consultant must still work through brokers and/or agents in order to secure coverage for their clients.

Limited Consumer Benefits

Economists and consumer advocates generally consider insurance to be worthwhile for low-probability, catastrophic losses, but not for high-probability, small losses. Because of this, consumers are advised to select high deductibles and to not insure losses which would not cause a disruption in their life. However, consumers have shown a tendency to prefer low deductibles and to prefer to insure relatively high-probability, small losses over low-probability, perhaps due to not understanding or ignoring the low-probability risk. This is associated with reduced purchasing of insurance against low-probability losses, and may result in increased inefficiencies from moral hazard.

Redlining

Redlining is the practice of denying insurance coverage in specific geographic areas, supposedly because of a high likelihood of loss, while the alleged motivation is unlawful discrimination. Racial profiling or redlining has a long history in the property insurance industry in the United States. From a review of industry underwriting and marketing materials, court documents, and research by government agencies, industry and community groups, and academics, it is clear that race has long affected and continues to affect the policies and practices of the insurance industry.

In July, 2007, The Federal Trade Commission (FTC) released a report presenting the results of a study concerning credit-based insurance scores in automobile insurance. The study found that these scores are effective predictors of risk. It also showed that African-Americans and Hispanics are substantially overrepresented in the lowest credit scores, and substantially underrepresented in the highest, while Caucasians and Asians are more evenly spread across the scores. The credit scores were also found to predict risk within each of the ethnic groups, leading the FTC to conclude that the scoring models are not solely proxies for redlining. The FTC indicated little data was available to evaluate benefit of insurance scores to consumers. The report was disputed by representatives of the Consumer Federation of America, the National Fair Housing Alliance, the National Consumer Law Center, and the Center for Economic Justice, for relying on data provided by the insurance industry.

All states have provisions in their rate regulation laws or in their fair trade practice acts that prohibit unfair discrimination, often called redlining, in setting rates and making insurance available.

In determining premiums and premium rate structures, insurers consider quantifiable factors, including location, credit scores, gender, occupation, marital status, and education level. However, the use of such factors is often considered to be unfair or unlawfully discriminatory, and the reaction against this practice has in some instances led to political disputes about the ways in which insurers determine premiums and regulatory intervention to limit the factors used.

An insurance underwriter's job is to evaluate a given risk as to the likelihood that a loss will occur. Any factor that causes a greater likelihood of loss should theoretically be charged a higher rate. This basic principle of insurance must be followed if insurance companies are to remain solvent. Thus, "discrimination" against (i.e., negative differential treatment of) potential insureds in the risk evaluation and premium-setting process is a necessary by-product of the fundamentals of insurance underwriting. For instance, insurers charge older people significantly higher premiums than they charge younger people for term life insurance. Older people are thus treated differently than younger people (i.e., a distinction is made, discrimination occurs). The rationale for the differential treatment goes to the heart of the risk a life insurer takes: Old people are likely to die sooner than young people, so the risk of loss (the insured's death) is greater in any given period of time and therefore the risk premium must be higher to cover the greater risk. However, treating insureds differently when there is no actuarially sound reason for doing so is unlawful discrimination.

What is often missing from the debate is that prohibiting the use of legitimate, actuarially sound factors means that an insufficient amount is being charged for a given risk, and there is thus a deficit in the system. The failure to address the deficit may mean insolvency and hardship for all of a company's insureds. The options for addressing the deficit seem to be the following: Charge the deficit to the other policyholders or charge it to the government (i.e., externalize outside of the company to society at large).

Insurance Patents

New assurance products can now be protected from copying with a business method patent in the United States.

A recent example of a new insurance product that is patented is Usage Based auto insurance. Early versions were independently invented and patented by a major U.S. auto insurance company, Progressive Auto Insurance (U.S. Patent 5,797,134) and a Spanish independent inventor, Salvador Minguijon Perez (EP 0700009).

Many independent inventors are in favour of patenting new insurance products since it gives them protection from big companies when they bring their new insurance products to market. Independent inventors account for 70% of the new U.S. patent applications in this area.

Many insurance executives are opposed to patenting insurance products because it creates a new risk for them. The Hartford insurance company, for example, recently had to pay $80 million to an independent inventor, Bancorp Services, in order to settle a patent infringement and theft of trade secret lawsuit for a type of corporate owned life insurance product invented and patented by Bancorp.

There are currently about 150 new patent applications on insurance inventions filed per year in the United States. The rate at which patents have issued has steadily risen from 15 in 2002 to 44 in 2006.

Inventors can now have their insurance U.S. patent applications reviewed by the public in the Peer to Patent program. The first insurance patent application to be posted was US2009005522 "Risk assessment company". It was posted on March 6, 2009. This patent application describes a method for increasing the ease of changing insurance companies.

The Insurance Industry and Rent-seeking

Certain insurance products and practices have been described as rent-seeking by critics. That is, some insurance products or practices are useful primarily because of legal benefits, such as reducing taxes, as opposed to providing protection against risks of adverse events. Under United States tax law, for example, most owners of variable annuities and variable life insurance can invest their premium payments in the stock market and defer or eliminate paying any taxes on their investments until withdrawals are made. Sometimes this tax deferral is the only reason people use these products. Another example is the legal infrastructure which allows life insurance to be held in an irrevocable trust which is used to pay an estate tax while the proceeds themselves are immune from the estate tax.

Religious Concerns

Muslim scholars have varying opinions about insurance. Insurance policies that earn interest are generally considered to be a form of *riba* (usury) and some consider even policies that do not earn interest to be a form of *gharar* (speculation). Some argue that *gharar* is not present due to the actuarial science behind the underwriting.

Jewish rabbinical scholars also have expressed reservations regarding insurance as an avoidance of God's will but most find it acceptable in moderation.

Some Christians believe insurance represents a lack of faith and there is a long history of resistance to commercial insurance in Anabaptist communities (Mennonites, Amish, Hutterites, Brethren in Christ) but many participate in community-based self-insurance programs that spread risk within their communities.

Risk Management

Risk management is the identification, assessment, and prioritization of risks (defined in ISO 31000 as *the effect of uncertainty on objectives*, whether positive or negative) followed by coordinated and economical application of resources to minimize, monitor, and control the probability and/or impact of unfortunate events or to maximize the realization of opportunities.

Risks can come from uncertainty in financial markets, project failures (at any phase in development, production, or sustainment life-cycles), legal liabilities, credit risk, accidents, natural causes and disasters as well as deliberate attack from an adversary or events of uncertain root-cause.

Several risk management standards have been developed including the Project Management Institute, the National Institute of Science and Technology, actuarial societies, and ISO standards. Methods, definitions and goals vary widely according to whether the risk management method is in the context of project management, security, engineering, industrial processes, financial portfolios, actuarial assessments, or public health and safety.

The strategies to manage risk include transferring the risk to another party, avoiding the risk, reducing the negative effect or probability of the risk, ov even accepting some or all of the consequences of a particular risk.

Certain aspects of many of the risk management standards have come under criticism for having no measurable improvement on risk, whether the confidence in estimates and decisions seem to increase.

Introduction

This section provides an introduction to the principles of risk management. The vocabulary of risk management is defined in ISO Guide 73, "Risk management. Vocabulary."

In ideal risk management, a prioritization process is followed whereby the risks with the greatest loss and the greatest probability of occurring are handled first, and risks with lower probability of occurrence and lower loss are handled in descending order. In practice the process can be very difficult, and balancing between risks with a high probability of occurrence but lower loss versus a risk with high loss but lower probability of occurrence can often be mishandled. Intangible risk management identifies a new type of a risk that has a 100% probability of occurring but is ignored by the organization due to a lack of identification ability. For example, when deficient knowledge is applied to a situation, a knowledge risk materializes. Relationship risk appears when ineffective collaboration occurs. Process-engagement risk may be an issue when ineffective operational procedures are applied.

These risks directly reduce the productivity of knowledge workers, decrease cost effectiveness, profitability, service, quality, reputation, brand value, and earnings quality. Intangible risk management allows risk management to create immediate value from the identification and reduction of risks that reduce productivity.

Risk management also faces difficulties in allocating resources. This is the idea of opportunity cost. Resources spent on risk management could have been spent on more profitable activities. Again, ideal risk management minimizes spending and minimizes the negative effects of risks.

Method

For the most part, these methods consist of the following elements, performed, more or less, in the following order.

1. identify, characterize, and assess threats
2. assess the vulnerability of critical assets to specific threats
3. determine the risk (i.e. the expected consequences of specific types of attacks on specific assets)
4. identify ways to reduce those risks
5. prioritize risk reduction measures based on a strategy.

Principles of Risk Management

The International Organization for Standardization (ISO) identifies the following principles of risk management:

Risk management should:

- create value
- be an integral part of organizational processes
- be part of decision making
- explicitly address uncertainty and assumptions
- be systematic and structured

- be based on the best available information
- be tailorable
- take into account human factors
- be transparent and inclusive
- be dynamic, iterative and responsive to change
- be capable of continual improvement and enhancement.

Process

According to the standard ISO 31000 "Risk management—Principles and guidelines on implementation," the process of risk management consists of several steps as follows:

Establishing the Context

Establishing the context involves:

1. Identification of risk in a selected domain of interest
2. Planning the remainder of the process.
3. Mapping out the following:
    - o the social scope of risk management
    - o the identity and objectives of stakeholders
    - o the basis upon which risks will be evaluated, constraints.
4. Defining a framework for the activity and an agenda for identification.
5. Developing an analysis of risks involved in the process.
6. Mitigation or Solution of risks using available technological, human and organizational resources.

Identification

After establishing the context, the next step in the process of managing risk is to identify potential risks. Risks are about events that, when triggered, cause problems. Hence, risk identification can start with the source of problems, or with the problem itself.

- Source analysis Risk sources may be internal or external to the system that is the target of risk management.

Examples of risk sources are: stakeholders of a project, employees of a company or the weather over an airport.

- Problem analysis Risks are related to identified threats. For example: the threat of losing money, the threat of abuse of privacy information or the threat of accidents and casualties. The threats may exist with various entities, most important with shareholders, customers and legislative bodies such as the government.

When either source or problem is known, the events that a source may trigger or the events that can lead to a problem can be investigated. For example: stakeholders withdrawing during a project may endanger funding of the project; privacy information may be stolen by employees even within a closed network; lightning striking an aircraft during takeoff may make all people on board immediate casualties.

The chosen method of identifying risks may depend on culture, industry practice and compliance. The identification methods are formed by templates or the development of templates for identifying source, problem or event. Common risk identification methods are:

- *Objectives-based risk identification Organizations and project teams have objectives:* Any event that may endanger achieving an objective partly or completely is identified as risk.
- *Scenario-based risk identification:* In scenario analysis different scenarios are created. The scenarios may be the alternative ways to achieve an objective, or an analysis of the interaction of forces in, for example, a market or battle. Any event that triggers an undesired scenario alternative is identified as risk.
- *Taxonomy-based risk identification:* The taxonomy in taxonomy-based risk identification is a breakdown of possible risk sources. Based on the taxonomy and knowledge of best practices, a questionnaire is compiled. The answers to the questions reveal risks.
- *Common-risk checking:* In several industries, lists with known risks are available. Each risk in the list can be checked for application to a particular situation.
- *Risk charting:* This method combines the above approaches by listing resources at risk, threats to those resources,

modifying factors which may increase or decrease the risk and consequences it is wished to avoid. Creating a matrix under these headings enables a variety of approaches. One can begin with resources and consider the threats they are exposed to and the consequences of each. Alternatively one can start with the threats and examine which resources they would affect, or one can begin with the consequences and determine which combination of threats and resources would be involved to bring them about.

Assessment

Once risks have been identified, they must then be assessed as to their potential severity of impact (generally a negative impact, such as damage or loss) and to the probability of occurrence. These quantities can be either simple to measure, in the case of the value of a lost building, or impossible to know for sure in the case of the probability of an unlikely event occurring. Therefore, in the assessment process it is critical to make the best educated decisions in order to properly prioritize the implementation of the risk management plan.

Even a short-term positive improvement can have long-term negative impacts. Take the "turnpike" example. A highway is widened to allow more traffic. More traffic capacity leads to greater development in the areas surrounding the improved traffic capacity. Over time, traffic thereby increases to fill available capacity. Turnpikes thereby need to be expanded in a seemingly endless cycles. There are many other engineering examples where expanded capacity (to do any function) is soon filled by increased demand. Since expansion comes at a cost, the resulting growth could become unsustainable without forecasting and management.

The fundamental difficulty in risk assessment is determining the rate of occurrence since statistical information is not available on all kinds of past incidents. Furthermore, evaluating the severity of the consequences (impact) is often quite difficult for intangible assets. Asset valuation is another question that needs to be addressed. Thus, best educated opinions and available statistics are the primary sources of information. Nevertheless, risk assessment should produce such information for the management of the organization that the primary risks are easy to understand and that the risk management decisions may be prioritized. Thus, there have been several theories and attempts to quantify risks. Numerous different risk formulae exist, but perhaps the most widely accepted formula for risk quantification is:

Rate (or Probability) of Occurrence Multiplied by the Impact of the Event Equals Risk Magnitude

Composite Risk Index

The above formula can also be re-written in terms of a Composite Risk Index, as follows:

Composite Risk Index = Impact of Risk event x Probability of Occurrence

The impact of the risk event is commonly assessed on a scale of 1 to 5, where 1 and 5 represent the minimum and maximum possible impact of an occurrence of a risk (usually in terms of financial losses). However, the 1 to 5 scale can be arbitrary and need not be on a linear scale.

The probability of occurrence is likewise commonly assessed on a scale from 1 to 5, where 1 represents a very low probability of the risk event actually occurring while 5 represents a very high probability of occurrence. This axis may be expressed in either mathematical terms (event occurs once a year, once in ten years, once in 100 years etc.) or may be expressed in "plain english"- event has occurred here very often; event has been known to occur here; event has been known to occur in the industry etc.). Again, the 1 to 5 scale can be arbitrary or non-linear depending on decisions by subject-matter experts.

The Composite Index thus can take values ranging (typically) from 1 through 25, and this range is usually arbitrarily divided into three sub-ranges. The overall risk assessment is then Low, Medium or High, depending on the sub-range containing the calculated value of the Composite Index. For instance, the three sub-ranges could be defined as 1 to 8, 9 to 16 and 17 to 25.

Note that the probability of risk occurrence is difficult to estimate, since the past data on frequencies are not readily available, as mentioned above. After all, probability does not imply certainty.

Likewise, the impact of the risk is not easy to estimate since it is often difficult to estimate the potential loss in the event of risk occurrence.

Further, both the above factors can change in magnitude depending on the adequacy of risk avoidance and prevention measures taken and due to changes in the external business environment.

Hence it is absolutely necessary to periodically re-assess risks and intensify/relax mitigation measures, or as necessary. Changes in procedures, technology, schedules, budgets, market conditions, political environment, or other factors typically require re-assessment of risks.

Risk Options

Risk mitigation measures are usually formulated according to one or more of the following major risk options, which are:

1. Design a new business process with adequate built-in risk control and containment measures from the start.
2. Periodically re-assess risks that are accepted in ongoing processes as a normal feature of business operations and modify mitigation measures.
3. Transfer risks to an external agency (e.g. an insurance company)
4. Avoid risks altogether (e.g. by closing down a particular high-risk business area).

Later research has shown that the financial benefits of risk management are less dependent on the formula used but are more dependent on the frequency and how risk assessment is performed.

In business it is imperative to be able to present the findings of risk assessments in financial, market, or schedule terms. Robert Courtney Jr. (IBM, 1970) proposed a formula for presenting risks in financial terms.

The Courtney formula was accepted as the official risk analysis method for the US governmental agencies. The formula proposes calculation of ALE (annualised loss expectancy) and compares the expected loss value to the security control implementation costs (cost-benefit analysis).

Potential Risk Treatments

Once risks have been identified and assessed, all techniques to manage the risk fall into one or more of these four major categories:

- Avoidance (eliminate, withdraw from or not become involved)
- Reduction (optimize-mitigate)
- Sharing (transfer-outsource or insure)
- Retention (accept and budget).

Ideal use of these strategies may not be possible. Some of them may involve trade-offs that are not acceptable to the organization or person making the risk management decisions. Another source, from the US Department of Defence, Defence Acquisition University, calls these categories ACAT, for Avoid, Control, Accept, or Transfer. This use of the ACAT acronym is reminiscent of another ACAT (for Acquisition Category) used in US Defence industry procurements, in which Risk Management figures prominently in decision making and planning.

Risk Avoidance

This includes not performing an activity that could carry risk. An example would be not buying a property or business in order to not take on the legal liability that comes with it. Another would be not flying in order not to take the risk that the airplane were to be hijacked. Avoidance may seem the answer to all risks, but avoiding risks also means losing out on the potential gain that accepting (retaining) the risk may have allowed. Not entering a business to avoid the risk of loss also avoids the possibility of earning profits.

Hazard Prevention

Hazard prevention refers to the prevention of risks in an emergency. The first and most effective stage of hazard prevention is the elimination of hazards. If this takes too long, is too costly, or is otherwise impractical, the second stage is mitigation.

Risk Reduction

Risk reduction or "optimization" involves reducing the severity of the loss or the likelihood of the loss from occurring. For example, sprinklers are designed to put out a fire to reduce the risk of loss by fire. This method may cause a greater loss by water damage and therefore may not be suitable. Halon fire suppression systems may mitigate that risk, but the cost may be prohibitive as a strategy.

Acknowledging that risks can be positive or negative, optimising risks means finding a balance between negative risk and the benefit of the operation or activity; and between risk reduction and effort applied. By an offshore drilling contractor effectively applying HSE Management in its organisation, it can optimise risk to achieve levels of residual risk that are tolerable.

Modern software development methodologies reduce risk by developing and delivering software incrementally. Early methodologies suffered from the fact that they only delivered software in the final phase of development; any problems encountered in earlier phases meant costly rework and often jeopardized the whole project. By developing in iterations, software projects can limit effort wasted to a single iteration.

Outsourcing could be an example of risk reduction if the outsourcer can demonstrate higher capability at managing or reducing risks. For example, a company may outsource only its software development, the manufacturing of hard goods, or customer support needs to another company, while handling the business management itself. This way, the company can concentrate more on business development without having to worry as much about the manufacturing process, managing the development team, or finding a physical location for a call center.

Risk Sharing

Briefly defined as "sharing with another party the burden of loss or the benefit of gain, from a risk, and the measures to reduce a risk."

The term of 'risk transfer' is often used in place of risk sharing in the mistaken belief that you can transfer a risk to a third party through insurance or outsourcing. In practice if the insurance company or contractor go bankrupt or end up in court, the original risk is likely to still revert to the first party. As such in the terminology of practitioners and scholars alike, the purchase of an insurance contract is often described as a "transfer of risk."

However, technically speaking, the buyer of the contract generally retains legal responsibility for the losses "transferred", meaning that insurance may be described more accurately as a post-event compensatory mechanism.

For example, a personal injuries insurance policy does not transfer the risk of a car accident to the insurance company. The risk still lies with the policy holder namely the person who has been in the accident. The insurance policy simply provides that if an accident (the event) occurs involving the policy holder then some compensation may be payable to the policy holder that is commensurate to the suffering/damage.

Some ways of managing risk fall into multiple categories. Risk retention pools are technically retaining the risk for the group, but spreading it over the whole group involves transfer among individual members of the group. This is different from traditional insurance, in that no premium is exchanged between members of the group up front, but instead losses are assessed to all members of the group.

Risk Retention

Involves accepting the loss, or benefit of gain, from a risk when it occurs. True self insurance falls in this category. Risk retention is a viable strategy for small risks where the cost of insuring against the risk would be greater over time than the total losses sustained. All risks that are not avoided or transferred are retained by default. This includes risks that are so large or catastrophic that they either cannot be insured against or the premiums would be infeasible.

War is an example since most property and risks are not insured against war, so the loss attributed by war is retained by the insured. Also any amounts of potential loss (risk) over the amount insured is retained risk. This may also be acceptable if the chance of a very large loss is small or if the cost to insure for greater coverage amounts is so great it would hinder the goals of the organization too much.

Create a Risk Management Plan

Select appropriate controls or countermeasures to measure each risk. Risk mitigation needs to be approved by the appropriate level of management. For instance, a risk concerning the image of the organization should have top management decision behind it whereas IT management would have the authority to decide on computer virus risks.

The risk management plan should propose applicable and effective security controls for managing the risks. For example, an observed high risk of computer viruses could be mitigated by acquiring and implementing antivirus software. A good risk management plan should contain a schedule for control implementation and responsible persons for those actions.

According to ISO/IEC 27001, the stage immediately after completion of the risk assessment phase consists of preparing a Risk Treatment Plan, which should document the decisions about how each of the identified risks should be handled. Mitigation of risks often means selection of security controls, which should be documented in a Statement of Applicability, which identifies which particular control objectives and controls from the standard have been selected, and why.

Implementation

Implementation follows all of the planned methods for mitigating the effect of the risks. Purchase insurance policies for the risks that have been decided to be transferred to an insurer, avoid all risks that can be avoided without sacrificing the entity's goals, reduce others, and retain the rest.

Review and Evaluation of the Plan

Initial risk management plans will never be perfect. Practice, experience, and actual loss results will necessitate changes in the plan and contribute information to allow possible different decisions to be made in dealing with the risks being faced.

Risk analysis results and management plans should be updated periodically. There are two primary reasons for this:

1. to evaluate whether the previously selected security controls are still applicable and effective, and
2. to evaluate the possible risk level changes in the business environment. For example, information risks are a good example of rapidly changing business environment.

Limitations

If risks are improperly assessed and prioritized, time can be wasted in dealing with risk of losses that are not likely to occur. Spending too much time assessing and managing unlikely risks can divert resources that could be used more profitably. Unlikely events do occur but if the risk is unlikely enough to occur it may be better to simply retain the risk and deal with the result if the loss does in fact occur. Qualitative risk assessment is subjective and lacks consistency. The primary justification for a formal risk assessment process is legal and bureaucratic.

Prioritizing the *risk management processes* too highly could keep an organization from ever completing a project or even getting started. This is especially true if other work is suspended until the risk management process is considered complete.

It is also important to keep in mind the distinction between risk and uncertainty. Risk can be measured by impacts x probability.

Areas of Risk Management

As applied to corporate finance, risk management is the technique for measuring, monitoring and controlling the financial or operational risk on a firm's balance sheet.

The Basel II framework breaks risks into market risk (price risk), credit risk and operational risk and also specifies methods for calculating capital requirements for each of these components.

Enterprise Risk Management

In enterprise risk management, a risk is defined as a possible event or circumstance that can have negative influences on the enterprise in question. Its impact can be on the very existence, the resources (human and capital), the products and services, or the customers of the enterprise, as well as external impacts on society, markets, or the environment. In a financial institution, enterprise risk management is normally thought of as the combination of credit risk, interest rate risk or asset liability management, market risk, and operational risk.

In the more general case, every probable risk can have a pre-formulated plan to deal with its possible consequences (to ensure *contingency* if the risk becomes a *liability*).

From the information above and the average cost per employee over time, or cost accrual ratio, a project manager can estimate:

- the cost associated with the risk if it arises, estimated by multiplying employee costs per unit time by the estimated time lost (*cost impact*, C where C = *cost accrual ratio* * S).
- the probable increase in time associated with a risk (*schedule variance due to risk*, Rs where Rs = P * S):
  - o Sorting on this value puts the highest risks to the schedule first. This is intended to cause the greatest risks to the project to be attempted first so that risk is minimized as quickly as possible.
  - o This is slightly misleading as *schedule variances* with a large P and small S and vice versa are not equivalent. (The risk of the RMS *Titanic* sinking vs. the passengers' meals being served at slightly the wrong time).
- the probable increase in cost associated with a risk (*cost variance due to risk*, Rc where Rc = P*C = P*CAR*S = P*S*CAR)
  - o sorting on this value puts the highest risks to the budget first.

Risk in a project or process can be due either to Special Cause Variation or Common Cause Variation and requires appropriate treatment. That is to re-iterate the concern about extremal cases not being equivalent in the list immediately above.

Risk Management Activities as Applied to Project Management

In project management, risk management includes the following activities:

- Planning how risk will be managed in the particular project. Plans should include risk management tasks, responsibilities, activities and budget.
- Assigning a risk officer-a team member other than a project manager who is responsible for foreseeing potential project problems. Typical characteristic of risk officer is a healthy skepticism.
- Maintaining live project risk database. Each risk should have the following attributes: opening date, title, short

description, probability and importance. Optionally a risk may have an assigned person responsible for its resolution and a date by which the risk must be resolved.

- Creating anonymous risk reporting channel. Each team member should have possibility to report risk that he/she foresees in the project.
- Preparing mitigation plans for risks that are chosen to be mitigated. The purpose of the mitigation plan is to describe how this particular risk will be handled – what, when, by who and how will it be done to avoid it or minimize consequences if it becomes a liability.
- Summarizing planned and faced risks, effectiveness of mitigation activities, and effort spent for the risk management.

Risk Management for Megaprojects

Megaprojects (sometimes also called "major programs") are extremely large-scale investment projects, typically costing more than US$1 billion per project. Megaprojects include bridges, tunnels, highways, railways, airports, seaports, power plants, dams, wastewater projects, coastal flood protection schemes, oil and natural gas extraction projects, public buildings, information technology systems, aerospace projects, and defence systems. Megaprojects have been shown to be particularly risky in terms of finance, safety, and social and environmental impacts. Risk management is therefore particularly pertinent for megaprojects and special methods and special education have been developed for such risk management.

Risk Management of Information Technology

Information technology is increasing pervasive in modern life in every sector.

IT risk is a risk related to information technology. This relatively new term due to an increasing awareness that information security is simply one facet of a multitude of risks that are relevant to IT and the real world processes it supports.

A number of methodologies have been developed to deal with this kind of risk.

ISACA's Risk IT framework ties IT risk to Enterprise risk management.

Risk Management Techniques in Petroleum and Natural Gas

For the offshore oil and gas industry, operational risk management is regulated by the safety case regime in many countries. Hazard identification and risk assessment tools and techniques are described in the international standard ISO 17776:2000, and organisations such as the IADC (International Association of Drilling Contractors) publish guidelines for HSE Case development which are based on the ISO standard. Further, diagrammatic representations of hazardous events are often expected by governmental regulators as part of risk management in safety case submissions; these are known as bow-tie diagrams. The technique is also used by organisations and regulators in mining, aviation, health, defence, industrial and finance.

Risk Management and Business Continuity

Risk management is simply a practice of systematically selecting cost effective approaches for minimising the effect of threat realization to the organization. All risks can never be fully avoided or mitigated simply because of financial and practical limitations. Therefore all organizations have to accept some level of residual risks.

Whereas risk management tends to be preemptive, business continuity planning (BCP) was invented to deal with the consequences of realised residual risks. The necessity to have BCP in place arises because even very unlikely events will occur if given enough time. Risk management and BCP are often mistakenly seen as rivals or overlapping practices.

In fact these processes are so tightly tied together that such separation seems artificial. For example, the risk management process creates important inputs for the BCP (assets, impact assessments, cost estimates etc.). Risk management also proposes applicable controls for the observed risks. Therefore, risk management covers several areas that are vital for the BCP process. However, the BCP process goes beyond risk management's preemptive approach and assumes that the disaster will happen at some point.

Risk Communication

Risk communication is a complex cross-disciplinary academic field. Problems for risk communicators involve how to reach the intended audience, to make the risk comprehensible and relatable to other risks, how to pay appropriate respect to the audience's values related to the risk, how to predict the audience's response to the communication, etc. A main goal of risk communication is to improve collective and individual decision making. Risk communication is somewhat related to crisis communication.

Bow Tie Diagrams

A popular solution to the quest to communicate risks and their treatments effectively is to use bow tie diagrams. These have been effective, for example, in a public forum to model perceived risks and communicate precautions, during the planning stage of offshore oil and gas facilities in Scotland. Equally, the technique is used for HAZID (Hazard Identification) workshops of all types, and results in a high level of engagement. For this reason (amongst others) an increasing number of government regulators for major hazard facilities (MHFs), offshore oil & gas, aviation, etc. welcome safety case submissions which use diagrammatic representation of risks at their core.

Communication advantages of bow tie diagrams:

- Visual illustration of the hazard, its causes, consequences, controls, and how controls fail.
- The bow tie diagram can be readily understood at all personnel levels.
- "A picture paints a thousand words."

Seven Cardinal Rules for the Practice of Risk Communication

(As first expressed by the U.S. Environmental Protection Agency and several of the field's founders)

- Accept and involve the public/other consumers as legitimate partners.
- Plan carefully and evaluate your efforts with a focus on your strengths, weaknesses, opportunities, and threats.
- Listen to the public's specific concerns.

- Be honest, frank, and open.
- Coordinate and collaborate with other credible sources.
- Meet the needs of the media.
- Speak clearly and with compassion.

Chief Risk Officer

The Chief Risk Officer (CRO) or chief risk management officer (CRMO) of a corporation is the executive accountable for enabling the efficient and effective governance of significant risks, and related opportunities, to a business and its various segments. Risks are commonly categorized as strategic, reputational, operational, financial, or compliance-related. CRO's are accountable to the Executive Committee and The Board for enabling the business to balance risk and reward. In more complex organizations, they are generally responsible for coordinating the organization's Enterprise Risk Management (ERM) approach.

The position became more common after the Basel Accord, the Sarbanes-Oxley Act, the Turnbull Report

A main priority for the CRO is to ensure that the organisation is in full compliance with applicable regulations (chief compliance officer). They may also deal with topics regarding insurance, internal auditing, corporate investigations, fraud, and information security. CRO's typically have post-graduate education and 20+ years of business experience, with actuarial, accounting, economics, and legal backgrounds common.

Financial Risk Management

Financial risk management is the practice of creating economic value in a firm by using financial instruments to manage exposure to risk, particularly credit risk and market risk. Other types include Foreign exchange, Shape, Volatility, Sector, Liquidity, Inflation risks, etc. Similar to general risk management, financial risk management requires identifying its sources, measuring it, and plans to address them.

Financial risk management can be qualitative and quantitative. As a specialization of risk management, financial risk management focuses on when and how to hedge using financial instruments to manage costly exposures to risk.

In the banking sector worldwide, the Basel Accords are generally adopted by internationally active banks for tracking, reporting and exposing operational, credit and market risks.

When to use Financial Risk Management

Finance theory (i.e., financial economics) prescribes that a firm should take on a project when it increases shareholder value. Finance theory also shows that firm managers cannot create value for shareholders, also called its investors, by taking on projects that shareholders could do for themselves at the same cost.

When applied to financial risk management, this implies that firm managers should not hedge risks that investors can hedge for themselves at the same cost. This notion was captured by the hedging irrelevance proposition: *In a perfect market, the firm cannot create value by hedging a risk when the price of bearing that risk within the firm is the same as the price of bearing it outside of the firm.* In practice, financial markets are not likely to be perfect markets.

This suggests that firm managers likely have many opportunities to create value for shareholders using financial risk management. The trick is to determine which risks are cheaper for the firm to manage than the shareholders. A general rule of thumb, however, is that market risks that result in unique risks for the firm are the best candidates for financial risk management.

The concepts of financial risk management change dramatically in the international realm. Multinational Corporations are faced with many different obstacles in overcoming these challenges. There has been some research on the risks firms must consider when operating in many countries, such as the three kinds of foreign exchange exposure for various future time horizons: transactions exposure, accounting exposure, and economic exposure.

Megaprojects (sometimes also called "major programs") have been shown to be particularly risky in terms of finance. Financial risk management is therefore particularly pertinent for megaprojects and special methods have been developed for such risk management.

2

Operational Risk Management

The term Operational Risk Management (ORM) is defined as a continual cyclic process which includes risk assessment, risk decision making, and implementation of risk controls, which results in acceptance, mitigation, or avoidance of risk. ORM is the oversight of operational risk, including the risk of loss resulting from inadequate or failed internal processes and systems; human factors; or external events.

Four Principles of ORM

The U.S. Department of Defence summarizes the principles of ORM as follows:

- Accept risk when benefits outweigh the cost.
- Accept no unnecessary risk.
- Anticipate and manage risk by planning.
- Make risk decisions at the right level.

Three Levels of ORM

In Depth : In depth risk management is used before a project is implemented, when there is plenty of time to plan and prepare. Examples of in depth methods include training, drafting instructions and requirements, and acquiring personal protective equipment.

Deliberate: Deliberate risk management is used at routine periods through the implementation of a project or process. Examples include quality assurance, on-the-job training, safety briefs, performance reviews, and safety checks.

Time Critical: Time critical risk management is used during operational exercises or execution of tasks. It is defined as the effective use of all available resources by individuals, crews, and teams to safely and effectively accomplish the mission or task using risk management concepts when time and resources are limited. Examples of tools used includes execution check-lists and change management. This requires a high degree of situational awareness.

ORM Process

In Depth

The International Organization for Standardization defines the risk management process in a four-step model:

1. Establish context
2. Risk assessment
    - o Risk identification
    - o Risk analysis
    - o Risk evaluation
3. Risk treatment
4. Monitor and review.

This process is cyclic as any changes to the situation (such as operating environment or needs of the unit) requires re-evaluation per step one.

Deliberate

The U.S. Department of Defence summarizes the deliberate level of ORM process in a five-step model:

1. Identify hazards
2. Assess hazards
3. Make risk decisions
4. Implement controls
5. Supervise (and watch for changes).

Time Critical

The U.S. Navy summarizes the time critical risk management process in a four-step model:

Assess the Situation

The three conditions of the Assess step are task loading, additive conditions, and human factors.

- Task loading refers to the negative effect of increased tasking on performance of the tasks.
- Additive factors refers to having a situational awareness of the cumulative effect of variables (conditions, etc.).
- Human factors refers to the limitations of the ability of the human body and mind to adapt to the work environment (e.g. stress, fatigue, impairment, lapses of attention, confusion, and willful violations of regulations).

Balance Uour Resources

This refers to balancing resources in three different ways:

- Balancing resources and options available. This means evaluating and leveraging all the informational, labor, equipment, and material resources available.
- Balancing Resources verses hazards. This means estimating how well prepared you are to safely accomplish a task and making a judgement call.
- Balancing individual verses team effort. This means observing individual risk warning signs. It also means observing how well the team is communicating, knows the roles that each member is supposed to play, and the stress level and participation level of each team member.

Communicate Risks and Intentions

- Communicate hazards and intentions.
- Communicate to the right people.
- Use the right communication style. Asking questions is a technique to opening the lines of communication. A direct and forceful style of communication gets a specific result from a specific situation.

Do and Debrief

This is accomplished in three different phases:

- Mission Completion is a point where the exercise can be evaluated and reviewed in full.

- Execute and Gauge Risk involves managing change and risk while an exercise is in progess.
- Future Performance Improvements refers to preparing a "lessons learned" for the next team that plans or executes a task.

Benefits of ORM

1. Reduction of operational loss.
2. Lower compliance/auditing costs.
3. Early detection of unlawful activities.
4. Reduced exposure to future risks.

Chief Operational Risk Officer

The role of the Chief Operational Risk Officer (CORO) continues to evolve and gain importance. In addition to being responsible for setting up a robust Operational Risk Management function at companies, the role also plays an important part in increasing awareness of the benefits of sound operational risk management.

Most complex financial institutions have a Chief Operational Risk Officer. The position is also required for Banks that fall into the Basel II Advanced Measurement Approach "mandatory" category.

ORM Software

The impact of the Enron failure and the implementation of the Sarbanes-Oxley Act has caused several software development companies to create enterprise-wide software packages to manage risk. These software systems allow the financial audit to be executed at lower cost.

Forrester Research has identified 115 Governance, Risk and Compliance vendors that cover operational risk management projects. Active Agenda is an open source project dedicated to operational risk management.

Risk

Risk is the potential that a chosen action or activity (including the choice of inaction) will lead to a loss (an undesirable outcome).

The notion implies that a choice having an influence on the outcome exists (or existed). Potential losses themselves may also be called "risks". Almost any human endeavour carries some risk, but some are much more risky than others.

Historical Background

The Oxford English Dictionary cites the earliest use of the word in English (in the spelling of *risque*) as from 1621, and the spelling as *risk* from 1655. It defines *risk* as: (Exposure to) the possibility of loss, injury, or other adverse or unwelcome circumstance; a chance or situation involving such a possibility.

For the sociologist Niklas Luhmann the term 'risk' is a neologism that appeared with the transition from traditional to modern society. "In the Middle Ages the term *risicum* was used in highly specific contexts, above all sea trade and its ensuing legal problems of loss and damage." In the vernacular languages of the 16th century the words *rischio* and *riezgo* were used. This was introduced to continental Europe, through interaction with Middle Eastern and North African Arab traders.

In the English language the term *risk* appeared only in the 17th century, and "seems to be imported from continental Europe." When the terminology of *risk* took ground, it replaced the older notion that thought "in terms of good and bad fortune." Niklas Luhmann (1996) seeks to explain this transition: "Perhaps, this was simply a loss of plausibility of the old rhetorics of *Fortuna* as an allegorical figure of religious content and of *prudentia* as a (noble) virtue in the emerging commercial society."

Scenario analysis matured during Cold War confrontations between major powers, notably the United States and the Soviet Union. It became widespread in insurance circles in the 1970s when major oil tanker disasters forced a more comprehensive foresight.

The scientific approach to risk entered finance in the 1960s with the advent of the capital asset pricing model and became increasingly important in the 1980s when financial derivatives proliferated. It reached general professions in the 1990s when the power of personal computing allowed for widespread data collection and numbers crunching.

Governments are using it, for example, to set standards for environmental regulation, e.g. "pathway analysis" as practiced by the United States Environmental Protection Agency.

Definitions of Risk

The many inconsistent and ambiguous meanings attached to "risk" lead to widespread confusion and also mean that very different approaches to risk management are taken in different fields. For example:

The ISO 31000 (2009)/ISO Guide 73 definition of risk is the 'effect of uncertainty on objectives'. In this definition, uncertainties include events (which may or not happen) and uncertainties caused by a lack of information or ambiguity. This definition also includes both negative and positive impacts on objectives.

Another definition is that risks are future problems that can be avoided or mitigated, rather than current ones that must be immediately addressed.

Risk can be seen as relating to the Probability of uncertain future events.. For example, according to Factor Analysis of Information Risk, risk is: the probable frequency and probable magnitude of future loss. In computer science this definition is used by The Open Group.

OHSAS (Occupational Health & Safety Advisory Services) defines risk as the product of the probability of a hazard resulting in an adverse event, times the severity of the event.

In information security risk is defined as "the potential that a given threat will exploit vulnerabilities of an asset or group of assets and thereby cause harm to the organization",

Financial risk is often defined as the unexpected variability or volatility of returns and thus includes both potential worse-than-expected as well as better-than-expected returns. References to negative risk below should be read as applying to positive impacts or opportunity (e.g., for "loss" read "loss or gain") unless the context precludes this interpretation.

The related term "hazard" is used to mean something that could cause harm.

As risk carries so many different meanings there are many formal methods used to assess or to "measure" risk. Some of the quantitative definitions of risk are well-grounded in statistics theory and lead naturally to statistical estimates, but some are more subjective. For example in many cases a critical factor is human decision making.

Even when statistical estimates are available, in many cases risk is associated with rare failures of some kind, and data may be sparse.

Often, the probability of a negative event is estimated by using the frequency of past similar events or by event tree methods, but probabilities for rare failures may be difficult to estimate if an event tree cannot be formulated. This makes risk assessment difficult in hazardous industries (for example nuclear energy) where the frequency of failures is rare and harmful consequences of failure are very high.

Statistical methods may also require the use of a Cost function, which in turn often requires the calculation of the cost of the loss of human life, a difficult problem. One approach is to ask what people are willing to pay to insure against death, and radiological release (e.g., GBq of radio-iodine), but as the answers depend very strongly on the circumstances it is not clear that this approach is effective.

Mathematical Formulations

In statistics, the notion of risk is often modelled as the expected value of some outcome seen as undesirable. This combines the probabilities of various possible events and some assessment of the corresponding harms into a single value. In a formula that can be used in the simple case of a binary possibility (accident or no accident), risk is then:

Risk=(probability of the accident occurring)×(cxccted loss in case of the accide)

For example: if activity X may suffer an accident of A at a probability of 0.01 with a loss of 1000, the total risk is a loss of 10, since that is the product of 0.01 and 1000.

One of the first major uses of this concept was at the planning of the Delta Works in 1953, a flood protection program in the Netherlands, with the aid of the mathematician David van Dantzig. The kind of risk analysis pioneered here has become common today in fields like nuclear power, aerospace and the chemical industry. In statistical decision theory, the risk function is defined as the expected value of a given loss function as a function of the decision rule used to make decisions in the face of uncertainty.

Risk Versus Uncertainty

Risk: Combination of the likelihood of an occurrence of a hazardous event or exposure(s) and the severity of injury or ill health that can be caused by the event or exposure(s)

In his seminal work *Risk, Uncertainty, and Profit,* Frank Knight (1921) established the distinction between risk and uncertainty.

> *"... Uncertainty must be taken in a sense radically distinct from the familiar notion of Risk, from which it has never been properly separated. The term "risk," as loosely used in everyday speech and in economic discussion, really covers two things which, functionally at least, in their causal relations to the phenomena of economic organization, are categorically different.... The essential fact is that "risk" means in some cases a quantity susceptible of measurement, while at other times it is something distinctly not of this character; and there are far-reaching and crucial differences in the bearings of the phenomenon depending on which of the two is really present and operating.... It will appear that a measurable uncertainty, or "risk" proper, as we shall use the term, is so far different from an unmeasurable one that it is not in effect an uncertainty at all. We... accordingly restrict the term "uncertainty" to cases of the non-quantitive type.:"*

Thus, Knightian uncertainty is immeasurable, not possible to calculate, while in the Knightian sense risk is measurable.

Another distinction between risk and uncertainty is proposed in *How to Measure Anything: Finding the Value of Intangibles in Business* and *The Failure of Risk Management: Why It's Broken and How to Fix It* by Doug Hubbard:

Uncertainty: The lack of complete certainty, that is, the existence of more than one possibility. The "true" outcome/state/result/ value is not known.

Measurement of Uncertainty: A set of probabilities assigned to a set of possibilities. Example: "There is a 60% chance this market will double in five years"

Risk: A state of uncertainty where some of the possibilities involve a loss, catastrophe, or other undesirable outcome.

Measurement of Risk: A set of possibilities each with quantified probabilities and quantified losses. Example: "There is a 40% chance the proposed oil well will be dry with a loss of $12 million in exploratory drilling costs".

In this sense, Hubbard uses the terms so that one may have uncertainty without risk but not risk without uncertainty. We can be uncertain about the winner of a contest, but unless we have some personal stake in it, we have no risk. If we bet money on the outcome of the contest, then we have a risk. In both cases there are more than one outcome. The measure of uncertainty refers only to the probabilities assigned to outcomes, while the measure of risk requires both probabilities for outcomes and losses quantified for outcomes.

Risk as a Vector Quantity

Hubbard also argues that defining risk as the product of impact and probability presumes (probably incorrectly) that the decision makers are risk neutral. Only for a risk neutral person is the "certain monetary equivalent" exactly equal to the probability of the loss times the amount of the loss. For example, a risk neutral person would consider 20% chance of winning $1 million exactly equal to $200,000 (or a 20% chance of losing $1 million to be exactly equal to losing $200,000). However, most decision makers are not actually risk neutral and would not consider these equivalent choices. This gave rise to Prospect theory and Cumulative prospect theory.

Hubbard proposes instead that risk is a kind of "vector quantity" that does not collapse the probability and magnitude of a risk by presuming anything about the risk tolerance of the decision maker. Risks are simply described as a set or function of possible loss amounts each associated with specific probabilities. How this array is collapsed into a single value cannot be done until the risk tolerance of the decision maker is quantified.

Risk can be both negative and positive, but it tends to be the negative side that people focus on. This is because some things can be dangerous, such as putting their own or someone else's life at risk. Risks concern people as they think that they will have a negative effect on their future.

Insurance and Health Risk

Insurance is a risk-reducing investment in which the buyer pays a small fixed amount to be protected from a potential large loss. Gambling is a risk-increasing investment, wherein money on hand is risked for a possible large return, but with the possibility of losing it all.

Purchasing a lottery ticket is a very risky investment with a high chance of no return and a small chance of a very high return. In contrast, putting money in a bank at a defined rate of interest is a risk-averse action that gives a guaranteed return of a small gain and precludes other investments with possibly higher gain.

Risks in personal health may be reduced by primary prevention actions that decrease early causes of illness or by secondary prevention actions after a person has clearly measured clinical signs or symptoms recognized as risk factors. Tertiary prevention reduces the negative impact of an already established disease by restoring function and reducing disease-related complications.

Ethical medical practice requires careful discussion of risk factors with individual patients to obtain informed consent for secondary and tertiary prevention efforts, whereas public health efforts in primary prevention require education of the entire population at risk. In each case, careful communication about risk factors, likely outcomes and certainty must distinguish between causal events that must be decreased and associated events that may be merely consequences rather than causes.

Information Technology Risk

Information technology risk, or IT risk, IT-related risk, is a risk related to information technology. This relatively new term due to an increasing awareness that information security is simply one facet of a multitude of risks that are relevant to IT and the real world processes it supports.

The increasing dependencies of modern society on information and computers networks (both in private and public sectors, including military) has led to a new terms like IT risk and Cyberwarfare.

Information Security Risk

Information security means protecting information and information systems from unauthorized access, use, disclosure, disruption, modification, perusal, inspection, recording or destruction.

Information security grew out of practices and procedures of computer security.

Information security has grown to information assurance (IA) i.e. is the practice of managing risks related to the use, processing, storage, and transmission of information or data and the systems and processes used for those purposes.

While focused dominantly on information in digital form, the full range of IA encompasses not only digital but also analog or physical form.

Information assurance is interdisciplinary and draws from multiple fields, including accounting, fraud examination, forensic science, management science, systems engineering, security engineering, and criminology, in addition to computer science.

So, *IT risk* is narrowly focused on computer security, while *information security* extends on risks related to other forms of information (paper, microfilm). *Information assurance* risks include the ones related to the consistency of the business information stored in IT systems and the one stored on other means and the relevant business consequences.

Economic Risk

Economic risks can be manifested in lower incomes or higher expenditures than expected. The causes can be many, for instance, the hike in the price for raw materials, the lapsing of deadlines for construction of a new operating facility, disruptions in a produciion process, emergence of a serious competitor on the market, the loss of key personnel, the change of a political regime, or natural disasters. Reference class forecasting was developed to eliminate or reduce economic risk.

In Business

Means of assessing risk vary widely between professions. Indeed, they may define these professions; for example, a doctor manages medical risk, while a civil engineer manages risk of structural failure. A professional code of ethics is usually focused on risk assessment and mitigation (by the professional on behalf of client, public, society or life in general).

In the workplace, incidental and inherent risks exist. Incidental risks are those that occur naturally in the business but are not part of the core of the business. Inherent risks have a negative effect on the operating profit of the business.

Risk-sensitive Industries

Some industries manage risk in a highly quantified and enumerated way. These include the nuclear power and aircraft industries, where the possible failure of a complex series of engineered systems could result in highly undesirable outcomes. The usual measure of risk for a class of events is then:

R = probability of the event × C

The total risk is then the product of the individual class-risks.

In the nuclear industry, consequence is often measured in terms of off-site radiological release, and this is often banded into five or six decade-wide bands.

The risks are evaluated using fault tree/event tree techniques. Where these risks are low, they are normally considered to be "Broadly Acceptable". A higher level of risk (typically up to 10 to 100 times what is considered Broadly Acceptable) has to be justified against the costs of reducing it further and the possible benefits that make it tolerable—these risks are described as "Tolerable if ALARP". Risks beyond this level are classified as "Intolerable".

The level of risk deemed Broadly Acceptable has been considered by regulatory bodies in various countries—an early attempt by UK government regulator and academic F. R. Farmer used the example of hill-walking and similar activities, which have definable risks that people appear to find acceptable. This resulted in the so-called Farmer Curve of acceptable probability of an event versus its consequence.

The technique as a whole is usually referred to as Probabilistic Risk Assessment (PRA) (or Probabilistic Safety Assessment, PSA).

In Finance

In finance, risk is the probability that an investment's actual return will be different than expected. This includes the possibility of losing some or all of the original investment. In a view advocated by Damodaran, risk includes not only "downside risk" but also "upside risk" (returns that exceed expectations).

Some regard a calculation of the standard deviation of the historical returns or average returns of a specific investment as providing some historical measure of risk; see modern portfolio theory. Financial risk may be market-dependent, determined by numerous market factors, or operational, resulting from fraudulent behavior (e.g. Bernard Madoff). Recent studies suggest that testosterone level plays a major role in risk taking during financial decisions.

In finance, *risk* has no one definition, but some theorists, notably Ron Dembo, have defined quite general methods to assess risk as an expected after-the-fact level of regret. Such methods have been uniquely successful in limiting interest rate risk in financial markets. Financial markets are considered to be a proving ground for general methods of risk assessment. However, these methods are also hard to understand.

The mathematical difficulties interfere with other social goods such as disclosure, valuation and transparency. In particular, it is not always obvious if such financial instruments are "hedging" (purchasing/selling a financial instrument specifically to reduce or cancel out the risk in another investment) or "speculation" (increasing measurable risk and exposing the investor to catastrophic loss in pursuit of very high windfalls that increase expected value).

As regret measures rarely reflect actual human risk-aversion, it is difficult to determine if the outcomes of such transactions will be satisfactory. Risk seeking describes an individual whose utility function's second derivative is positive. Such an individual would willingly (actually pay a premium to) assume all risk in the economy and is hence not likely to exist.

In financial markets, one may need to measure credit risk, information timing and source risk, probability model risk, and legal risk if there are regulatory or civil actions taken as a result of some "investor's regret". Knowing one's risk appetite in conjunction with one's financial well-being are most crucial.

A fundamental idea in finance is the relationship between risk and return. The greater the potential return one might seek, the greater the risk that one generally assumes. A free market reflects this principle in the pricing of an instrument: strong demand for a safer instrument drives its price higher (and its return proportionately lower), while weak demand for a riskier instrument drives its price lower (and its potential return thereby higher).

"For example, a US Treasury bond is considered to be one of the safest investments and, when compared to a corporate bond, provides a lower rate of return. The reason for this is that a corporation is much more likely to go bankrupt than the U.S. government. Because the risk of investing in a corporate bond is higher, investors are offered a higher rate of return."

The most popular, and also the most vilified lately risk measurement is Value-at-Risk (VaR). There are different types of VaR-Long Term VaR, Marginal VaR, Factor VaR and Shock VaR The latter is used in measuring risk during the extreme market stress conditions.

In Public Works

In a peer reviewed study of risk in public works projects located in twenty nations on five continents, Flyvbjerg, Holm, and Buhl (2002, 2005) documented high risks for such ventures for both costs and demand. Actual costs of projects were typically higher than estimated costs; cost overruns of 50% were common, overruns above 100% not uncommon. Actual demand was often lower than estimated; demand shortfalls of 25% were common, of 50% not uncommon.

Due to such cost and demand risks, cost-benefit analyses of public works projects have proved to be highly uncertain.

The main causes of cost and demand risks were found to be optimism bias and strategic misrepresentation. Measures identified to mitigate this type of risk are better governance through incentive alignment and the use of reference class forecasting.

In Human Services

Huge ethical and political issues arise when human beings themselves are seen or treated as 'risks', or when the risk decision making of people who use human services might have an impact on that service. The experience of many people who rely on human services for support is that 'risk' is often used as a reason to prevent them from gaining further independence or fully accessing the community, and that these services are often unnecessarily risk averse.

Risk in Psychology

Regret

In decision theory, regret (and anticipation of regret) can play a significant part in decision-making, distinct from risk aversion (preferring the status quo in case one becomes worse off).

Framing

Framing is a fundamental problem with all forms of risk assessment. In particular, because of bounded rationality (our brains get overloaded, so we take mental shortcuts), the risk of extreme events is discounted because the probability is too low to evaluate intuitively. As an example, one of the leading causes of death is road accidents caused by drunk driving—partly because any given driver frames the problem by largely or totally ignoring the risk of a serious or fatal accident.

For instance, an extremely disturbing event (an attack by hijacking, or moral hazards) may be ignored in analysis despite the fact it has occurred and has a nonzero probability. Or, an event that everyone agrees is inevitable may be ruled out of analysis due to greed or an unwillingness to admit that it is believed to be inevitable. These human tendencies for error and wishful thinking often affect even the most rigorous applications of the scientific method and are a major concern of the philosophy of science.

All decision-making under uncertainty must consider cognitive bias, cultural bias, and notational bias: No group of people assessing risk is immune to "groupthink": acceptance of obviously wrong answers simply because it is socially painful to disagree, where there are conflicts of interest. One effective way to solve framing problems in risk assessment or measurement (although some argue that risk cannot be measured, only assessed) is to raise others' fears or personal ideals by way of completeness.

Neurobiology of Framing

Framing involves other information that affects the outcome of a risky decision. The right prefrontal cortex has been shown to take a more global perspective while greater left prefrontal activity relates to local or focal processing

From the Theory of Leaky Modules McElroy and Seta proposed that they could predictably alter the framing effect by the selective manipulation of regional prefrontal activity with finger tapping or monaural listening.

The result was as expected. Rightward tapping or listening had the effect of narrowing attention such that the frame was ignored. This is a practical way of manipulating regional cortical activation to affect risky decisions, especially because directed tapping or listening is easily done.

Fear as Intuitive Risk Assessment

For the time being, people rely on their fear and hesitation to keep them out of the most profoundly unknown circumstances.

In *The Gift of Fear*, Gavin de Becker argues that "True fear is a gift. It is a survival signal that sounds only in the presence of danger. Yet unwarranted fear has assumed a power over us that it holds over no other creature on Earth. It need not be this way."

Risk could be said to be the way we collectively measure and share this "true fear"—a fusion of rational doubt, irrational fear, and a set of unquantified biases from our own experience.

The field of behavioral finance focuses on human risk-aversion, asymmetric regret, and other ways that human financial behavior varies from what analysts call "rational". Risk in that case is the degree of uncertainty associated with a return on an asset.

Recognizing and respecting the irrational influences on human decision making may do much to reduce disasters caused by naive risk assessments that pretend to rationality but in fact merely fuse many shared biases together.

Risk Assessment and Management

Because planned actions are subject to large cost and benefit risks, proper risk assessment and risk management for such actions are crucial to making them successful.

Since risk assessment and management is essential in security management, both are tightly related. Security assessment methodologies like CRAMM contain risk assessment modules as an important part of the first steps of the methodology. On the other hand, risk assessment methodologies like Mehari evolved to become security assessment methodologies. A ISO standard on risk management (Principles and guidelines on implementation) was published under code ISO 31000 on 13 November 2009.

Risk and Size

In the book *Megaprojects and Risk,* Professor Bent Flyvbjerg (with Nils Bruzelius and Werner Rothengatter) demonstrates that big ventures (big construction projects, big capital investments, etc.) are highly risky. For instance, such ventures typically have high cost overruns, benefit shortfalls, and schedule delays, plus negative and unanticipated social and environmental impacts.

Risk in Auditing

The audit risk model expresses the risk of an auditor providing an inappropriate opinion of a commercial entity's financial statements. It can be analytically expressed as:

$$AR = IR \times CR \times DR$$

Where AR is *audit risk,* IR is *inherent risk,* CR is *control risk* and DR is *detection risk.*

Optimism Bias

Optimism bias is the demonstrated systematic tendency for people to be overly optimistic about the outcome of planned actions. This includes over-estimating the likelihood of positive events and under-estimating the likelihood of negative events. Along with the illusion of control and illusory superiority, it is one of the positive illusions to which people are generally susceptible. Excessive optimism can result in cost overruns, benefit shortfalls, and delays when plans are implemented or expensive projects are built. More generally, they are related to the initiation of military conflicts and the creation of economic bubbles.

Experimental Demonstration

Armor and Taylor review a number of studies that have found optimism bias in different kinds of judgment. These include:

- Second-year MBA students overestimated the number of job offers they would receive and their starting salary.
- Students overestimated the scores they would achieve on exams.
- Almost all newlyweds in a US study expected their marriage to last a lifetime, even while aware of the divorce statistics.
- Professional financial analysts consistently overestimated corporate earnings.
- Most smokers believe they are less at risk of developing smoking-related diseases than others who smoke.

Students in one study rated themselves as much less likely than their peers (students of the same sex at the same college) to experience negative life events such as developing a drinking problem, having a heart attack, being fired from a job, or divorcing a few years after getting married. This effect, called unrealistic personal optimism, has been replicated and extended in between-subject research. This research shows that optimistic bias is more prevalent in people with greater left-prefrontal activation.

Optimism bias does not apply universally. For example, people overestimate their chances of experiencing very rare events, including negative events.

Possible Effects of Overconfidence

Increased Risk Taking and Insufficient Preventive Care

Optimism bias can induce people to underinvest in primary and preventive care and other risk-reducing behaviors, such as abstinence from smoking. The overconfident may also inadequately react to legal threats and incentives, undermining the deterrent effect of liability rules.

Increased Risk for Financial Problems

Overconfidence causes many people to grossly underestimate their odds of making a payment late. Statistically, many people are quite likely to make at least one payment late due to the normal range of difficulties and delays in day-to-day life. Overconfidence bias causes these people to grossly underestimate the odds of this happening and therefore to accept grossly punitive fees and rates (e.g., an interest rate of nearly 30% on a credit card or similar line of credit) as a result of otherwise minor transgressions such as a late payment. Companies have exploited this bias by increasing interest rates to punitive rates for any late payment, even if it is to another creditor. Overconfidence bias makes these terms more acceptable to borrowers than if they were accurately calibrated.

Overconfidence bias also causes many people to substantially underestimate the probability of having serious financial or liquidity problems, such as from a sudden job loss or severe illness. This can cause them to take on excessive debt under the expectation that they will do better than average in the future and be readily able to pay it off.

Overconfidence, Locus of Control, and Depression

Overconfidence bias may cause many people to overestimate their degree of control and their odds of success. This may be protective against depression—since Seligman and Maier's model of depression includes a sense of learned helplessness and loss of predictability and control. Depressives tend to be more accurate and less overconfident in their assessments of the probabilities of good and bad events occurring to others, but they tend to overestimate the probability of bad events happening to them. This has caused some researchers to consider that overconfidence bias may be adaptive or protective in some situations.

Optimism Bias and Planning

Optimism bias arises in relation to estimates of costs and benefits and duration of tasks. It must be accounted for explicitly in appraisals if these are to be realistic. Optimism bias typically results in cost overruns, benefit shortfalls, and delays when plans are implemented.

The UK government explicitly acknowledges that optimism bias is a problem in planning and budgeting and has developed measures for dealing with optimism bias in government (HM Treasury 2003). The UK Department for Transport requires project planners to use so-called optimism bias uplifts for large transport projects in order to arrive at accurate budgets for planned ventures (Flyvbjerg and Cowi 2004).

In a debate in Harvard Business Review, between Daniel Kahneman, Dan Lovallo, and Bent Flyvbjerg, Flyvbjerg (2003)—while acknowledging the existence of optimism bias—pointed out that what appears to be optimism bias may actually be strategic misrepresentation. Planners may deliberately underestimate costs and overestimate benefits in order to get their projects approved, especially when projects are large and when organizational and political pressures are high. Kahneman and Lovallo (2003) maintained that optimism bias is the main problem.

Optimism Bias and Reference Class Forecasting

Reference class forecasting was developed to eliminate or reduce optimism bias in forecasting, planning, and decision making.

Mechanisms

A brain-imaging study found that, when imagining negative future events, signals in the amygdala, an emotion centre of the brain, are weaker than when remembering past negative events. This weakened consideration of possible negative outcomes is one possible mechanism for optimism bias. The activity of brain regions that are known to malfunction in psychological depression also predict the optimism bias.

Precautionary Principle

The precautionary principle or precautionary approach states that if an action or policy has a suspected risk of causing harm to the public or to the environment, in the absence of scientific consensus that the action or policy is harmful, the burden of proof that it is *not* harmful falls on those taking the action.

This principle allows policy makers to make discretionary decisions in situations where there is the possibility of harm from taking a particular course or making a certain decision when extensive scientific knowledge on the matter is lacking. The principle implies that there is a social responsibility to protect the public from exposure to harm, when scientific investigation has found a plausible risk. These protections can be relaxed only if further scientific findings emerge that provide sound evidence that no harm will result.

In some legal systems, as in the law of the European Union, the application of the precautionary principle has been made a statutory requirement.

Formulations of the Precautionary Principle

Many definitions of the precautionary principle exist. Precaution may be defined as "*caution in advance*," "*caution practised in the context of uncertainty*," or *informed prudence*. All definitions have two key elements.

1. an expression of a need by decision-makers to anticipate harm before it occurs. Within this element lies an implicit reversal of the onus of proof: under the precautionary principle it is the responsibility of an activity proponent to establish that the proposed activity will not (or is very unlikely to) result in significant harm.
2. the establishment of an obligation, if the level of harm may be high, for action to prevent or minimise such harm even when the absence of scientific certainty makes it difficult to predict the likelihood of harm occurring, or the level of harm should it occur. The need for control measures increases with both the level of possible harm and the degree of uncertainty.

One of the primary foundations of the precautionary principle, and globally accepted definitions, results from the work of the Rio Conference, or "Earth Summit" in 1992. Principle #15 of the Rio Declaration notes:

> *"In order to protect the environment, the precautionary approach shall be widely applied by States according to their capabilities. Where there are threats of serious or irreversible damage, lack of full scientific certainty shall not be used as a reason for postponing cost-*

effective measures to prevent environmental degradation."

This definition is important for several reasons. First, it explains the idea that scientific uncertainty should not preclude preventative measures to protect the environment. Second, the use of "cost-effective" measures indicates that costs can be considered. This is different from a "no-regrets" approach, which ignores the costs of preventative action.

The 1998 Wingspread Statement on the Precautionary Principle summarizes the principle this way: "When an activity raises threats of harm to human health or the environment, precautionary measures should be taken even if some cause and effect relationships are not fully established scientifically." (The Wingspread Conference on the Precautionary Principle was convened by the Science and Environmental Health Network).

The February 2, 2000 European Commission Communication on the Precautionary Principle notes: "The precautionary principle applies where scientific evidence is insufficient, inconclusive or uncertain and preliminary scientific evaluation indicates that there are reasonable grounds for concern that the potentially dangerous effects on the environment, human, animal or plant health may be inconsistent with the high level of protection chosen by the EU".

The January 29, 2000 Cartagena Protocol on Biosafety says: "Lack of scientific certainty due to insufficient relevant scientific information. . . shall not prevent the Party of import, in order to avoid or minimize such potential adverse effects, from taking a decision, as appropriate, with regard to the import of the living modified organism in question."

It is important to emphasize that, although this principle operates in the context of scientific uncertainty, it is considered by its proponents to be applicable only when, on the basis of the best scientific advice available, there is good reason to believe that harmful effects might occur.

The precautionary principle is most often applied in the context of the impact of human actions on the environment and human health, as both involve complex systems where the consequences of actions may be unpredictable.

As applied to environmental policy, the precautionary principle stipulates that for practices such as the release of radiation or toxins or massive deforestation the burden of proof lies with the advocates.

Concerning potential risks to public health, examples of cases in which the precautionary principle has been advocated (but not always accepted) are: the commercialization of genetically modified foods, the use of growth hormones in cattle raising, measures to prevent the "mad cow" disease, health claims linked to phthalates in PVC toys, among many others.

An important element of the precautionary principle is that its most meaningful applications pertain to those that are potentially irreversible, for example where biodiversity may be reduced. With respect to bans on substances like mercury in thermometers, freon in refrigeration, or even carbon dioxide exhaust from automobile engines and power plants, it implies:

A willingness to take action in advance of scientific proof [or] evidence of the need for the proposed action on the grounds that further delay will prove ultimately most costly to society and nature, and, in the longer term, selfish and unfair to future generations.

The concept includes an implicit ethical responsibility towards maintaining the integrity of natural systems, and acknowledges the fallibility of human understanding.

Origins and Theory

The formal concept evolved out of the German socio-legal tradition in the 1930s, centering on the concept of good household management. In German the concept is *Vorsorgeprinzip,* which translates into English as *precaution principle.*

Many of the concepts underpinning the precautionary principle pre-date the term's inception. For example, the essence of the principle is captured in a number of cautionary aphorisms such as "an ounce of prevention is worth a pound of cure", "better safe than sorry", and "look before you leap". The precautionary principle may also be interpreted as the evolution of the ancient medical principle of "first, do no harm" to apply to institutions and institutional decision-making processes rather than individuals.

The precautionary principle is in some ways an expansion of the English common law concept of 'duty of care' originating in the decisions of the judge Lord Esher in the late 1800s. According to Lord Esher: "Whenever one person is by circumstances placed in such a position with regard to another that everyone of ordinary sense who did think, would at once recognise that if he did not use ordinary care and skill in his own conduct with regard to those circumstances, he would cause danger or injury to the person, or property of the other, a duty arises to use ordinary care and skill to avoid such danger".

This statement clearly contains elements of foresight and responsibility, but does not refer to a lack of certainty, as the word "would" is used rather than "might", or "could". The other important difference is that the duty of care applies only to people and property, not to the environment.

In economics, the precautionary principle has been analysed in terms of the effect on rational decision-making of the interaction of irreversibility and uncertainty. Authors such as Epstein (1980) and Arrow and Fischer (1974) show that irreversibility of possible future consequences creates a quasi-option effect which should induce a "risk-neutral" society to favour current decisions that allow for more flexibility in the future. Gollier et al. (2000) conclude that "more scientific uncertainty as to the distribution of a future risk– that is, a larger variability of beliefs– should induce Society to take stronger prevention measures today."

Application

The application of the precautionary principle is hampered by both lack of political will, as well as the wide range of interpretations placed on it. One study identified 14 different formulations of the principle in treaties and nontreaty declarations. R.B. Stewart (2002) reduced the precautionary principle to four basic versions:

1. Scientific uncertainty should not automatically preclude regulation of activities that pose a potential risk of significant harm (Non-Preclusion PP).
2. Regulatory controls should incorporate a margin of safety; activities should be limited below the level at which no adverse effect has been observed or predicted (Margin of Safety PP).

3. Activities that present an uncertain potential for significant harm should be subject to best technology available requirements to minimize the risk of harm unless the proponent of the activity shows that they present no appreciable risk of harm (BAT PP).
4. Activities that present an uncertain potential for significant harm should be prohibited unless the proponent of the activity shows that it presents no appreciable risk of harm (Prohibitory PP).

In deciding how to apply the principle, analysis may use a cost-benefit analysis that factors in both the opportunity cost of not acting, and the option value of waiting for further information before acting. One of the difficulties of the application of the principle in modern policy-making is that there is often an irreducible conflict between different interests, so that the debate necessarily involves politics.

Strong vs. Weak

Strong precaution holds that regulation is required whenever there is a possible risk to health, safety, or the environment, even if the supporting evidence is speculative and even if the economic costs of regulation are high. In 1982, the United Nations World Charter for Nature gave the first international recognition to the strong version of the principle, suggesting that when "potential adverse effects are not fully understood, the activities should not proceed." The widely publicized Wingspread Declaration, from a meeting of environmentalists in 1998, is another example of the strong version. 'Strong precaution' can also be termed as a "no-regrets" principle, where costs are not considered in preventative action.

Weak precaution holds that lack of scientific evidence does not preclude action if damage would otherwise be serious and irreversible. Humans practice weak precaution every day, and often incur costs, to avoid hazards that are far from certain: we do not walk in moderately dangerous areas at night, we exercise, we buy **smoke detectors**, we buckle our seatbelts.

The **weak version** [of the Precautionary Principle] is the least restrictive and allows preventive measures to be taken in the face of uncertainty, but does not require them (eg, Rio Declaration 1992; United Nations Framework Convention of Climate Change 1992). To satisfy the threshold of harm, there must be some evidence relating to both the likelihood of occurrence and the severity of consequences.

Some, but not all, require consideration of the costs of precautionary measures. Weak formulations do not preclude weighing benefits against the costs. Factors other than scientific uncertainty, including economic considerations, may provide legitimate grounds for postponing action. Under weak formulations, the requirement to justify the need for action (the burden of proof) generally falls on those advocating precautionary action. No mention is made of assignment of liability for environmental harm.

Strong versions justify or require precautionary measures and some also establish liability for environmental harm, which is effectively a strong form of "polluter pays". For example, the Earth Charter states: "When knowledge is limited apply a precautionary approach .... Place the burden of proof on those who argue that a proposed activity will not cause significant harm, and make the responsible parties liable for environmental harm." Reversal of proof requires those proposing an activity to prove that the product, process or technology is sufficiently "safe" before approval is granted.

Requiring proof of "no environmental harm" before any action proceeds implies the public is not prepared to accept any environmental risk, no matter what economic or social benefits may arise (Peterson, 2006). At the extreme, such a requirement could involve bans and prohibitions on entire classes of potentially threatening activities or substances (Cooney, 2005). Over time, there has been a gradual transformation of the precautionary principle from what appears in the Rio Declaration to a stronger form that arguably acts as restraint on development in the absence of firm evidence that it will do no harm.

International Agreements and Declarations

The World Charter for Nature, which was adopted by the UN General Assembly in 1982, was the first international endorsement of the precautionary principle. The principle was implemented in an international treaty as early as the 1987 Montreal Protocol, and among other international treaties and declarations [6] is reflected in the 1992 Rio Declaration on Environment and Development (signed at the United Nations Conference on Environment and Development).

"Principle" vs. "Approach"

No introduction to the precautionary principle would be complete without brief reference to the difference between the precautionary principle and the precautionary approach. Principle 15 of the Rio Declaration 1992 states that: "in order to protect the environment, the precautionary approach shall be widely applied by States according to their capabilities.

Where there are threats of serious or irreversible damage, lack of full scientific certainty shall be not used as a reason for postponing cost-effective measures to prevent environmental degradation." As Garcia (1995) pointed out, "the wording, largely similar to that of the principle, is subtly different in that: (1) it recognizes that there may be differences in local capabilities to apply the approach, and (2) it calls for cost-effectiveness in applying the approach, e.g., taking economic and social costs into account." The 'approach' is generally considered a softening of the 'principle'.

"As Recuerda has noted, the distinction between the ′precautionary principle` and a ′precautionary approach` is diffuse and, in some contexts, controversial. In the negotiations of international declarations, the United States has opposed the use of the term ′principle` because this term has special connotations in legal language, due to the fact that a ′principle of law` is a source of law.

This means that it is compulsory, so a court can quash or confirm a decision through the application of the precautionary principle. In this sense, the precautionary principle is not a simple idea or a desideratum but a source of law. This is the legal status of the precautionary principle in the European Union. On the other hand, an ′approach` usually does not have the same meaning,16 although in some particular cases an approach could be binding. A precautionary approach is a particular ′lens` used to identify risk that every prudent person possesses (Recuerda, 2008)

European Commission

On 2 February 2000, the European Commission issued a Communication on the precautionary principle, in which it adopted a procedure for the application of this concept, but without giving a detailed definition of it. Paragraph 2 of article 191 of the Lisbon Treaty states that;

> *"Union policy on the environment shall aim at a high level of protection taking into account the diversity of situations in the various regions of the Union. It shall be based on the precautionary principle and on the principles that preventive action should be taken, that environmental damage should as a priority be rectified at source and that the polluter should pay."*

After the adoption of the European Commission's Communication on the precautionary principle, the principle has come to inform much EU policy, including that in areas beyond that of environmental policy. It is implemented, for example, in the EU food law and also affects, among others, policies relating to consumer protection, trade and research, and technological development.

While a comprehensive definition of the precautionary principle was never formally adopted by the EU, a working definition and implementation strategy for the EU context has been proposed by Rene von Schomberg in Fisher et al. (2006):

> *"Where, following an assessment of available scientific information, there are reasonable grounds for concern for the possibility of adverse effects but scientific uncertainty persists, provisional risk management measures based on a broad cost/benefit analysis whereby priority will be given to human health and the environment, necessary to ensure the chosen high level of protection in the Community and proportionate to this level of protection, may be adopted, pending further scientific information for a more comprehensive risk assessment, without having to wait until the reality and seriousness of those adverse effects become fully apparent".*

USA

On July 18, 2005, the City of San Francisco passed a Precautionary Principle Purchasing ordinance, which requires the city to weigh the environmental and health costs of its $600 million in annual purchases–for everything from cleaning supplies to computers. Members of the Bay Area Working Group on the Precautionary Principle including the Breast Cancer Fund, helped bring this to fruition.

Japan

In 1997, Japan tried to use the consideration of the precautionary principle in a WTO SPS Agreement on the Application of Sanitary and Phytosanitary Measures case, as Japan's requirement to test each variety of agricultural products (apples, cherries, peaches, walnuts, apricots, pears, plums and quinces) for the efficacy of treatment against codling moths was challenged.

This moth is a pest that does not occur in Japan, and whose introduction has the potential to cause serious damage. The United States claimed that it was not necessary to test each variety of a fruit for the efficacy of the treatment, and that this varietal testing requirement was unnecessarily burdensome.

Australia

The most important Australian court case so far, due to its exceptionally detailed consideration of the precautionary principle, is Telstra Corporation Limited v Hornsby Shire Council. The case was heard in the New South Wales Land and Environment Court under Justice CJ Preston (24 April 2006).

The Principle was summarised by reference to the NSW *Protection of the Environment Administration Act 1991*, which itself provides a good definition of the principle:

> *"If there are threats of serious or irreversible environmental damage, lack of full scientific certainty should not be used as a reasoning for postponing measures to prevent environmental degradation. In the application of the principle... decisions should be guided by: (i) careful evaluation to avoid, wherever practicable, serious or irreversible damage to the environment; and*

(ii) an assessment of risk-weighted consequence of various options".

The most significant points of Justice Preston's decision are the following findings:

1. The principle and accompanying need to take precautionary measures is "triggered" when two prior conditions exist: a threat of serious or irreversible damage, and scientific uncertainty as to the extent of possible damage.
2. Once both are satisfied, "a proportionate precautionary measure may be taken to avert the anticipated threat of environmental damage, but it should be proportionate."
3. The threat of serious or irreversible damage should invoke consideration of five factors: the scale of threat (local, regional etc.); the perceived value of the threatened environment; whether the possible impacts are manageable; the level of public concern, and whether there is a rational or scientific basis for the concern.
4. The consideration of the level of scientific uncertainty should involve factors which may include: what would constitute sufficient evidence; the level and kind of uncertainty; and the potential to reduce uncertainty.
5. The principle shifts the burden of proof. If the principle applies, the burden shifts: "a decision maker must assume the threat of serious or irreversible environmental damage is... a reality [and] the burden of showing this threat... is negligible reverts to the proponent..."
6. The precautionary principle invokes preventative action: "the principle permits the taking of preventative measures without having to wait until the reality and seriousness of the threat become fully known".
7. "The principle should not be used to try to avoid all risks."
8. The precautionary measures appropriate will depend on the combined effect of "the degree of seriousness and irreversibility of the threat and the degree of uncertainty... the more significant and uncertain the threat, the

greater...the precaution required". "...measures should be adopted... proportionate to the potential threats".

Corporate

The Body Shop International, a UK-based cosmetics company, recently included the Precautionary Principle in their 2006 Chemicals Strategy.

Environment/Health

Fields typically concerned by the precautionary principle are the possibility of:

- Global warming or abrupt climate change in general
- Extinction of species
- Introduction of new and potentially harmful products into the environment, threatening biodiversity (e.g., genetically modified organisms)
- Threats to public health, due to new diseases and techniques (e.g., AIDS transmitted through blood transfusion)
- Persistent or acute pollution (asbestos, endocrine disruptors...)
- Food safety (e.g., Creutzfeldt-Jakob disease)
- Other new biosafety issues (e.g., artificial life, new molecules).

The precautionary principle is often applied to biological fields because changes cannot be easily contained and have the potential of being global. The principle has less relevance to contained fields such as aeronautics, where the few people undergoing risk have given informed consent (e.g., a test pilot). In the case of technological innovation, containment of impact tends to be more difficult if that technology can self-replicate. Bill Joy emphasized the dangers of replicating genetic technology, nanotechnology, and robotic technology in his article in *Wired Magazine*, "Why the future doesn't need us", though he does not specifically cite the precautionary principle. The application of the principle can be seen in the public policy of requiring pharmaceutical companies to carry out clinical trials to show that new medications are safe.

Oxford based philosopher Nick Bostrom discusses the idea of a future powerful superintelligence, and the risks that we/it face should it attempt to gain atomic level control of matter.

Application of the principle modifies the status of innovation and risk assessment: it is not the risk that must be avoided or amended, but a potential risk that must be prevented. Thus, in the case of regulation of scientific research, there is a third party beyond the scientist and the regulator: the consumer.

In an analysis concerning application of the precautionary principle to nanotechnology, Chris Phoenix and Mike Treder posit that there are *two forms* of the principle, which they call the "strict form" and the "active form".

The former "requires inaction when action might pose a risk", while the latter means "choosing less risky alternatives when they are available, and taking responsibility for potential risks."The academic Thomas Alured Faunce has argued for stronger application of the precautionary principle by chemical and health technology regulators particularly in relation to TI02 and ZNO nanoparticles in sunscreens, biocidal nanosilver in waterways and products whose manufacture, handling or recycling exposes humans to the risk of inhaling multi-walled carbon nanotubes.

Change of Laws Controlling Societal Norms

Associate Justice Martha Sosman's dissent in Goodridge v. Department of Public Health, the decision of the Supreme Judicial Court of Massachusetts that mandated legalization of same sex marriage, is an example of the precautionary principle as applied by analogy to changes in culturally significant social policy. She describes the myriad societal structures that rest on the institution of marriage, and points out the uncertainty of how they will be affected by this re-definition.

The disagreement of the majority illustrates the difficulty of reaching agreement on the value of competing perspectives. Although the Goodridge case involved interpreting the state constitution, the substantive canon in Anglo-American jurisprudence that derogations of fundamental societal values should be narrowly construed is analogous to the precautionary principle favoring a statutory interpretation that comports with rather than damages the common law and established norms.

Resource Management

Several natural resources like fish stocks are now managed by precautionary approach, through Harvest Control Rules (HCR) based upon the precautionary principle. The figure indicates how the principle is implemented in the cod fisheries management proposed by the International Council for the Exploration of the Sea.

In classifying endangered species, the precautionary principle means that if there is doubt about an animal's or plant's exact conservation status, the one that would cause the strongest protective measures to be realized should be chosen. Thus, a species like the Silvery Pigeon that might exist in considerable numbers and simply be under-recorded or might just as probably be long extinct is not classified as "data deficient" or "extinct" (which both do not require any protective action to be taken), but as "critically endangered" (the conservation status that confers the need for the strongest protection), whereas the increasingly rare, but probably not yet endangered Emerald Starling is classified as "data deficient", because there is urgent need for research to clarify its status rather than for conservation action to save it from extinction.

If, for example, a large ground-water body that many people use for drinking water is contaminated by bacteria (e-coli 0157 H7, campylobacter or leptospirosis) and the source of contamination is strongly suspected to be dairy cows but the exact science is not yet able to provide absolute proof, then the cows should be removed from the environment until they are proved, by the dairy industry, not to be the source or until that industry ensures that such contamination will not recur.

Criticisms

Threshold of Plausibility

The Wingspread Statement version of the PP takes the form "When an activity raises threats of harm to human health or the environment, precautionary measures should be taken even if some cause and effect relationships are not fully established scientifically". When applying this principle, it is recommended that society establish a minimal threshold of scientific certainty or plausibility before undertaking precautions. Normally, no minimal threshold of plausibility is specified as a "triggering" condition, so that any indication that a proposed product or activity might harm health or the environment is sufficient to invoke the principle. Often the only precaution taken is a ban on the product or activity.

In Sancho vs. DOE, Helen Gillmor, Senior District Judge, wrote in a dismissal of Wagner's lawsuit which included a popular worry that the LHC could cause "destruction of the earth" by a black hole:

Injury in fact requires some "credible threat of harm." *Cent. Delta Water Agency v. United States*, 306 F.3d 938, 950 (9th Cir. 2002). At most, Wagner has alleged that experiments at the Large Hadron Collider (the "Collider") have "potential adverse consequences." Speculative fear of future harm does not constitute an injury in fact sufficient to confer standing. *Mayfield*, 599 F.3d at 970.

Negative Consequences of Application

The Precautionary Principle may cause resentment, since people are more aware of negative changes than they are positive changes (i.e. a ban is more noted than allowing a proposal to proceed). Because of this effect, a technology which brings advantages may be banned by PP because of its potential for negative impacts, leaving the positive benefits unrealized.

The Hazardous Air Pollutant provisions in the 1990 amendments to the U.S. Clean Air Act are an example of the Precautionary Principle where the onus is now on showing a listed compound is harmless. Under this rule no distinction is made between those air Pollutants that provide a higher or lower risk, so operators tend to choose less-examined agents that are not on the existing list.

A California researcher has pointed out the fallacy of extrapolating possible risk of a proposed product or action, without examining equally closely the possible risks of *not* adopting the proposal. When looking at the proposal, policymakers tend to apply PP to that proposal while assuming the alternative(s) to be risk-free, which places an unfair burden on the proponents of the new product or activity.

Internal Inconsistency

The Precautionary Principle, applied to itself as a policy decision, may rule out its own use depending on the precise definition used; for example, Prohibitory PP as a policy decision would need to demonstrate that no substantial damage would result from the prohibition of products and technologies. For a potential example of this, the uncertain safety and long-term environmental effects of nuclear power led to its disfavor by precautionary groups, which may have resulted in greater carbon emissions through the use of coal power.

Michael Crichton wrote: The "precautionary principle," properly applied, forbids the precautionary principle. It is self-contradictory. The precautionary principle therefore cannot be spoken of in terms that are too harsh.

Perspective

- Critics of the principle argue that it is impractical, since every implementation of a technology carries some risk of negative consequences. For example, when the arrival of amplified music came on the scene, the risk of electrocution and deafness arose. However, this did not prevent it from becoming an artistic and cultural norm.
- A summary of some representative objections to the precautionary principle are described in a Reason article by Ronald Bailey which, using the Wingspread consensus as a starting point, argues the possibilities for misapplication of the principle.

Process Safety Management

Process Safety Management is a regulation, promulgated by the U.S. Occupational Safety and Health Administration (OSHA). A process is any activity or combination of activities including any use, storage, manufacturing, handling or the on-site movement of Highly Hazardous Chemicals (HHCs) as defined by OSHA and the Environmental Protection Agency.

Definition

Process Safety Management is an analytical tool focused on preventing releases of any substance defined as a "Highly Hazardous Chemicals" by the EPA or OSHA.dfs

Compliance

A process includes any group of vessels which are interconnected or separate and contain Highly Hazardous Chemicals (HHC's) which could be involved in a potential release. A process safety incident is the "Unexpected release of toxic, reactive, or flammable liquids and gases in processes involving highly hazardous chemicals. Incidents continue to occur in various industries that use highly hazardous chemicals which exhibit toxic, reactive, flammable, or even explosive properties, or may exhibit a combination of these properties.

Regardless of the industry that uses these highly hazardous chemicals, there is a potential for an accidental release any time they are not properly controlled. This, in turn, creates the possibility of disaster. To help assure safe and healthy workplaces, OSHA has issued the Process Safety Management of Highly Hazardous Chemicals regulation (Title 29 of CFR Section 1910.119) which contains requirements for the management of hazards associated with processes using highly hazardous chemicals."

Any facility that stores or uses a defined "highly hazardous chemical" must comply with OSHA's Process Safety Management (PSM) regulations as well as the quite similar United States Environmental Protection Agency (EPA) Risk Management Program (RMP) regulations (Title 40 CFR Part 68). The EPA has published a model RMP plan for an ammonia refrigeration facility which provides excellent guidance on how to comply with either OSHA's PSM regulations or the EPA's RMP regulations.

The Center for Chemical Process Safety (CCPS) of the American Institute of Chemical Engineers (AIChE) has published a widely used book that explains various methods for identifying hazards in industrial facilities and quantifying their potential severity. Appendix D of the OSHA's PSM regulations endorses the use of the methods explained in that book.

Risk Governance

Risk governance is a systemic approach to decision making processes associated to natural and technological risks, based on the principles of cooperation, participation, mitigation and sustainability, adopted to achieve more effective risk management, that is convergent with other public and private policies. It seeks to reduce risk exposure and vulnerability by filling gaps in risk policy, in order to avoid or reduce human and economic costs caused by disasters.

Risk Perception

Risk perception is the subjective judgment that people make about the characteristics and severity of a risk. The phrase is most commonly used in reference to natural hazards and threats to the environment or health, such as nuclear power. Several theories have been proposed to explain why different people make different estimates of the dangerousness of risks. Three major families of theory have been developed: psychology approaches (heuristics and cognitive), anthropology/sociology approaches (cultural theory) and interdisciplinary approaches (social amplification of risk framework).

Early Theories

The study of risk perception arose out of the observation that experts and lay people often disagreed about how risky various technologies and natural hazards were.

The mid 1960's saw the rapid rise of nuclear technologies and the promise for clean and safe energy. However, public perception shifted against this new technology. Fears of both longitudinal dangers to the environment as well as immediate disasters creating radioactive wastelands turned the public against this new technology. The scientific and governmental communities asked why public perception was against the use of nuclear energy when all of the scientific experts were declaring how safe it really was. The problem, from the perspectives of the experts, was a difference between scientific facts and an exaggerated public perception of the dangers.

A key early paper was written in 1969 by Chauncey Starr. Starr used a revealed preference approach to find out what risks are considered acceptable by society. He assumed that society had reached equilibrium in its judgment of risks, so whatever risk levels actually existed in society were acceptable. His major finding was that people will accept risks 1,000 greater if they are voluntary (e.g. driving a car) than if they are involuntary (e.g. a nuclear disaster).

This early approach assumed that individuals behave in a rational manner, weighing information before making a decision. Individuals have exaggerated fears due to inadequate or incorrect information. Implied in this assumption is that additional information can help people understand true risk and hence lessen their opinion of danger. While researchers in the engineering school did pioneer research in risk perception, by adapting theories from economics, it has little use in a practical setting. Numerous studies have rejected the belief that additional information, alone, will shift perceptions.

Psychology Approach

The psychology approach began with research in trying to understand how people process information. These early works maintain that people use cognitive heuristics in sorting and simplifying information which lead to biases in comprehension. Later work built on this foundation and became the psychometric paradigm. This approach identifies numerous factors responsible for influencing individual perceptions of risk, including dread, newness, stigma, and other factors.

Heuristics and Biases

The earliest psychometric research was done by psychologists Daniel Kahneman and Amos Tversky, who performed a series of gambling experiments to see how people evaluated probabilities. Their major finding was that people use a number of heuristics to evaluate information. These heuristics are usually useful shortcuts for thinking, but they may lead to inaccurate judgments in some situations – in which case they become cognitive biases.

- Representativeness: is usually employed when people are asked to judge the probability that an object or event belongs to a class/processes by its similarity:
    - insensitivity to prior probability
    - insensitivity to sample size
    - misconception of chance (gambler fallacy)
    - insensitivity to predictability

  * illusion of validity
  * misconception of regression.

- Availability heuristic: events that can be more easily brought to mind or imagined are judged to be more likely than events that could not easily be imagined:
  * biases due to retrievability of instances
  * biases due to the effectivenss of research set
  * biases of imaginability
  * illusiory correlation.
- Anchoring and Adjustment heuristic: people will often start with one piece of known information and then adjust it to create an estimate of an unknown risk – but the adjustment will usually not be big enough:
  * insufficient adjustment
  * biases in the evaluation of conjunctive and disjunctive event
  * anchoring in the assessment of subjective probability distributions.
- Asymmetry between gains and losses: People are risk averse with respect to gains, preferring a sure thing over a gamble with a higher expected utility but which presents the possibility of getting nothing. On the other hand, people will be risk-seeking about losses, preferring to hope for the chance of losing nothing rather than taking a sure, but smaller, loss (e.g. insurance).
- Threshold effects: People prefer to move from uncertainty to certainty over making a similar gain in certainty that does not lead to full certainty. For example, most people would choose a vaccine that reduces the incidence of disease A from 10% to 0% over one that reduces the incidence of disease B from 20% to 10%.

Another key finding was that the experts are not necessarily any better at estimating probabilities than lay people. Experts were often overconfident in the exactness of their estimates, and put too much stock in small samples of data.

Cognitive Psychology

The majority of people in the general public express a greater concern for problems which appear to possess an immediate effect on everyday life such as hazardous waste or pesticide-use than for long-term problems that may affect future generations such as climate change or population growth. People greatly rely on the scientific community to assess the threat of environmental problems because they usually do not directly experience the effects of phenomena such as climate change. The exposure most people have to climate change has been impersonal; most people only have virtual experience though documentaries and news media in what may seem like a "remote" area of the world. However, coupled with the population's wait-and-see attitude, people do not understand the importance of changing environmentally destructive behaviors even when experts provide detailed and clear risks caused by climate change.

Psychometric Paradigm

Research within the psychometric paradigm turned to focus on the roles of affect, emotion, and stigma in influencing risk perception. Melissa Finucane and Paul Slovic have been among the key researchers here. These researchers first challenged Starr's article by examining expressed preference – how much risk people say they are willing to accept. They found that, contrary to Starr's basic assumption, people generally saw most risks in society as being unacceptably high. They also found that the gap between voluntary and involuntary risks was not nearly as great as Starr claimed.

Slovic and team found that perceived risk is quantifiable and predictable. People tend to view current risk levels as unacceptably high for most activities. All things being equal, the greater people perceived a benefit, the greater the tolerance for a risk. If a person derived pleasure from using a product, people tended to judge its benefits as high and its risks as low. If the activity was disliked, the judgments were opposite. Research in psychometrics has proven that risk perception is highly dependent on intuition, experiential thinking, and emotions.

Psychometric research identified a broad domain of characteristics that may be condensed into three high order factors:

1) the degree to which a risk is understood, 2) the degree to which it evokes a feeling of dread, and 3) the number of people exposed to the risk. A dread risk elicits visceral feelings of terror, uncontrollable, catastrophe, inequality, and uncontrolled. An unknown risk is new and unknown to science. The more a person dreads an activity, the higher its perceived risk and the more that person wants the risk reduced.

Anthropology/Sociology Approach

The anthropology/sociology approach posits risk perceptions as produced by and supporting social institutions. In this view, perceptions are socially constructed by institutions, cultural values, and ways of life.

Cultural Theory

"The Cultural Theory of risk" (with capital C and T). Cultural Theory is based on the work of anthropologist Mary Douglas and political scientist Aaron Wildavsky first published in 1982.

In Cultural Theory, Douglas and Wildavsky outline four "ways of life" in a grid/group arrangement. Each way of life corresponds to a specific social structure and a particular outlook on risk. Grid categorizes the degree to which people are constrained and circumscribed in their social role. The tighter binding of social constraints limits individual negotiation. Group refers to the extent to which individuals are bounded by feelings of belonging or solidarity. The greater the bonds, the less individual choice are subject to personal control. Four ways of life include: Hierarchical, Individualist, Egalitarian, and Fatalist.

Risk perception researchers have not widely accepted Cultural theory. Even Douglas says that the theory is controversial; it poses a danger of moving out of the favored paradigm of individual rational choice of which many researchers are comfortable.

Interdisciplinary Approach

Social Amplification of Risk Framework

The Social Amplification of Risk Framework (SARF), combines research in psychology, sociology, anthropology, and communications theory. SARF outlines how communications of risk events pass from the sender through intermediate stations to a receiver and in the process serve to amplify or attenuate perceptions of risk. All links in the communication chain, individuals, groups, media, etc., contain filters through which information is sorted and understood.

The framework attempts to explain the process by which risks are amplified, receiving public attention, or attenuated, receiving less public attention. The framework may be used to compare responses from different groups in a single event, or analyze the same risk issue in multiple events. In a single risk event, some groups may amplify their perception of risks while other groups may attenuate, or decrease, their perceptions of risk.

The main thesis of SARF states that risk events interact with individual psychological, social and other cultural factors in ways that either increase or decrease public perceptions of risk. Behaviors of individuals and groups then generate secondary social or economic impacts while also increasing or decreasing the physical risk itself.

These ripple effects caused by the amplification of risk include enduring mental perceptions, impacts on business sales, and change in residential property values, changes in training and education, or social disorder. These secondary changes are perceived and reacted to by individuals and groups resulting in third-order impacts. As each higher-order impacts are reacted to, they may ripple to other parties and locations. Traditional risk analyses neglect these ripple effect impacts and thus greatly underestimate the adverse effects from certain risk events. Public distortion of risk signals provides a corrective mechanism by which society assesses a fuller determination of the risk and its impacts to such things not traditionally factored into a risk analysis.

Risk Homeostasis

Risk homeostasis is a hypothesis about risk, developed by Gerald J.S. Wilde, a professor emeritus of psychology at Queen's University, Kingston, Ontario, Canada. This hypothesis is elucidated in Wilde's book. The idea of risk homeostasis has garnered criticism.

The hypothesis of risk homeostasis holds that everyone has his or her own fixed level of acceptable risk. When the level of risk in one part of the individual's life changes, there will be a corresponding rise or fall in risk elsewhere to bring the overall risk back to that individual's equilibrium. Wilde argues that the same is true of larger human systems, e.g. a population of drivers.

For example, in a Munich study, half a fleet of taxicabs were equipped with anti-lock brakes (ABS), while the other half had conventional brake systems. The crash rate was the same for both types of cab, and Wilde concludes this was owing to drivers of ABS-equipped cabs taking more risks, assuming that ABS would take care of them, while the non-ABS drivers drove more carefully since ABS would not be there to help in case of a dangerous situation.

Likewise, it's been found that drivers behave less carefully around bicyclists wearing helmets than around unhelmeted riders

Wilde states that the massive increase in car safety features has had little effect on the rate or costs of crashes overall, and argues that safety campaigns tend to shift rather than reduce risk.

Risk Management Agency

The Risk Management Agency (RMA) of the U.S. Department of Agriculture helps producers manage their business risks through effective, market-based risk management solutions. RMA's mission is to promote, support, and regulate sound risk management solutions to preserve and strengthen the economic stability of America's agricultural producers. As part of this mission, RMA operates and manages the Federal Crop Insurance Corporation (FCIC). RMA was created in 1996; the FCIC was founded in 1938.

RMA employs approximately 530 people in offices around the country. The administrative budget is nearly US$79 million (FY 2008). Meanwhile, the size of the program has grown tremendously. In FY 2008, RMA is estimated to have managed nearly US$90 billion worth of insurance liabilities.

RMA Administrator William J. Murphy was appointed in July 2009. He also serves as the manager of the FCIC. Located within the Office of the Administrator are the Director of External Affairs, the Director of Civil Rights and Outreach, the Director of Program Support and Chief Information Officer, the Chief Financial Officer, and the Secretary to the Board of Directors of the FCIC.

The agency currently has three divisions: Insurance Services, Product Management, and Risk Compliance. Insurance Services Division is responsible for program delivery (e.g., managing the contracts with the companies that sell and service the policies), and local program administration and support.

Product Management is responsible for overseeing product development. Risk Compliance monitors compliance with program provisions by both producers and the insurance companies that sell and services policies.

RMA, via the FCIC, provides crop and livestock insurance to American producers. Fifteen private-sector insurance companies sell and service the policies. RMA develops and/or approves the premium rate, administers premium and expense subsidy, approves and supports products, and reinsures the 15 companies. In addition, RMA sponsors educational and outreach programs and seminars on the general topic of risk management.

Additional information about RMA can be found on its web site, including agency news, state profiles and other publications, summaries of insurance sales, information on pilot programs, downloadable crop policies, and agency-sponsored events. The site also features online tools, calculator, and applications. The most popular applications are the Agent Locator, Actuarial Document Browser, Premium Calculator, and Summary of Business.

Risk Management Authority

The Risk Management Authority is a Scottish public body, established by the Criminal Justice (Scotland) Act 2003. Its functions relate to the risk assessment of offenders whose liberty presents a risk to the public at large and minimising risk in respect of a small number of serious violent and sexual offenders who may be or have been sentenced to the Order for Lifelong Restriction.

The Authority is to be the recognised expert authority on risk assessment and risk management and will:

- develop policy and carry out research into the risk assessment and risk management of offenders whose liberty presents a risk to the public at large

- set standards for, and issue guidance to those involved in the assessment and management of risk
- accredit practitioners and risk management plans and monitor risk management plans for those offenders who receive an Order for Lifelong Restriction sentence from the High Court of Justiciary.

The Authority is based in Paisley.

Risk Management Information Systems

Risk Management Information Systems (RMIS) are typically computerized systems that assist in consolidating property values, claims, policy, and exposure information and provide the tracking and management reporting capabilities to enable you to monitor and control your overall cost of risk.

General Overview

The management of risk data and information is key to the success of any risk management effort regardless of an organization's size or industry sector. Risk management information systems/services (RMIS) are used to support expert advice and cost-effective information management solutions around key processes such as:

- Risk identification and assessment
- Risk control
- Risk financing.

Typically, RMIS facilitates the consolidation of insurance related information, such as claims from multiple sources,property values, policy information, and exposure information, into one system. Often, Risk Management Information Services/Systems (RMIS) applies primarily to "casualty" claims/loss data systems. Such casualty coverages include Auto Liability, Auto Physical Damage, Workers' Compensation, General Liability and Products Liability.

RMIS products are designed to provide their insured organizations and their brokers with basic policy and claim information via electronic access, and most recently, via the Internet. This information is essential for managing individual claims, identifying trends, marketing an insurance program, loss forecasting, actuarial studies and internal loss data communication within a client organization. They may also provide the tracking and management reporting capabilities to enable one to monitor and control overall cost of risk in an efficient and cost-effective manner.

In the context of the acronym RMIS, the word "risk" pertains to an insured or self-insured organization. This is important because prior to the advent of RMIS, insurance company loss information reporting typically organized loss data around insurance policy numbers. The historical focus on insurance policies detracted from a clear, coherent and consolidated picture of a single customer's loss experience.

The advent of RMIS in the 1980s was a breakthrough step in the insurance industry's evolution toward persistent and focused understanding of their end-customer needs. Typically, the best solution for your organization depends on whether it is enhancing an existing RMIS system, ensuring the highest level of data quality, or designing and implementing a new system while maintaining a focus on state-of-the-art technology.

Common Types of RMIS

Most major insurance companies (carriers), broker/agents, and Third Party Administrators (TPAs)offer/provide at least one external RMIS product to their insureds (clients) and any brokers involved in the insurance program. Most commonly, RMIS products allow individual claim detail look-up, basic trend report production, policy summaries and ad hoc queries. The resulting information can then be shared throughout the client's organization, usually for insurance program cost allocation, loss prevention and effective claim management at the local level.

More advanced products allow multiple claim data sources to be consolidated into one "Master RMIS," which is essential for most large client organizations with complex insurance programs.

The primary users of RMIS are risk/insurance departments of insured organizations and any insurance broker involved. Interestingly, it is much less common for the insured's safety department and vehicle operations department to have access to RMIS despite similar interest in the data. In fact, safety and vehicle operations of larger organizations typically maintain their own separate database systems of "accidents/incidents," many of which will correlate to RMIS claim data.

Insurance companies normally use a different version of externally provided RMIS for internal use, such as by underwriting and loss control personnel. Occasionally, there could be timing or other differences that could cause data discrepancies between the internal system and externally provided RMIS.

Insurance brokers have a similar need for access to their insured client's claim data. Brokers are normally added as an additional user to the RMIS product provided to their clients by the insurance carrier and TPAs.

The information available from RMIS is critical to the broker for interfacing effectively with their counterparts in the insurance carrier and TPAs. Additionally, effectively presented RMIS information that shows trends and analysis is essential to successfully marketing their clients' insurance programs.

Insurance carrier and Third-Party Administer (TPA) claim adjusters traditionally use claims management systems to collect and manage claim information and to administer claims. Some client organizations, however, may choose to manage certain types of claims or those within a loss retention layer and thus use this type of system as well.

Typically, the claims management system provides the primary data to RMIS products. RMIS products in turn provide an externally accessed view into the client's claims data. RMIS products are commonly available directly from larger insurance carriers and TPAs, but the most advanced systems are often offered by independent RMIS vendors. Independent RMIS vendor systems are most desirable when a client organization needs to consolidate claims data from multiple current insurance programs and/or past programs with current program information.

Key Vendor Attributes and Differences

Along with insurance carriers, broker/agents and TPAs that offer their own proprietary systems, there are a variety of direct RMIS technology companies who sell to direct insureds and even the carriers, broker/agents and TPAs themselves.

Major differences among RMIS vendors include:

- Currency of technology (Internet-based vs. Internet-accessible);
- System speed (response time for screen changes, report generation time, etc.);
- Flexibility in meeting client requirements (custom screen views, client-defined data fields, special reports, etc.);
- Ongoing support service quality (availability of senior/quality technical support, help desk availability, dedicated staff and stability, etc.);
- Data quality control (data conversion accuracy, data source cleanup, etc.);
- Pricing (first-year cost, ongoing cost, custom programming charges, data record storage fees);
- Availability of related modules (property exposure management, policy management, claim/incident setup, Occupational Safety and Health Administration (OSHA) record keeping, claims audits, etc.);
- Turnaround time for data loads;
- Foreign conversion/support (financial fields, language, fluent support staff, etc.)

RMIS system compatibility varies among carriers, broker/agents and TPAs. However, quality independent RMIS vendors by design can take almost any claim data source and convert or map the data to their particular system's file structure. A few major insurance carriers offer similar consolidation services, i.e., combining the insured client's current claim data with another carrier's or TPA's data for the same insured client. The other data sources can be for current separate insurance programs or from expired insurance programs. Usually, this type of consolidation service is performed to accommodate their major policyholder organizations. Major TPAs, however, more commonly offer such data consolidation services.

Average RMIS Costs and RMIS Market Drivers

The cost of a typical independent RMIS product varies from $60,000 to $150,000 for the first year, and ongoing annual charges are slightly less. Insurance company RMIS product lines typically average around $50,000 for the first user, but they often offer less expensive light-weight versions for claim look-up only. More costly full-featured products are sometimes available with more advanced reporting systems. The products are usually priced on a per-user basis on a sliding scale for a larger number of users. Insured clients' brokers are given access at no cost or occasionally for a flat annual fee for multiple insured clients with a particular broker.

TPAs commonly include one or two RMIS access IDs within their claims management pricing to encourage both the client's broker and the client to use their claim look-up product. Normally, beyond the first two access IDs, the pricing follows the same per-user range of the insurance companies. The cost drivers of RMIS include:

- Number of user/access IDs
- Number of outside claim data sources that must be converted (carriers and TPAs do not have to convert their own data)
- Frequency of outside claim data updates
- Special programming/report development charges
- Training of users (initial and annual users' conferences).

Clearly, higher cost systems do not always correlate to better performance in terms of both usefulness and speed. While most carrier and TPA RMIS systems are similarly priced; the independent RMIS vendors' price range varies significantly, as previously mentioned.

Risk Management Programme

Risk Management is a research programme set up by the Geneva Association, also known as the International Association for the Study of Insurance Economics. The focus of this programme is manifold and address the following issues: fostering the use of the tools of risk assessment and risk management in new fields of application such as policy making; providing a platform between the insurance community, the engineering and academic communities and policy makers to discuss risk issues; promoting the concept of the insurability of risks as the natural borderline between State legislation and the market economy; identifying new opportunities for insurers in the emerging sustainability concept in order to enlarge the field of insurable risks.

Selected Key Issues

- What are the vulnerabilities in our industrial and services value-added processes?
- Where are the mechanisms for understanding, managing and mitigating these risks?
- How can insurance cope with a more complex and demanding risk scenario?
- What is the new risk environment that has been created in recent years?
- What about technologies being a new source of vulnerability?

Publications

- *Risk Management,* Geneva Association Information Newsletter, The Geneva Association
- *Etudes et Dossiers,* Working Paper Series, The Geneva Association
- *The Geneva Risk and Insurance Review,* formerly The Geneva Papers on Risk and Insurance Theory (until March 2005), The Geneva Association & Springer
- *Pensions and Life Insurance* and *Risk Management/M.O.R.E,* The Geneva Papers on Risk and Insurance-Issues and Practice, Vol.29-No.3/July 2004, Palgrave Macmillan
- *Special Issue on Risk Management,* The Geneva Papers on Risk and Insurance-Issues and Practice, Vol.27-No.2/April 2002, Palgrave Macmillan
- *Strategic Issues in Risk Management and Insurance,* The Geneva Papers on Risk and Insurance-Issues and Practice, Vol.24-No.3/July 1999, Palgrave Macmillan
- *Issues in Risk Management and Insurance,* The Geneva Papers on Risk and Insurance-Issues and Practice, Vol.24-No.2/April 1999, Palgrave Macmillan.

- *Risk Management Strategies*, The Geneva Papers on Risk and Insurance-Issues and Practice, No.80/July 1996
- *Risk Management Issues*, The Geneva Papers on Risk and Insurance-Issues and Practice, No.76/July 1995
- *1973-1993 Twenty Years of Initiatives and Research on the Economic Role of Insurance and Risk Management in Modern Society*, The Geneva Papers on Risk and Insurance-Issues and Practice, No.68/July 1993
- *Risk Management Studies*, The Geneva Papers on Risk and Insurance-Issues and Practice, No.64/July 1992
- *Hazardous Waste Management*, The Geneva Papers on Risk and Insurance-Issues and Practice, No.51/April 1989
- *Risk and Society, The Discount Rate* and *Risk and Insurance Issues*, The Geneva Papers on Risk and Insurance-Issues and Practice, No.48/July 1988
- *Risk and Insurance Issues*, The Geneva Papers on Risk and Insurance-Issues and Practice, No.44/July 1987.

Risk Management Tools

Risk Management is a non-intuitive field of study, where the most simple of models consist of a probability multiplied by an impact. Even understanding individual risks is difficult as multiple probabilities can contribute to Risk total probability, and impacts can be "units" of cost, time, events (for example, a catastrophe), market states, etc. This is further complicated by there being no straightforward approach to consider how multiple risks will influence one another or increase the overall risk of the subject of analysis.

Risk management tools allow planners to explicitly address uncertainty by identifying and generating metrics, parameterizing, prioritizing, and developing mitigations, and tracking risk. These capabilities are very difficult to track without some form of documentation or, with the advent of information technology, software application. Simple risk management tools allow documentation. More sophisticated tools provide a visual display of risks, while the most cutting edge, such as those developed by Air Force Research Laboratory Headquarters, are able to aggregate risks into a coherent picture. A few tools have predictive capability, which, through collaboration between partners allow fair partition of risks and improvement of business relations.

The following is a list of risk management tools.

Risk-performs risk analysis using Monte Carlo simulation to show many possible outcomes in Microsoft Excel spreadsheet—and predicts how likely they are to occur.

Active Risk Manager-(ARM), addresses enterprise-wide risk management (ERM) and governance, risk and compliance (GRC) requirements, enabling the identification, communication, analysis and mitigation of risks and opportunities in both quantitative and qualitative formats.

The Aggregate Risk Tool-(ART), generates predictive financial data from any probability-impact model.

Bow tie diagrams-a fault identifying visual tool.

Capital asset pricing model-(CAPM) is used to determine the appropriate required rate of return of an asset, if that asset be added to an already well diversified portfolio, based on non-diversifiable risk.

Control Estratégico de Riesgo (CERO)-Software tool with specific tools for each activity of the risk management process. With clients mostly in Latin America.

Cost/Risk Identification & Management System (CRIMS)-Integrated Probabilistic risk assessment model with cost and other variables.

Crystal Ball-performs risk analysis using Monte Carlo simulation, analyzes time series and creates statistical forecasts, and determines the best values of decision variables based on stochastic optimization, all in a Microsoft Excel spreadsheet.

Cura Enterprise-Cura's GRC platform is a highly configurable solution that meets organizational requirements, and provides a balance between qualified and quantified data, all of which can be normalized and reported on across the entire organization.

Cura Quants-Is a quantitative modelling solution designed to integrate with the existing Enterprise GRC Platform. Cura Quants enables customers to quickly and easily quantify the impact of capital and project related risks as well as the effects of accompanying treatment strategies.

Dymonda-Dymonda is a software tool that enables Dynamic Flowgraph Methodology (DFM) modelling and analysis. The model explicitly identifies the cause-and-effect and timing relationships between parameters and states that are best suited to describe a particular system behavior.

Resolve by RPM'"-Cloud software toolbox to manage, track and audit processes associated with risk and safety areas within corporations.

IBM OpenPages GRC Platform-Integrated enterprise governance, risk and compliance solution that includes modules for operational risk management, policy and compliance management, financial controls management, IT governance, and internal audit management

Methodware-Methodware's ERA is a GRC solution that is a scalable,and flexible tool to automate,identify and track risk across departments, regions, and business units effectively.transparency

Operational risk management-The continual cyclic process which includes risk assessment, risk decision making, and implementation of risk controls, which results in acceptance, mitigation, or avoidance of risk.

PIMS Risk-Is a complete risk framework for identifying, analysing and evaluate threats and opportunities. Created for and used by major companies in oil and energy sector.

Probabilistic risk assessment (PRA), Probability Consequence (P/C) or Probability Impact Model-Simple model where estimates of probability of occurrence are multiplied by the consequence (cost, schedule delay, etc.). This is the most common tool, examples are RiskNav and RiskMatrix.

Reference class forecasting – Predicts the outcome of a planned, risky action based on actual outcomes in a reference class of similar actions to that being forecast.

RiskAid products-collaborative web/intranet-based risk management software environments for projects, operations and Enterprise Risk Management (ERM), developed by Risk Reasoning.

RiskAoA – A predictive tool used to discriminate between proposals, choices or alternatives, by expressing risk for each as a single number, so a proposal's trade-space between cost, scheduled time and risk from its desired characteristics can be compared instantly.

RiskAoA and variations of PRA are the only approved tools for United States Department of Defence Military Acquisition.

RiskComplete-Tracks project risk from planning approached to measuring tasks, from concept to manufacture.

RiskIssue.com-An online risk management tool for business, projects, teams and processes.

RiskLike'Con-A free probabilistic risk assessment tool. Displays risks in the industry-standard matrix; Probability vs. Consequence.

Risk register-A project planning and organizational risk assessment tool. It is often referred to as a Risk Log.

RiskPath-An improvement of RiskAoA, available to the public, where forecasts are quantified for each alternative.

Safety case-An assessment of the potential risks in a project and of the measures to be taken to minimize them.

SAPHIRE-A probabilistic risk and reliability assessment software tool. SAPHIRE stands for Systems Analysis Programs for Hands-on Integrated Reliability Evaluations.

SCHRAM-The Schedule Risk Assessment Manager; allows the generation of risk-adjusted schedules; the time of least risk, consequence of rushed/broken schedules. Allows realistic planning based on operational realities.

TRIMS-Provides insight as a knowledge-based tool that measures technical risk management rather than cost and schedule.

Unified Risk Assessment and Regulatory Compliance-A standards based end-to-end comprehensive cloud service from Unisys that performs model based risk assessment and also provides a real time dashboard for Regulatory & Policy Compliance traceability and transparency.

Xero Risk-Web based enterprise risk governance tool to identify, track and balance risks across an organization using user definable assessment and impact criteria.

Risk Register

A risk register is a tool commonly used in project planning and organisational risk assessments. It is often referred to as a Risk Log (for eg in PRINCE2).

This tool is widely used within Risk Management for identifying, analysing and managing risks. In this context a project risk is essentially an uncertain event that, should it occur, will have an impact on the project (this could be positive or negative).

It contains the information on the identified and collected project risks that the project team identifies when estimating and adjusting the activity durations for risks.

The project team considers the extent to which the effects of risks are included in the baseline duration estimate for each schedule activity, particularly the risks with high impact.

Example Contents

A wide range of contents for a risk register exist and recommendations are made by the Project Management Institute Body of Knowledge (PMBOK) and PRINCE2 among others. In addition many companies provide software tools that act as risk registers. Typically a risk register contains:

- A description of the risk
- The impact should this event actually occur
- The probability of its occurrence
- Risk score is multiplication of Probability and Impact
- A summary of the planned response should the event occur
- A summary of the mitigation (the actions taken in advance to reduce the probability and/or impact of the event)
- The risks are often given a ranking with the highest priority risks clearly identified to all involved.

Useful Terminology

In a "qualitative" risk register descriptive terms are used: for example a risk might have a "High" impact and a "Medium" probability.

In a "quantitative" risk register the descriptions are enumerated: for example a risk might have a "$1m" impact and a "50%" probability.

Contingent response-the actions to be taken should the risk event actually occur.

Contingency-the budget allocated to the contingent response

Trigger-an event that itself results in the risk event occurring (for example the risk event might be "flooding" and "heavy rainfall" the trigger)

Roy's Safety-first Criterion

Roy's safety-first criterion is a risk management technique that allows an investor to select one portfolio rather than another based on the criterion that the probability of the the portfolio's return falling below a minimum desired threshold is minimized.

For example, suppose there are two available investment strategies-portfolio A and portfolio B, and suppose the investor's threshold return level (the minimum return that the investor is willing to tolerate) is-1%. then the investor would choose the portfolio that would provide the maximum probability of the portfolio return being at least as high as "1%.

Thus, Roy's safety criterion can be summarized symbolically as:

Minimize $P(R_a < R_m)$,

Where $P(R_a < R_m)$ is the probability of R_a (the actual return) being less than R_m (the minimum acceptable return).

Normally Distributed Return

If the portfolios under consideration have normally distributed returns, Roy's safety-first criterion can be reduced to:

Maximize the SFRatio (safety-first ratio).

Where SFRatio is defined as $[E(R_a)$ " $R_m]$/(standard deviation of portfolio return) where $E(R_a)$ is the expected return (the mean return) of the portfolio and R_m is the minimum acceptable return.

Example

Thus if Portfolio A has a mean return of 10% and standard deviation of 15%, while portfolio B has a mean return of 8% and a standard deviation of 5%, and the investor is willing to invest in a portfolio that maximizes the probability of a return no lower than 0%:

SFRatio(A) = [10 " 0]/15 = 0.67,

SFRatio(B) = [8 " 0]/5 = 1.6

By Roy's safety-first criterion, the investor would choose portfolio B as the correct investment opportunity.

Similarity to Sharpe Ratio

Under normality:

SFRatio = (expected return " minimum return)/(standard deviation of return).

In contrast, the Sharpe ratio is defined as excess return per unit of risk, or in other words:

Sharpe ratio = (expected return " risk-free return)/(standard deviation of return).

SFRatio has a striking similarity to the Sharpe ratio: for normally distributed returns, Roy's Safety-first criterion with the minimum acceptable return assumed to equal the risk-free rate provides the same conclusion about which portfolio to invest in as does the criterion of maximizing the Sharpe Ratio. However, this partial equivalence no longer holds in the absence of normally distributed returns.

Social Risk Management

Social risk management (SRM) is a new conceptual framework assigned and designed by the World Bank. The objective of SRM is to extend the traditional framework of social policy to the non-market based social protection of which its three primary strategies include prevention, mitigation, and coping. It is now well understood that social unrest is positively parallel to the poverty. Assisting individuals, households and communities to elevate living standard above the poverty level will harmonize global economy and strengthen the social security.

Strategies : Prevention Strategies

Prevention strategies are those implemented to avert a risk. Some typical measures could be:

- In the labor market, SRM intervention targets skill training or job function improvement to reduce the risk of un/under-employment or low wages which are probably man-made.
- In the financial market, SRM emphasize on optimizing macroeconomic policies to reduce the shocks of financial crisis, such as oil price surges, or unpredictable market moves on currencies, indices and blue chip stocks.
- For natural disasters and environment degradation, SRM are gear to deploy a networked warning system or sustainable, renewable and environmental friendly eco-system to minimize the impact of the consequences.
- In health care, SRM focuses on the prevention of pandemic illnesses by implementing vaccination and public health education programs. Setting up rehabilitation centers to help drug addicts.
- In the public social security, establishing a community-based insurance schemes to compensate pensioners, disability or chronic illness person's living expenses. Building up nursing homes for elderlies and setting up public housing for homelesses and orphans.

Mitigation Strategies

Mitigation strategies focus on reducing the risk. Common practices are:

- In the financial market, diversifying portfolios or hedging stocks to decrease the exposure of the financial risks.
- Microfinance to the poor or jobless people.

Coping Strategies

Coping strategies are designed to relieve the impact of the risk event once it has occurred. The typical examples are

- Issuing government relieve fund or publicly raising money.
- Setting up unemployment benefit schemes.

Vulnerability Assessment

A vulnerability assessment is the process of identifying, quantifying, and prioritizing (or ranking) the vulnerabilities in a system. Examples of systems for which vulnerability assessments are performed include, but are not limited to, nuclear power plants, information technology systems, energy supply systems, water supply systems, transportation systems, and communication systems. Such assessments may be conducted on behalf of a range of different organisations, from small businesses up to large regional infrastructures.

Vulnerability from the perspective of disaster management means assessing the threats from potential hazards to the population and to infrastructure. It may be conducted in the political, social, economic or environmental fields.

Vulnerability assessment has many things in common with risk assessment. Assessments are typically performed according to the following steps:

1. Cataloging assets and capabilities (resources) in a system.
2. Assigning quantifiable value (or at least rank order) and importance to those resources
3. Identifying the vulnerabilities or potential threats to each resource
4. Mitigating or eliminating the most serious vulnerabilities for the most valuable resources.

"Classical risk analysis is principally concerned with investigating the risks surrounding physical plant (or some other object), its design and operations. Such analyses tend to focus on causes and the direct consequences for the studied object. Vulnerability analyses, on the other hand, focus both on consequences for the object itself and on primary and secondary consequences for the surrounding environment. It also concerns itself with the possibilities of reducing such consequences and of improving the capacity to manage future incidents." In general, a vulnerability analysis serves to "categorize key assets and drive the risk management process."

In the United States, guides providing valuable considerations and templates for completing a vulnerability assessment are available from numerous agencies including the Department of Energy, the Environmental Protection Agency, and the United States Department of Transportation, just to name a few.

Supply Chain Risk Management

Supply Chain Risk Management (SCRM) is a discipline of Risk Management which attempts to identify potential disruptions to continued manufacturing production and thereby commercial financial exposure..

Supply Chain Exposures

SCRM attempts to reduce supply chain vulnerability via a coordinated holistic approach, involving all supply chain stakeholders, which identifies and analyses the risk of failure points within the supply chain. Mitigation plans to manage these risks can involve logistics, finance and risk management disciplines; the ultimate goal being to ensure supply chain continuity in the event of a scenario which otherwise have interrupted normal business and thereby profitability.

Sometimes, it's possible for Supply Chain Logistics techniques such as Supply chain optimization to prejudice contingency planning which would otherwise reduce the overall risk level for that particular supply chain.

Contingency Options

Some options to engineer an acceptable risk level include:

- Managing stock
- Considering alternative sourcing arrangements
- Business Interruption/Contingency Insurance.

3

Enterprise Risk Management

Enterprise risk management (ERM) in business includes the methods and processes used by organizations to manage risks and seize opportunities related to the achievement of their objectives. ERM provides a framework for risk management, which typically involves identifying particular events or circumstances relevant to the organization's objectives (risks and opportunities), assessing them in terms of likelihood and magnitude of impact, determining a response strategy, and monitoring progress. By identifying and proactively addressing risks and opportunities, business enterprises protect and create value for their stakeholders, including owners, employees, customers, regulators, and society overall. (ERM)

ERM can also be described as a risk-based approach to managing an enterprise, integrating concepts of internal control, Sarbanes–Oxley Act, and strategic planning. ERM is evolving to address the needs of various stakeholders, who want to understand the broad spectrum of risks facing complex organizations to ensure they are appropriately managed. Regulators and debt rating agencies have increased their scrutiny on the risk management processes of companies.

ERM Frameworks Defined

There are various important ERM frameworks, each of which describe an approach for identifying, analysing, responding to, and monitoring risks and opportunities, within the internal and external environment facing the enterprise. Management selects a *risk response strategy* for specific risks identified and analyzed, which may include:

1. Avoidance: exiting the activities giving rise to risk
2. Reduction: taking action to reduce the likelihood or impact related to the risk
3. Share or insure: transferring or sharing a portion of the risk, to finance it
4. Accept: no action is taken, due to a cost/benefit decision.

Monitoring is typically performed by management as part of its internal control activities, such as review of analytical reports or management committee meetings with relevant experts, to understand how the risk response strategy is working and whether the objectives are being achieved.

Casualty Actuarial Society Framework

In 2003, the Casualty Actuarial Society (CAS) defined ERM as the discipline by which an organization in any industry assesses, controls, exploits, finances, and monitors risks from all sources for the purpose of increasing the organization's short-and long-term value to its stakeholders." The CAS conceptualized ERM as proceeding across the two dimensions of *risk type* and *risk management processes.* The risk types and examples include:

- Hazard risk
- Liability torts, Property damage, Natural catastrophe.
- Financial risk
- Pricing risk, Asset risk, Currency risk, Liquidity risk.
- Operational risk
- Customer satisfaction, Product failure, Integrity, Reputational risk.
- Strategic risks
- Competition, Social trend, Capital availability.

The risk management process involves:

1. Establishing Context: This includes an understanding of the current conditions in which the organization operates on an internal, external and risk management context.
2. Identifying Risks: This includes the documentation of the material threats to the organization's achievement of its

objectives and the representation of areas to the organization may exploit for competitive advantage.

3. Analysing/Quantifying Risks: This includes the calibration and, if possible, creation of probability distributions of outcomes for each material risk.
4. Integrating Risks: This includes the aggregation of all risk distributions, reflecting correlations and portfolio effects, and the formulation of the results in terms of impact on the organization's key performance metrics.
5. Assessing/Prioritizing Risks: This includes the determination of the contribution of each risk to the aggregate risk profile, and appropriate prioritization.
6. Treating/Exploiting Risks: This includes the development of strategies for controlling and exploiting the various risks.
7. Monitoring and Reviewing: This includes the continual measurement and monitoring of the risk environment and the performance of the risk management strategies.

COSO ERM Framework

The COSO "Enterprise Risk Management-Integrated Framework" published in 2004 defines ERM as a "...process, effected by an entity's board of directors, management, and other personnel, applied in strategy setting and across the enterprise, designed to identify potential events that may affect the entity, and manage risk to be within its risk appetite, to provide reasonable assurance regarding the achievement of entity objectives."

The COSO ERM Framework has eight Components and four objectives categories. It is an expansion of the COSO Internal Control-Integrated Framework published in 1992 and amended in 1994. The eight components-additional components highlighted-are:

- Internal Environment
- Objective Setting
- Event Identification
- Risk Assessment

- Risk Response
- Control Activities
- Information and Communication
- Monitoring.

The four objectives categories-additional components highlighted-are:

- Strategy-high-level goals, aligned with and supporting the organization's mission
- Operations-effective and efficient use of resources
- Financial Reporting-reliability of operational and financial reporting
- Compliance-compliance with applicable laws and regulations.

Implementing an ERM Program

Goals of an ERM Program

Organizations by nature manage risks and have a variety of existing departments or functions ("risk functions") that identify and manage particular risks. However, each risk function varies in capability and how it coordinates with other risk functions. A central goal and challenge of ERM is improving this capability and coordination, while integrating the output to provide a unified picture of risk for stakeholders and improving the organization's ability to manage the risks effectively.

Typical Risk Functions

The primary risk functions in large corporations that may participate in an ERM program typically include:

- Strategic planning-identifies external threats and competitive opportunities, along with strategic initiatives to address them
- Marketing-understands the target customer to ensure product/service alignment with customer requirements
- Compliance & Ethics-monitors compliance with code of conduct and directs fraud investigations

- Accounting/Financial compliance-directs the Sarbanes-Oxley Section 302 and 404 assessment, which identifies financial reporting risks
- Law Department-manages litigation and analyzes emerging legal trends that may impact the organization
- Insurance-ensures the proper insurance coverage for the organization
- Treasury-ensures cash is sufficient to meet business needs, while managing risk related to commodity pricing or foreign exchange
- Operational Quality Assurance-verifies operational output is within tolerances
- Operations management-ensures the business runs day-to-day and that related barriers are surfaced for resolution
- Credit-ensures any credit provided to customers is appropriate to their ability to pay
- Customer service-ensures customer complaints are handled promptly and root causes are reported to operations for resolution
- Internal audit-evaluates the effectiveness of each of the above risk functions and recommends improvements.

Common Challenges in ERM Implementation

Various consulting firms offer suggestions for how to implement an ERM program. Common topics and challenges include:

- Identifying executive sponsors for ERM.
- Establishing a common risk language or glossary.
- Describing the entity's risk appetite (i.e., risks it will and will not take)
- Identifying and describing the risks in a "risk inventory".
- Implementing a risk-ranking methodology to prioritize risks within and across functions.
- Establishing a risk committee and or Chief Risk Officer (CRO) to coordinate certain activities of the risk functions.

- Establishing ownership for particular risks and responses.
- Demonstrating the cost-benefit of the risk management effort.
- Developing action plans to ensure the risks are appropriately managed.
- Developing consolidated reporting for various stakeholders.
- Monitoring the results of actions taken to mitigate risk.
- Ensuring efficient risk coverage by internal auditors, consulting teams, and other evaluating entities.
- Developing a technical ERM framework that enables secure participation by 3rd parties and remote employees.

Internal audit Role

In addition to information technology audit, internal auditors play an important role in evaluating the risk management processes of an organization and advocating their continued improvement. However, to preserve its organizational independence and objective judgment, Internal Audit professional standards indicate the function should not take any direct responsibility for making risk management decisions for the enterprise or managing the risk management function.

Internal auditors typically perform an annual risk assessment of the enterprise, to develop a plan of audit engagements for the upcoming year. This plan is updated at various frequencies in practice. This typically involves review of the various risk assessments performed by the enterprise (e.g., strategic plans, competitive benchmarking, and SOX top-down risk assessment), consideration of prior audits, and interviews with a variety of senior management. It is designed for identifying audit projects, not to identify, prioritize, and manage risks directly for the enterprise.

Current Issues in ERM

The risk management processes of U.S. corporations are under increasing regulatory and private scrutiny. Risk is an essential part of any business. Properly managed, it drives growth and opportunity. Executives struggle with business pressures that may be partly or completely beyond their immediate control, such as distressed financial markets; mergers, acquisitions and restructurings; disruptive technology change; geopolitical instabilities; and the rising price of energy.

Sarbanes-Oxley Act Requirements

Section 404 of the Sarbanes-Oxley Act of 2002 required U.S. publicly-traded corporations to utilize a control framework in their internal control assessments. Many opted for the COSO Internal Control Framework, which includes a risk assessment element.

In addition, new guidance issued by the Securities and Exchange Commission (SEC) and PCAOB in 2007 placed increasing scrutiny on top-down risk assessment and included a specific requirement to perform a fraud risk assessment. Fraud risk assessments typically involve identifying scenarios of potential (or experienced) fraud, related exposure to the organization, related controls, and any action taken as a result.

NYSE Corporate Governance Rules

The New York Stock Exchange requires the Audit Committees of its listed companies to "discuss policies with respect to risk assessment and risk management." The related commentary continues: "While it is the job of the CEO and senior management to assess and manage the company's exposure to risk, the audit committee must discuss guidelines and policies to govern the process by which this is handled.

The audit committee should discuss the company's major financial risk exposures and the steps management has taken to monitor and control such exposures. The audit committee is not required to be the sole body responsible for risk assessment and management, but, as stated above, the committee must discuss guidelines and policies to govern the process by which risk assessment and management is undertaken.

Many companies, particularly financial companies, manage and assess their risk through mechanisms other than the audit committee. The processes these companies have in place should be reviewed in a general manner by the audit committee, but they need not be replaced by the audit committee."

ERM and Corporate Debt Ratings

Standard & Poor's (S&P), the debt rating agency, plans to include a series of questions about risk management in its company evaluation process. This will rollout to financial companies in 2007. The results of this inquiry is one of the many factors considered in debt rating, which has a corresponding impact on the interest rates lenders charge companies for loans or bonds. On May 7, 2008 S&P also announced that it would begin including an ERM assessment in its ratings for non-financial companies starting in 2009, with initial comments in its reports during Q4 2008.

ISO 31000 : The New International Risk Management Standard

ISO 31000 is an International Standard for Risk Management which was published last November 13, 2009. An accompanying standard, ISO 31010-Risk Assessment Techniques, soon followed publication (December 1, 2009) together with the updated Risk Management vocabulary ISO Guide 73.

Actuarial Response : Casualty Actuarial Society

In 2003, the Enterprise Risk Management Committee of the Casualty Actuarial Society (CAS) issued its overview of ERM. This paper laid out the evolution, rationale, definitions, and frameworks for ERM from the casualty actuarial perspective, and also included a vocabulary, conceptual and technical foundations, actual practice and applications, and case studies.

The CAS has specific stated ERM goals, including being "a leading supplier internationally of educational materials relating to Enterprise Risk Management (ERM) in the property casualty insurance arena," and has sponsored research, development, and training of casualty actuaries in that regard. The CAS has refrained from issuing its own credential; instead, in 2007, the CAS Board decided that the CAS should participate in the initiative to develop a global ERM designation, and make a final decision at some later date.

Society of Actuaries

In 2007, the Society of Actuaries developed the Chartered Enterprise Risk Analyst (CERA) credential in response to the growing field of enterprise risk management. This is the first new professional credential to be introduced by the SOA since 1949. A CERA studies to focus on how various risks, including operational, investment, strategic, and reputational combine to affect organizations.

CERAs work in environments beyond insurance, reinsurance and the consulting markets, including broader financial services, energy, transportation, media, technology, manufacturing and healthcare.

It takes approximately three to four years to complete the CERA curriculum which combines basic actuarial science, ERM principles and a course on professionalism. To earn the CERA credential, candidates must take five exams, fulfill an educational experience requirement, complete one online course, and attend one in-person course on professionalism. CERAs are members of the Society of Actuaries.

Institute and Faculty of Actuaries

The Institute and Faculty of Actuaries (the merged body formed in 2010 from the Institute of Actuaries and the Faculty of Actuaries) is the professional body representing actuaries in the United Kingdom. In March 2008, Enterprise Risk Management was adopted as one of the six actuarial practice areas, reflecting the increased involvement of actuaries in the ERM field.

A regular newsletter communicates the ongoing work that the profession performs in respect of ERM.

Some of the key areas that the profession works on are summarised below (together with some of the recent outcomes in each area):

Education, CPD, Career Support and Development

From April 2010 actuaries were able to study ERM as one of the Specialist Technical Stage exams (ST9 course information), which (with other exam passes) gives candidates the Chartered Enterprise Risk Actuary (CERA) qualification. In July 2010 the first nine actuaries to obtain the CERA qualification were announced. The CERA qualification is offered by 13 participating actuarial associations, with further information available at a global or UK level.

Various events (eg networking evenings and webinars) are available to actuaries and other interested parties. The main event is the Risk and Investment Conference, which is often held during the summer months (eg 2011 Risk & Investment Conference). There is also some regularly reviewed material available from the profession which may be of use in developing knowledge of ERM.

Research & Thought Leadership

A committee has been established to consider research and thought leadership in the ERM field (including what the "elevator speech" on ERM issues might be, definition of the scope of ERM and demonstration of the value of ERM).

Some areas in which work has been completed include:

- ERM-A guide to Implementation
- A survey on actuaries in risk management
- A suggested common risk classification system for the actuarial profession.

Research topics will be categorised and subject to a number of tests before proceeding with the research.

- enterprise-wide test (not just topic-specific/silo-based)
- risk management test (management = taking actions, not just modelling)
- director test (important enough for the Board, not just line managers).

Communications & Marketing

Actuaries continue to look to demonstrate and promote the value of actuaries and the CERA qualification in the field of ERM-including through publication of articles in the Actuary.

The Actuarial Profession also liases with other professions where appropriate-eg the Institution of Civil Engineers on considering ERM in the context of Risk Analysis and Management for Projects (RAMP).

Companies Increasingly Focusing on ERM

It is clear that companies recognize ERM as a critical management issue. This is demonstrated through the prominence assigned to ERM within organizations and the resources devoted to building ERM capabilities. In a 2008 survey by Towers Perrin, at most life insurance companies, responsibility for ERM resides within the C-suite. Most often, the chief risk officer (CRO) or the chief financial officer (CFO) is in charge of ERM, and these individuals typically report directly to the chief executive officer. From their vantage point, the CRO and CFO are able to look across the organization and develop a perspective on the risk profile of the firm and how that profile matches its risk appetite.

They act as drivers to improve skills, tools and processes for evaluating risks and to weigh various actions to manage those exposures. Companies are also actively enhancing their ERM tools and capabilities. Three quarters of responding companies said they have tools for specifically monitoring and managing enterprise-wide risk. These tools are used primarily for identifying and measuring risk and for management decision making. Respondents also reported that they have made good progress in building their ERM capabilities in certain areas.

In this study, more than 80% of respondents reported that they currently have adequate or better controls in place for most major risks. In addition, about 60% currently have a coordinated process for risk governance and include risk management in decision making to optimize risk adjusted returns.

In another survey conducted in May and June 2008, against the backdrop of the developing financial crisis, six major findings came to light regarding risk and capital management among insurers worldwide:

- Embedding ERM is proving to be a significant challenge
- Company size matters
- European insurers are better positioned
- ERM is influencing important strategic decisions
- Economic capital standards are gaining ground
- Operational risk remains a weak spot.

Total Security Management

Total Security Management (TSM) is the business practice of developing and implementing comprehensive risk management and security practices for a firm's entire value chain. This business process improvement strategy seeks to create added value for companies by managing security and resilience requirements as core business functions rather than as reactionary expenditures. TSM implementation involves a thorough evaluation of key internal and external stakeholders, distribution channels, and policies and procedures in terms of a firm's level of preparedness for a variety of disruptive events.

TSM encourages companies to manage security initiatives as investments with a measurable return and seeks to transform security from a net cost to a net benefit. In applying TSM, the theory holds that companies may be able to realize cost savings, improve business processes, reduce theft, enhance asset management, increase brand equity and goodwill, and improve preparedness and resiliency.

Formulation

The concept of Total Security Management was first introduced in the book *Securing Global Transportation Networks: A Total Security Management Approach*, published by McGraw Hill in 2006. This title was co-authored by Luke Ritter, J Michael Barrett, and Rosalyn Wilson, with the Foreword written by Governor Tom Ridge, the first U.S. Secretary of Homeland Security. According to Secretary Ridge, the book offers a, "comprehensive solution for approaching security in the context of sound business practices."

According to Dr. Kent N. Gourdin of the National Defence Transportation Association, "This book reflects the changing view of management regarding security. Still seen by many as both an additional cost and an impediment to good service, security is emerging as another competitive variable that firms can use to add customer value."

The TSM approach built upon scholarly research on the issue that stressed the importance of security as a key component of the supply chain. An April 2004 report for the IBM Center for The Business of Government noted, "Just as a chain is no stronger than its weakest link, a supply chain is only as secure as its weakest link, which includes the suppliers, manufacturers, wholesalers, retailers, carriers, terminals, and governmental institutions that plan, manage, facilitate, and monitor the global movement of goods. Additionally, the conclusions in a July 2006 Stanford Graduate School of Business report titled, "Supply Chain Security: Better Security Drives Business Valùe," state that, "...when properly leveraged, investments in supply chain security may not only be offset to some extent by benefits...but, in fact,...can overall have a positive impact on a company's bottom line."

Relation to Total Quality Management

The TSM name borrows from the management concept Total Quality Management (TQM), an approach made famous by the work of W. Edwards Deming. The TQM concept revolutionized the manner in which quality was perceived in industry, encouraging it to be integrated into the core business processes of a firm.

In the Foreword to *Securing Global Transportation Networks*, Secretary Tom Ridge writes: "The paradigm that now exists in transportation security is similar to the paradigm that existed when the now revered Dr. W. Edwards Deming tried to convince the business world in the 1960s that quality mattered. The now well-accepted theory of Total Quality Management was not initially met with open arms in the United States. I suspect that there are many professionals in the transportation industry today who may not endorse security management as a core business function that can create value. My hope is that readers will embrace the concepts of the TSM approach offered within *Securing Global Transportation Networks* and act upon them."

Companies Employing TSM

A company using the TSM methodology is meant to be able to establish a framework of focus points, metrics and feedback loops in order to elevate risk management from a non-core objective to an essential business function. This process includes establishing and creating a compliance management plan, implementing operational processes, evaluating the effectiveness of those operational plans, making appropriate changes as necessary, sharing successful lessons learned with internal and external stakeholders, and pursuing continual, incremental improvement.

Securing Global Transportation Networks details case studies of many large companies that benefited from the implementation of aspects of the TSM approach, including FedEx, Home Depot,

Hutchison Port Holdings, Maersk, Procter & Gamble, and Target, amongst others.

Criticism

Some suggest that the TSM approach, while containing merit, may be too complicated for companies to put into practice. "The difficulty of TSM is that it relies on a level of commitment and coordination that may be difficult to achieve...Reluctance to adopt TSM is not capitulation to mediocrity but rather an acceptance that the role that security plays within a company should not be any more than is needed. There are some useful ideas in the book, but the overall program may be too ambitious for many corporations to realistically consider," writes Ross Johnson in a 2007 *Security Management* review.

Other Developments

On December 16, 2009, the U.S. Securities and Exchange Commission (SEC) approved Rule No. 33-9089, which went into effect on February 28, 2010. This rule requires companies to increase their reporting of risk management practices, including details about the manner in which risk oversight is administered. The ruling has generated increased interest in implementing the TSM approach to ensure compliance with the updated SEC guidelines. In January 2010, ISO 28000 (ISO/PAS 28000 – Specification for security management systems for the supply chain) was updated to include an explicit reference to the Plan-Do-Check-Act model of quality management popularized by Deming.

Hospitality Industry Business Risk Management: Hotel Owners Must Have "Business Interruption Insurance" In Place To Protect Property From Disasters and Unforeseen Events

Business interruption insurance (also known as business income coverage) helps businesses in situations like this. Many businesses without the business income coverage, shut down their business operations after their business is completely shuttered due to some unforeseen event. It covers the loss of income and helps a business return to the financial position as it was in prior to the disaster.

Hence, a business in hospitality industry should understand the importance of business interruption insurance and should go for this insurance. Critical aspects of business interruption insurance Business owners from hospitality industry should be aware of some of the critical aspects of business interruption insurance. Here, we will take a look at some critical aspects of hotel business interruption coverage and understand why it is very useful for businesses in hospitality sector.

Business interruption period: The business interruption period is the length of period for which the benefits are payable under an insurance policy. This period is the most critical part of quantifying the business interruption loss. It covers a business from loss of income for a specified period till the damaged business property is repaired or reopened. Some hotels being aware of the losses that may persist even after repairs are done; opt for "extended period of indemnity". As it may take some time for the hotel to regain bookings and rebuild market share.

Loss of rooms revenues: The business in the hospitality or the lodging industry may suffer financial performance as two of its main functions, occupancy percentage and average daily rate (ADR) may get affected. In simpler terms, a hotel damaged by a hurricane or fire or stuck in a deep local recession will not be able to generate any revenues because of closed rooms, especially in hotels and lodges. Business interruption insurance compensates you for lost income due to loss of rooms. It covers the profits you would have earned, based on your financial records.

Other lost revenues: Revenues from food and beverage, conferences, golf, spa, etc., can constitute a significant portion of a hotel's income. When a business is interrupted, not only revenues through rooms are affected, some or all of these sources of income are typically interrupted. The business interruption insurance covers all the profits that would have been earned.

Ordinary payroll: Even if the business activities are temporarily stalled, operating expenses, and other costs such as rent, electricity bill, taxes, interest payable on bank loans, payroll costs etc., cannot be ignored. The business still needs to retain some employees such as accountants, front office executives etc. The business owner needs to pay salaries to them. In this kind of situations business interruption insurance is very helpful as ordinary payroll coverage is a common endorsement in many policies.

Extra expenses: Business interruption policies generally allow an insured hotel to claim extra expenses incurred during the period of indemnity. It reimburses for reasonable expenses that allow the business to continue operation while the property is being rebuilt. Some policies also cover the extra costs required for moving the business to a different (temporary) location.

Business interruption insurance is one of the most important insurance policies that help in minimizing the adverse consequences of some unwanted events for the businesses in the hospitality industry. A well-thought out risk strategy by hotel owners or operators can make a significant difference at the most crucial times.

Hospitality Industry Accident Risk Management: Falls From Slips And Trips Represent One Of The Most Common Hazards In Restaurants

Slips trips and falls can result in head injuries, back injuries, broken bones, cuts and lacerations, or sprained muscles. In the years 2007-2008, the average workers' compensation cost for a slip/trip/fall was $21,500. This exceeds the average cost of other injuries by 14%!

The following are some simple ways to reduce the probability of a slip and/or fall on wet or slippery floors:

- Install slip-resistant floor surface or use anti-skid adhesive tape in high traffic areas.
- Use absorbent matting in entrance ways during inclement weather or in areas where walkers may pass through puddles. (Note: unanchored mats may cause slip hazards themselves. Make sure that matting lays flat and that the backing material is slip resistant.).
- Maintain good housekeeping throughout all work areas. Utilize trash receptacles for the disposing of trash, food debris and other items which might wind up on floors.
- Immediately clean up spills and leaks. Place caution signs to warn employees and/or patrons of slippery surfaces or other slip/trip hazards.

- Develop written procedures to handle spills and ensure they are reported and cleaned up immediately. Regular, frequent inspections of working and walking areas should be conducted to identify hazards which could cause slips, trips and falls.
- Wear proper footwear for better traction on slippery surfaces.
- Use handrails or other stable objects that you can hold on to in paths of travel.

Hospitality Industry Security Risks: "Extended-Stay" Hotels Can Be "Havens For Crime" Unless Extra Security Measures Are Implemented Including Use Of Off-Duty Police Officers And Criminal Record And Sex Offender Background Checks

City officials were fed up and threatened to revoke the hotel's business license. But a recent agreement to curtail crime at the 124-unit hotel is working, authorities say.

"By word of mouth, one tells the other this is a place where you can set up shop and be unencumbered," Unrein said. Police had been called to Value Place about 230 times since it opened, Unrein said. That's more than triple the number of calls to the city's three other hotels combined, he said.

Problems reached a head this month. The hotel is offering a free hotel room where an Arnold police officer can live and have allowed police dogs to roam the halls this month, said Gina-Lynne Smith, president of Value Place.

The chain has a hotel in St. Charles. Police get more calls for service at that hotel than others in town, but it's certainly not a nuisance, said Sgt. Todd Wilson of the city's police department.

The hotels are not popular everywhere. Subdivision residents in Oakand Park, Fla., launched a campaign to keep a Value Place from being built nearby. So far, they have succeeded.

Their guests range from those who can't afford a lease to professionals away from home for a temporary job assignment or extended training.

Kell Stovall of Memphis, an estimator for a roofing company, said he is spending his third week at the Arnold Value Place. He plans to move to an apartment at the end of the month.

He considered staying elsewhere after hearing about the hotel's history but opted not to leave because he hasn't had any problems. He said police officers knock on his truck windows to check on him when he talks on his phone on the hotel's lot.

Hospitality Industry Information Security Risks: Hotel Computer Systems Are Increasingly "Breached" Through "Privileged Users" Who Have Total Access To Sensitive Data

One solution that is emerging to this problem is to carefully monitor everything (e.g. every key stroke and every mouse click) that a privileged user does on the network, while also putting more granular limits on what they can do. Basically "trust but verify," with the goal being detecting any anomalies in a privileged user's computing usage (e.g. why is this person downloading the source code at 3 a.m.?). This is not uncommon as it relates to other privileged users in other jobs – the "Eye in the Sky" in the casinos in Las Vegas is equally monitoring the gamblers for cheating but is also monitoring the dealers, and at a bank the CCTV is not only looking for robbers but the teller slipping some money in their pocket.

Instructive of the value of this new approach is that immediately after its breach, the RSA division of EMC acquired private company Netwitness for a reported large premium. Netwitness is known for analysing user activity monitoring at the network layer. In addition, the latest security vendor to file for an IPO, Imperva, has as its core solution the ability to monitor database access and usage by Database Administrators, another type of privileged user.

Catastrophe Risk and Your Insurance Policy

Catastrophic events such as hurricanes, terrorist plots and power outages affect all businesses but have a disproportionate impact on the hospitality industry. A guest's primary objective is often the safe and quiet enjoyment of a room and the hotel's grounds. When catastrophic events alter this formula, hotel owners and operators stand to lose significant profits or incur increased expenses, sometimes much greater than the cost of physical restoration. Short-and long-term economic consequences often permeate well after the property has returned to its pre-loss physical condition.

In response to the financial risk of catastrophic events, hoteliers have paid more attention to disaster recovery planning, including emergency response, guest safety, back-up of critical records, advance retention of construction contractors and a host of employee issues. Having a disaster recovery plan helps mitigate potential losses, but certainly doesn't eliminate them.

The residual economic losses, however, are often the subject of insurance claims, which could become a lengthy, sometimes-disagreeable process that is alien to many hotel operators and owners. This article highlights some of the insurance claim-related surprises encountered by hoteliers over the past few years. Many of these issues remain controversial today. By understanding these issues, you can be better prepared for the true financial risks from catastrophic events.

Limits on Coverage

There is often a limit to the duration of insurance coverage for lost income from a catastrophic event. Physical damage is the most common trigger for business interruption coverage, although there are other perils, such as civil authority, ingress/egress and service interruption that often result in lost income to hotels. The most commonly insured period of indemnity ends with the physical restoration of the property. As history has shown, a hotel may take years to recover from a catastrophic event. Frequent and loyal customers may migrate to competitors. Long-term employees may move to other properties and, worst of all, the hotel's reputation can be tarnished. Insurance policies rarely cover the full duration of such long-term losses. Instead, income losses are generally limited to the stated time limit in the policy. The hotel must absorb subsequent losses.

Loss of Market

After a catastrophe, insurance underwriters and their adjusters often argue that the economic effects from non-physical damage to the surrounding community is not covered under the business interruption policy. For example, if potential convention business diverts to another city, despite the completion of physical repairs to your property, insurers often argue that some or all of the resulting loss of income is a result of a "loss of market." Insurance carriers may assert this position irrespective of whether a loss of market exclusion is present in your policy. Underwriters argue that they insure a hotel and not the entire city or town.

Make-up or Recovered Business by Another Entity

Diversion of business from one commonly owned hotel to another may not be considered a compensable loss. For example, if Hotel A, which is owned by Owner 1, loses a group booking to Hotel B, also owned by Owner 1, Hotel A is unlikely to be compensated for its loss. Complications arise when hotels are insured under different policies, and operators are different while ownership overlaps. Other make-up scenarios include the re-booking of a group in the future. Not all re-bookings qualify as "make-up." If the re-booked party causes displacement of potential guests in the future, the re-booking should not be considered "make-up."

Deductibles, Self-retention Limits and Co-insurance

Deductibles, self-retention and co-insurance may significantly reduce your compensable loss. Many in the hospitality industry, especially those in catastrophe-prone locations, must absorb large deductibles in order to procure affordable coverage. Deductibles for business interruption may be expressed in hours, days or percentages and often exceed the amount contemplated by the insured. Another misunderstanding arises when the insured is under-insured and the policy carries a co-insurance penalty. The co-insurance penalty serves to make the insured proportionately liable for losses to the extent of their under-insurance. In its simplest term, if the insured only insures 50 percent of the total value, then the underwriters will only indemnify 50 percent of otherwise covered losses.

Subjectivity of Business Interruption Losses

Business interruption losses are subjective, and reasonable accountants may disagree on the quantification of lost income. If the hotel maintains detailed booking records, including historical pick-up data, turndown data and historical forecasts, the exercise may become more objective. Hotels with inconsistent performance, newly renovated facilities or start-ups, as well as an unreliable history of revenue projections, further complicate the exercise.

The development of a disaster recovery plan, including appropriate and timely modifications to account for current and anticipated business conditions as well as periodic testing of the plan, will help mitigate some but not all of the risk.

When insuring the residual risk, a thorough understanding of your insurance policy and the positions often taken by underwriters and their adjusters following catastrophic losses will help hotels to properly measure the total risk of loss from catastrophic events.

Understanding Claims Process Critical for Gulf Coast Hotels

The BP oil spill has wreaked havoc on the people of the Gulf region, the environment and businesses both small and large that operate on or near the coast. Hotels and motels in the region face significant uncertainty about the full scope of the impact on their business. It's critical to know what options there are for recouping business losses, especially considering that rules, protocols and procedures are a work in process.

The Current Environment

BP has acknowledged that millions of gallons of oil have leaked into the Gulf from the Deepwater Horizon explosion on April 20, 2010. It has pledged $20 billion to an independently administered fund to compensate victims of the oil spill, but there is still uncertainty around the handling and resolving of claims. Kenneth Feinberg, the fund's independent administrator, has promised a swift evaluation and processing procedure for claims, but as we write this article, his specific protocols are still under review by the House Judiciary Committee.

Several unanticipated claim scenarios, the speed and depth of the region's recovery, and the rate of opt-outs from the independently administered plan are all factors that will contribute to the evolution of the plan's protocols.

Challenges and Uncertainties for the Hospitality Industry

There are several scenarios specific to the hospitality industry that could lead to confusion for hotel operating executives, and to some difficult decisions for Feinberg.

It's a very real possibility hotels may have to close due to reduced revenue and a shortage of working capital, with no foreseeable recovery. This creates business valuation complexities that are inherently subjective, which prompts the question: for how long a period of time can hotel owners and operators expect to be compensated? Second, if a hotel hasn't suffered any direct physical damage to its property, and still suffers significant losses of income, will it be indemnified for its lost income from BP?

We believe Feinberg will treat these businesses the same as those that suffered direct physical damage, given the vast majority of economic impact occurring without damage to owned property. Finally, substantial claims will likely come from hotels located farther away from the Gulf coast. Hundreds of properties have suffered lost income as a result of lower demand for their services from vacationers who are reluctant to visit the Gulf region this summer.

How will Feinberg compensate these hoteliers, if at all? What supporting documentation will be needed? Will he follow state law to determine how a business is compensated, as he has said, when there is established federal law? Will he indemnify businesses differently depending upon the respective state residence of the claimant?

Avenues of Recovery

With so many uncertainties swirling, it's crucial for hotel managers and operating executives of impacted properties to fully understand the options available to them for potential loss compensation. Generally, they have three choices:

- File a claim with BP, which will ultimately evolve into a claim under the independently administered fund.
- Retain counsel and sue BP and or other culpable parties. With this option, they will likely end up in class action litigation that could take several years to resolve.

- File a business interruption insurance claim with their insurance carrier.

These three avenues of recovery are not mutually exclusive. Feinberg has indicated the independently administered fund will initially compensate victims for up to six months of losses. A business may file a claim for all or part of such losses without losing its option to also sue the culpable parties. However, he has stated subsequent claims beyond the six-month period will require claimants to give up their right to sue. The insurance claim process is full of its own challenges as well. Many standard property policies have pollution exclusions and only cover owned or used property, and hotels may face coverage hurdles on both of these issues.

Business interruption will only cover a hotel for the time it takes to restore the property to its pre-loss condition plus a pre-determined ramp-up period (extended period of indemnity). If property is defined as the beach and not the Gulf of Mexico itself, the claim clock may stop ticking when the beach has been cleaned and restored to its pre-loss condition. In addition, insurance companies are certain to offset insurable lost income by payments from either the fund or via class action litigation.

Macro and Micro Approaches to Preparing a Claim

So what is the best course of action for hotels that have lost business due to the oil spill? Irrespective of the preferred avenue(s) of recovery, hotels should document their losses in the most detailed fashion possible.

In documenting lost income we often refer to the "Macro Approach" and the "Micro Approach." Most hotels will require a Macro Approach to quantify and document their losses—at the very least as a supplement to the Micro Approach. Several steps should be considered in documenting losses via the Macro Approach:

> *Consider the recent history of the hotel. Was the income of the business expected to vary significantly from historical results? If so, document expected variations with a Micro Approach and other Macro-based methodologies (ordinary course of business forecasts, booking trends, comparable properties that were not impacted by the spill).*

Consider seasonality. If the claim is for a period of less than one year, does the lost revenue calculation reflect the seasonality of the business?

Review ordinary course of business forecasts and budgets. Assess their credibility and accuracy over recent history. Are they consistent with prior forecasts and budgets? Have any loss-period factors other than the oil spill impacted your revenues?

Identify independent sources of information (yardsticks or comparables) for similar properties that have not been impacted by the spill. Compare loss-period performance of the yardstick to the impacted property and quantify the relationship. Do the same for the pre-loss period and use the change in the relationship to quantify the loss.

Consider, document and claim extra expenses. Many Gulf area hotels are expending large sums of money to retain their guests via advertising, guarantees of clean beaches and additional amenities. In fact, the cost of assessing and documenting damages both physical and financial is a cost that should be considered and claimed.

The Micro Approach identifies and documents specific losses such as cancelled reservations and cancelled events. It provides the most compelling evidence of a loss, but may not be a practical methodology if a hotel derives its revenues from less predictable sources (such as transient guests, walk-ins or last-minute bookings), or if losses continue for a prolonged period of time. A Micro approach may be more appropriate for a hotel or motel that books guests and groups months in advance. These hotels and motels should:

- Train sales and administrative employees to track cancelled bookings and preserve its documentation as part of their everyday responsibilities.
- Modify ordinary course of business accounting systems to account for Gulf-related cancellations, including adding Gulf-related reason codes for tracking cancellations.
- Log calls with guests to account for and document cancellations.
- Retain emails documenting cancellations for Gulf-related reasons.

- Require guests to commit cancellations to writing in order to document Gulf-related losses.
- Identify specific group discounts or special accommodations to either appease a group, maintain an existing group booking or to convert a tentative booking into a definitive one.
- Track alternative stays by guests.
- Quantify lost revenues based on the above documentation.
- Determine whether the entirety of losses is captured by the above evidence or whether a Macro Approach should be used to supplement the calculation.

In addition to the accounting records required to support lost income, we also recommend to hotels that are directly on the beach to take water and sand sample for evaluation. This will provide a baseline to document the quality of water and sand surrounding your property today. If the oil does affect the property in the upcoming months, you will have proof as to the reduction in the quality of the beach, which may give rise to future lost income this fall and possibly into 2011.

Hotels affected by the Gulf oil spill face a myriad of uncertainties in filing claims for their lost income. Following some or all of the suggestions above may help in facing those. As the claims process evolves the rules may change, but one principle should be relied upon throughout: A claim that is well documented and properly calculated will stand a better chance of success, indemnification and ultimately, recovery for its owners.

Hotel Risk Management is Critical

One of the most important aspects of owning and operating a hotel is minimizing the various physical and liability risks associated with this type of business. Risk management is the process of evaluating a hotel's risk exposure and developing strategies for mitigating those. It incorporates a program for reducing exposure supplemented by insurance protection should an incident occur. A hotel owner and operator would be far better off if they could eliminate all the possibilities of an incident occurring on their property. Since this is not always possible, particularly incidents they have no control over, adequate insurance protection provides a way to reduce exposure to a financial loss.

When reviewing your hotel's risk management strategies, it is essential you understand all the potential areas of exposure and exactly how insurance policies are structured to handle the unfortunate incidents that could occur.

The primary areas of concern include the property itself, premises liability, automobile liability, worker's compensation, fidelity, boiler & machinery and umbrella. An effective risk management strategy will also reduce a hotel's insurance cost. Saving money on insurance requires not only a good broker who fully understands the unique risk exposure of a hotel, but one who can also advise on a strategy that will reduce the chance of an incident.

Let's look at some of the unique risks faced by hotels:

Property Risk

Property risk exposures in the industry are primarily due to the high combustibility of contents and multiple sources of ignition that exist in a hotel. Managing these as well as updating building electrical wiring, plumbing and heating systems must be a top priority to mitigate the potential for a fire loss. Additionally, smoke alarms and sprinklers should be installed in all areas of the building and kitchen equipment must meet all National Fire Protection Association requirements. For resort areas, storm damage is always a concern and needs to be addressed.

It is always essential to insure a hotel's buildings and furniture, fixtures and equipment to replacement cost. Replacement cost is the cost to repair or re-build to like kind and quality in today's dollars. Another major component of your property insurance is the BI (Business Interruption) exposure. BI exposure can be substantial due to lack of backup facilities and the seasonal natures of certain hotel operations. A hotel must be sure to complete a business income worksheet to ensure proper insurance proceeds for a loss of profits and continuing expenses. An accurate account of annual revenues by type such as room, food, and beverage will be advantageous for insurance brokers when they are researching the best and least expensive coverage.

Premises Liability

A hotel's premises liability exposure is high due to the number of guests typically in the property at any given time. High-rise hotels pose unique life-safety issues. Hotels should implement every safety code possible to ensure guest safety. Stairways, elevators, railings and floor coverings should all be in good condition. Exits should be clearly marked, and lighting should be available in the event of a power outage. Balconies should be regularly inspected and maintained. Guestrooms should be accessed by magnetic keys or other similar systems that are unique for each new guest. Services and recreational facilities, such as exercise rooms, swimming pools, laundry facilities, gift shops, barber, beauty and other personal services, require separate review. It is important to identify all the potential liabilities and develop a risk management strategy to reduce the chance of an incident.

Products Liability

Products liability exposures can be high if the hotel has a restaurant or lounge serving alcohol. Employees should be trained in the proper handling of food to prevent food poisoning or the spread of other transmissible diseases. Liquor liability exposures can be high if employees are not property trained to recognize the effects of excessive alcohol consumption.

Automobile Liability

Automobile liability exposure is also high for some properties, like airport hotels, when it is necessary to pick up and deliver guests to and from the hotel. Valet services present garage-keepers exposure for damages to guest's vehicles. With automobile exposures, pre-approval of acceptable MVR's (driving history report), and restricting driving duties to those between the ages of 18-65, are effective methods in managing this type of risk.

Workers Compensation

Workers compensation exposure is also high within the hospitality industry. Cleaning and maintenance operations can cause workers to experience lung, eye or skin irritations and reactions. Slip and falls, as well as lifting, back injury, hernia, sprain and strain, are all common occurrences.

Every hotel should have a risk management strategy that works to reduce the exposure and then provides adequate insurance to cover unfortunate incidents that were not prevented. Your hotel insurance broker can assist in finding an insurance company that has the extensive experience in evaluating unique hotel risks so you don't end up paying more for your coverage because the company overestimated the exposure and charged too much. The broker should also find you an insurance company with a hotel-oriented loss-control department, which will survey your hotel and assist in identifying areas of risk that can be addressed in your strategy.

When shopping for insurance, your broker will assist in obtaining adequate underwriting information to get you the best insurance at the lowest rate. COPE (Construction Occupancy Protection Information) should be organized per location, and include items such as buildings' square footage, construction materials, year built, number of stories, swimming pools, sprinklers, smoke alarms, key system, buildings contents, business income, hotel receipts, food receipts, liquor receipts and total receipts. Along with this information, obtaining up to five years of loss history is crucial for your broker to get your insurance program the best coverage, at the best price and with the best terms and conditions.

Bridging Troubled Waters

Popular vacation destinations such as California, Hawaii and Florida offer travelers picturesque coastlines, warm weather and sandy beaches. For those seeking to take advantage of those attractions, hotels on or near the water offer ideal accommodations. While these picturesque coastlines can be beautiful places to relax and sunbathe, hidden below the surface can be dangerous natural hazards. Although these beaches are often owned and managed by the city or county in which they are located, under certain circumstances, a hotel can be held liable for failing to warn guests of these naturally occurring, dangerous conditions.

Injuries caused by natural conditions, such as sandbars or riptides, constitute the basis for many of the lawsuits brought against hotels for injuries sustained on beachfront property.

The majority of courts hold that in order for a hotel to have a legal duty to warn of dangerous conditions at a beach—for example, the prevalence of rip currents—the hotel must exercise sufficient control over the beach. Control in this context does not mean actual ownership of the beach property; rather, control will be implied where the hotel possesses an area and demonstrates intent to control it. Although the question of control will depend on the facts of each case, there are certain factors a court will generally consider in making its determination.

These factors include who has the authority to dictate who may use the beach; whether guests were invited by the hotel to use the beach; whether the hotel facilitated the use of the beach; whether the hotel sets up chairs, umbrellas or the like on the beach; and whether the hotel derives revenue from the beach. Generally, courts have been reluctant to imply control of beach property by a hotel, even when the hotel encourages the use of the beach by guests. Most cases that have found a duty to warn based on control have either been brought against the municipality that actually owns or controls the beach or have been based on implied control of the land portion of the beach rather than the water portion.

Even if a hotel is found to exhibit the requisite control over the beach area, it does not have a duty to warn beachgoers of every possible danger. Generally, the danger must be foreseeable, in that the hotel must have notice of the condition, in order for the duty to warn to arise. An example involves a claim brought by a swimmer who sustained injuries when he executed a surface dive in the ocean and struck a sandbar. The court ruled the defendant could not anticipate a danger to swimmers simply from the existence of the natural shifting condition of sandbars and the fact three similar incidents had occurred in a 24-year period did not give the defendant notice.

The second theory of hotel liability employs a test of foreseeability. In these cases, courts have found a hotel operator has a duty to warn of foreseeable dangers at the beach, regardless of whether the hotel has any control over the area. In order to be foreseeable, the hotel must have some knowledge of the dangerous condition. In one such case, a guest at a hotel walked to the beach across the street. While in the ocean, the guest suffered serious injury. The court stated it was not a question of whether the hotel had control over the beach, but whether the injury sustained by the guest was foreseeable. If it was foreseeable that the guests would go to the beach and be injured by dangers that the hotel knew or should have known of, the hotel would have a duty to warn of these dangers.

Nonetheless, many courts hold there is no duty to warn of naturally occurring conditions. In a case employing this theory, the plaintiff sued a hotel for the drowning death of her husband off the coast of Brazil, which she alleged was due to the hotel's failure to warn of treacherous ocean water. In dismissing the plaintiff's lawsuit, the court found that even if the hotel had exhibited control over the beach area and could have foreseen the dangerous surf conditions, there was no duty to warn of a natural phenomena occurring in ocean beaches.

Although the case law is not nationally uniform as to exactly when a hotel has to warn guests of naturally occurring conditions, some states have enacted statutes that directly address the issue. For example, Hawaii enacted a statute to determine liability for beachfront hotels, which states:

In a claim alleging injury or loss on account of a hazardous condition on a beach or in the ocean, a hotelkeeper shall be liable to a hotel guest for damages ... resulting from the hotel guest going onto the beach or into the ocean for a recreational purpose ... only when such loss or injury is caused by the hotelkeeper's failure to warn against a hazardous condition on a beach or in the ocean, known, or which should have been known to a reasonably prudent hotelkeeper, and when the hazardous condition is not known to the guest or would not have been known to a reasonably prudent guest.

Because of the uncertainty surrounding a hotel's duty to warn, precautionary measures may be the most appropriate form of action for hotels and other accommodation providers to take. Even simple steps, like erecting a sign on the beach, may be successful and cost-effective ways to warn guests of possible beach dangers. One court even suggested a simple warning from a hotel pool attendant that the beach water was rough will satisfy a hotel's duty to warn. However, because the law is different in every state, contacting a local attorney is the best way to find out the extent of hotel liability in that particular area and how a duty to warn can be satisfied.

Hospitality Industry Employment Risks: Hospitality Management Must Have "Valid" Reasons to Fire Employees

- *Make sure that you have a valid reason for firing (or laying off) the employee.* Some invalid reasons include: retaliation, complaining about OSHA violations, discrimination, alien status, and any violation of public policy.
- *Keep it confidential*: a company-wide Eblast is probably not the best approach to alerting others in the company of the employees' situation. Rather, only telling those individuals that need to know is the best approach to ensuring that the employee does not hear about his firing before it happens.
- *Plan ahead*: sounds simple enough, but by considering all the legal requirements you need to comport with before firing the employee, you will also alleviate a lot of legal concerns that may occur post-firing. This may include: severance offers, monies due, terms in the employment contract, company policies, etc.
- *Keep a paper trail*: keeping copies of performance reviews, relevant correspondence, and other personnel documents will help protect you should there be a lawsuit later on.
- *The employee should not be completely surprised by the firing or lay-off.* Whether it is keeping employees abreast of the struggling finances of the company, or alerting the worker to poor job performance, there should be a dialogue before the employment termination.

Although a majority of the American workforce is based on "at will" employment, essentially meaning that the employer-employee relationship can be severed at any time, there are still some viable concerns over a wrongful termination suit in any situation. Making sure you have a valid reason for firing an employee, and planning the conversation ahead of time will help with the actual firing and protect your company from many of the legal issues that follow.

In the end, honesty is almost always the best policy, and usually appreciated as the employee can take your reasons with them as they job hunt.

The Epsilon Data Breach and the Risk for Hotel Companies

Customers of Hilton HHonours, Marriott Rewards, Ritz-Carlton Rewards, Red Roof Inns and Disney Destinations have been exposed to the risk of targeted phishing attacks after a data breach disclosed last Friday involving online marketer Epsilon of Alliance Data Systems Corp, which said some clients' customer names and email addresses were obtained via an "unauthorized entry."

Epsilon assures that compromised files did not include payment card data, yet it is clear that with just having email addresses-plus knowing where someone shops – helps online criminals design more sophisticated and targeted 'phishing' campaigns to steal financial data or spread malicious software, or malware.

The practice of using emails that appear to come from a trustworthy source to get users to divulge information about themselves is also known as 'spear-phishing' because such emails are more focused than traditional 'phishing' emails.

This type of data breach may be considered a 'light' one, however, the companies involved are responsible to take appropriate action as they may considered liable for the data breach – even if this occurred by a third party – or, at the very least, they may lose their customers' trust in handling their personal data.

Data Breach Risk in Hotels: High Probability – High Impact

In 2010 Trustwave's SpiderLabs compiled a list of 218 data breach investigations in organizations across 24 countries. The hotel sector accounted for 38% of these cases as opposed to financial services companies which accounted for only 19 percent. A whopping 98 percent of targeted data was payment card information.

Last September HEI Hotels & Resorts, owner and operator of a number of branded (Westin, Marriott, Hilton, Embassy Suites, Le Meridien, Sheraton, Renaissance and Crowne Plaza) hotels, announced that a "vulnerability in an information system at certain of its hotel properties may have been exploited, and credit card information related to certain transactions occurring between March 25 and April 17, 2010 may have been compromised." According to a source, this incident involved data of around 3400 customers.

Previously, a number of data breaches have shaken the hospitality sector. In July 2008 an incident involving 41 Wyndham Hotels and Resorts may have affected as many as 21,000 customers in Florida according to that state's attorney general. In February 2009 Hilton became aware that the Hilton Grand Vacations credit applications or Vacation Introduction Program databases were hacked and that names, social security number, and dates of birth of as many as 2,304 individuals have been compromised. In August 2009 Radisson admitted data breach of significant dimensions in the company's servers and compromise of unknown number of customer credit card details.

These incidents show a clear vulnerability of hospitality operations and a risk that companies operating franchise and management agreements need to consider quite seriously. More often than not these risks are far more than just IT risks and cannot only be attributed to IT security 'holes'. There are plenty of cases where breaches are due to plain negligence at operational level (e.g., password sharing, people forgetting to log out when using public computers, misplaced data storage devices, forgotten laptops in taxis, etc.). The consequences of a breach may also cause serious reputational and financial damage for the company and the aftermath needs to be very carefully handled.

Data Breach Risk Treatment

Hacker attacks range from very sophisticated to relatively basic and can be dealt with to a good extent with appropriate IT security measures and policies. The area of major concern for hoteliers however is the 'negligent practice' at operational level. Developing appropriate risk awareness culture and enforcing the policy controls with periodic audits and training (password control, anti-phishing and social engineering training, etc.) is one of the key measures against data breaches at this level.

Attacks against point of sale systems have been an area of growing concern for the Payment Card Industry (PCI) Security Standards Council, the body that administers the payment industry's PCI security rules. Hotel risk managers are strongly advised to comply with these standards.

However, one needs to make the difference between being compliant from just being PCI certified. The two most important data breaches in the history took place on TJX and Heartland Financial, both PCI certified by a QSA at some point in time. However, these companies were compromised after they stopped being or practicing PCI compliance or when they stopped performing best practice, state of the art, and best of breed information security on a daily basis.

Post-Incident Response

There are many ways to address a post-breach incident but disclosure is necessary in all cases. The accepted 'best practice' for companies in this case is to:

1. Publically acknowledge the data breach, apologise and assure everyone that they are putting every possible effort to prevent this from happening again and list specific measures that are being put in place.
2. Release information regarding which businesses were affected, as "full disclosure" is one of the major tenets of crisis communications.
3. Establish a "hotline" to answer any questions of consumers that might have been affected and offer a free credit monitoring package for cases where there is suspicion of data compromise. (In a similar case, in 2006, Expedia and Hotels.com did exactly that when the data of 243,000 Hotels.com customers were compromised). Depending on the type of breach, this may be a minimal cost measure, with hugely positive reputational effect.

The 2010 Trustwave report indicates that in the more than 70 post-breach investigations in the hospitality industry it performed, the majority of the companies involved have not publicised their data losses or warned customers.

What needs to be noted here is that non-response or partial response exposes the company to the risk of a class action lawsuit where general public may be invited by 'consumer protection specialist law firms' to contact them, if they have been notified that their debit card, credit card, or other information may have been compromised as a result of a data breach. The complaint may a claim pursuant to local Consumer Fraud Act (or equivalent) and assert causes of action for negligence, breach of implied contract, breach of contracts to which plaintiffs and class members were intended third party beneficiaries, breach of fiduciary duty, and negligence per se.

In the case of Epsilon, Marriott responded by a post on its website on Monday, saying that "the unauthorized person(s) had access to names and email addresses only. They did not have access to sensitive customer information, such as physical addresses, point balances, account logins and passwords, credit card information or other personal data."

Hilton notified its customers by email on Monday that their names and email addresses were part of the breach. "The files accessed did not include any customer financial information.... The most likely impact, if any, would be receipt of unwanted e-mails," Hilton noted. They also reminded the customers that Hilton will never ask for sensitive personal data-credit card numbers, social security numbers and the like-to be transmitted over email.

Apart from the hospitality companies reported here, the Epsilon data breach involved customer emails of companies such as: JP Morgan Chase & Co, the second-largest U.S. bank; Citigroup Inc, the third-largest U.S. bank; Capital One Financial Corp, a bank and credit card lender; Kroger Co, the biggest U.S. supermarket operator; Walgreen Co, the largest U.S. drugstore and Best Buy Co, the largest U.S. consumer electronics chain.

4

Hotel Lifecycle and Risk Components

In line with any type of real estate investment (and probably any investment!), a hotel's lifecycle has three main phases: development, operation and exit.

It takes approximately one to three years to develop a hotel asset (depending on the type of property), and a typical investor would hold the asset for a period of between five and 25 years. At the end of the lifecycle (or holding period), an investor would sell the property or redevelop it; a process that takes a minimum of one year and may, infrequently, never materialise.

Development Risk

Development risk is the economic threat that a developer/investor is exposed to upon converting a vacant piece of land or an existing building into a fully operational hotel asset. Obviously, the more complicated the type of asset is, the higher the development risk would be. In other words, this risk is the probability that a setback takes place during the development process that has a negative effect on the development cost or any aspect that influences the future investment returns (location of the asset, positioning, type of operator, physical characteristics, construction and design, timing of completion, capital structuring and so forth). There is sometimes a great difference between how a hotel asset should look and how it actually does when it is built!

Developing hotels is highly capital intensive and requires the ultimate harmony between all parties involved in order to secure an economically viable investment. Any setback during the development would severely impact the investment returns.

Full service and luxury hotels are, by nature, complicated hotels to develop, when compared to other hotel assets. Such properties require more time to develop, necessitate complicated space planning and design, are highly capital intensive and face high market expectations in terms of the physical product offering (which, again, makes it increasingly critical for the developer to ensure an appropriate end product). Therefore, such an asset class is exposed to a high level of development risk when compared to other hotel derivatives.

As with full service hotels, serviced apartments/extended stay units have different 'grades' that span the budget, mid-market and luxury sectors. In general, all can be said to provide more spacious accommodation than traditional hotel rooms of a similar standard, with the benefit of kitchen facilities allowing for self-catering. While such an asset class is less complicated to develop than full service/luxury hotels, given its limited amount of public space, such properties (irrespective of their grade) are more complicated to develop when compared to limited service/budget hotels.

Shared ownership properties vary widely in terms of product offering, grade and so forth. For example, products range from an upmarket timeshare development in a beach resort (hence requiring complicated designs, space planning and so forth) to condominium units (second home/residential/investment) in a city (which are easier to develop). Therefore, the development risk associated with this asset class varies considerably. For the purpose of this paper, we have assumed that this asset class is prone to a medium level of development risk, when compared to other hotel derivatives.

Ownership's Operating Risk

The total 'holding period return' of any type of investment is the combination of the cash flow earned throughout the holding period as well as the capital appreciation (or depreciation) of the asset. Depending on the type of hotel property (and its holding period), the operating cash flow returns represent between 30 and 70 per cent of the overall returns. Typically, the operating risk of a hotel asset is higher during the first years of operation of the property, when compared to the level of risk attributed to its operation once it reaches a stabilised level of trading performance.

The operating risk is simply the ability of the asset (and its management) to generate sufficient levels of cash flow in order to produce a certain level of financial returns to justify the investment and/or catalyse an exit.

Owners are significantly exposed to the operating risk in a hotel investment. Any fluctuation in the operating performance of a hotel asset has a significant impact over the net operating income available to its owner to service the hotel mortgage/senior debt and secure a level of capital to justify a return on the investment. A severe economic downturn, for example, could potentially force the business (and its owner) into liquidation and result in a lender's step in, pulling the owner out of business. Obviously, the uplift is equally positively rewarding.

The main operating risk factor in a hotel property is the volatility of its net operating income (EBITDA) throughout the holding period. The more the net operating income is likely to fluctuate over a specific period of time, the higher the operating risk.

Given the operating structure of a hotel asset, this risk can be attributed to two main characteristics: revenues and the fixed cost structure of the operation. Various dynamics and business characteristics, whether controllable or uncontrollable, impact on these operating risk factors.

There are fundamental operating differences between the various types of hotel asset. For example, while a conventional full service hotel typically requires a balanced and broadly based business mix (segmentation), an extended stay property is less dependent on such an operating dynamic. Furthermore, while the room inventory of a full service hotel is highly perishable (each room needs to be sold to different guests on a continuing basis), an extended stay unit inventory is less perishable given the long average length of stay of such an asset class (in both cases, however, you cannot sell yesterday's available room!). Other operating differences include the fact that the fixed cost structure of a full service hotel operation is greater than that of a limited service hotel or an extended stay property (due to food and beverage facilities, revenue mix, service quality expectations and so forth). Moreover, our assessment of historical trading data of various hotel categories and classifications suggests that limited service hotels and extended stay units tend to be less vulnerable to economic shocks and external factors than full service and luxury hotels.

Some of the external factors that also impact the operating performance of a hotel asset include the demand and supply dynamics in a given market, as well as the barriers of entry for a specific asset class. An overly supplied market will undoubtedly hamper the trading performance of a hotel asset. Yet, barriers of entry such as scarcity of land, capital liquidity, zoning restrictions, planning regulations, bureaucracy and so forth typically serve as a hedge against such a risk. While most hotel asset classes are equally exposed to this risk, one could argue that full service hotels tend to be, on occasions, hedged against that risk due to the barriers of entry associated with this asset class.

In terms of the shared ownership asset class, despite the cash flow volatility of such a business model, the operating risk of this type of hotel derivative is considerably reduced (to the original developer/investor), as the room inventory is typically sold before (or upon) completion of the development, which either transfers this risk to the individual owners of the units or significantly dilutes/eliminates this risk. The level of return associated with the operation of a shared ownership property is lower than that of other asset classes (between 10 and 20 per cent of total holding period returns), given the initial inventory exit/sale of the units. Therefore, the operating risk of a shared ownership development is minimal (unless the developer provides guaranteed returns), from the original developer's perspective.

Obsolescence/Exit Risk

This risk impacts the ability of the owner of the hotel property to exit the investment or extend its economic life. This risk involves the potential decrease in a property's value as at the envisaged exit period. It is the uncertainty of the future value of the hotel asset.

Obsolescence is an incurable economic depreciation that has a considerable impact on the holding period returns of a hotel asset. There are various types of obsolescence that can impact hotel real estate but generally they are classified as either internal or external obsolescence.

Internal Obsolescence

Typically this is functional obsolescence that occurs when a hotel no longer functions/operates the way it did when it was initially built; it is a change in the fitness for purpose. This includes the physical deterioration of the building, which can be either curable via repairs and capital expenditure or incurable if the basic structure of the building has been heavily damaged over time. While most types of physical deterioration of a hotel asset can be curable, sometimes it makes no economic sense to do so.

For example, while the physical deterioration of the external appearance (exterior, public areas and so forth) or the internal specifications (services, finishes and so forth) can be cured, the property can become obsolete if the configuration of the building is no longer appropriate (style, plan layout, floor to ceiling heights, structural damages and so forth). In general, most hotel assets are equally prone to this type of obsolescence; however, service/budget hotels are more exposed to this risk given the initial economical approach to the building and low-cost layout/structure.

External Obsolescence

This is the loss in income and value resulting from external factors. Various economic, demographic, environmental, legal and social factors may impact the economic viability of a hotel which may not be curable. For example, new legislation regarding safety may render a property obsolete if it impacts the layout of the hotel. A shift in the economic, demographic or social gravity of the immediate area of the hotel can also render a property obsolete, especially if the hotel is located in a secondary location (as is usually the case with limited service and budget hotels with the aim to reduce the initial cost of land to boost economic viability) or if the area in which it was originally built migrates from primary to secondary over time.

Given the structural design, layout, building structure, style and location of limited service hotels, they are exposed to the highest risk of internal and eternal obsolescence when compared to other types of hotel properties. Extended stay properties are less exposed to obsolescence risk than limited service hotels (given their typical locations, layout and so forth), but are more exposed to this risk than full service and luxury hotel assets (especially from a 'fitness for purpose' perspective).

The success of a shared ownership property investment depends heavily on the ability of the developer to sell the units during the development phase (or during the few years following the completion of the development). Therefore, this risk factor has a dual risk potential (in terms of its impact on investment returns) when compared to other asset classes: while the property itself may not become physically obsolete after a period of time, given the emerging nature of the shared ownership sector, the complexity of the exit process (heavy administrative and marketing overheads) and the heterogeneity of potential investors this asset class inherits a high level of exit risk. This exit risk occurs in two phases: initial exit of the units and exit upon transfer of ownership back to the developer in Year 20 or thereafter.

Synthesis and Implications

Various asset classes within the hotel sector have different risk profiles throughout their cycles. While full service and luxury hotels inherit higher levels of development and operating risks than limited service and extended stay properties, upscale hotel properties are less exposed to the obsolescence/exit risk. Furthermore, while shared ownership developments have a lower operating risk than other hotel derivatives, this asset class probably inherits a high exit risk.

Therefore, the fundamental differences in the various asset classes have different implications for their investment evaluation, lending characteristics and asset management.

Typically, when evaluating a hotel investment, one would project the property's cash flow over a specific period of time, and would then apply various financing parameters to assess the value of the investment in today's prices. Usually, a property yield is applied to those cash flows in order to compute the investment value of the asset as at a specific date.

The property yield is usually the combination of the cost of capital as well as the potential property appreciation or depreciation. Practically, the main variables that form the property yield include the cost of debt, the cost of equity, an optimum/ market specific financing structure and a terminal capitalisation rate (the residual/reversionary value upon exit). These variables each impact the various time cycles in the cash flow differently.

The simplified illustration of an investment assessment:

- The developer's profit reflects the development risk associated with that phase; the higher the development risk, the greater the required profit percentage. Upon making investment decisions, the total development cost (including developer's profit – and taking into account the development risk) is then compared with the net present value of the cash flow (taking into account the time value of money).
- The cost of capital is typically applied to the operating cash flow during the holding period as well as upon discounting the exit/residual value of the investment to Year 1. This parameter reflects the operating risk (and other risks inherited from the development phase) of a hotel asset. A high operating risk would fuel the debt and equity yields and would therefore imply a higher weighted cost of capital.
- The terminal capitalisation rate reflects the value of a hotel property at exit, taking into account economic cycles as well as capital appreciation/depreciation. In a conventional valuation, this rate is usually the adjusted cost of capital less inflation. In practice, however, the terminal capitalisation rate can fluctuate in order to reflect future capital appetite, yield compressions, cycles or, in some instances, obsolescence. A higher obsolescence risk in an asset class would therefore necessitate a higher terminal capitalisation rate (hence a lower exit value).

Assuming identical market and economic conditions and based on the preceding assessments, we make the following observations:

- A lower developer's profit (in percentage and quantum) could be applied to extended stay properties and limited service hotels, when compared to full service and luxury hotel assets, given their lower development risk.

- A lower cost of capital could be applied to extended stay and limited service hotel properties, when compared to full service and luxury hotel assets, in order to reflect their lower operating risk profile.
- Given the lower exit risk of five-star and luxury hotels, a lower terminal capitalisation rate should therefore be applied to this type of hotel property, when compared to limited service and extended stay properties.
- Due to the comparatively higher obsolescence risk of limited service/budget hotels, it should be no surprise when lenders resist long-term bullet/balloon financing for such an asset class.
- While the asset manager of a typical full service/luxury hotel continuously aims at maximising the value of the hotel asset and improving its operating cash flow, the asset management objective of limited service or extended stay properties should mainly focus on maximising the operating cash flow throughout the economic life cycle of the asset.

Unfortunately, no generalisation can be made or concluded in terms of what is the safest or least risky type of hotel property to invest in, given the various risk profiles of the asset classes throughout their economic cycle. It is certain, however, that risk diversification can be achieved within the industry (from a portfolio perspective or by combining two or more asset classes within one development), which would enhance the risk-adjusted returns to the owners.

We would highlight that this approach of risk assessment is theoretical/fundamental, and that various market dynamics as well as characteristics and levels of investor appetite must always be considered upon appraising a hotel property.

Capital markets can have diverse characteristics and risk profiles and would oftentimes view the risk of a hotel investment differently; a fact that must always be considered upon appraising an investment, as long as it represents the market participants. As in the theory of equity markets, the 'market efficiency' of the hotel transaction sector is a debatable topic.

Finally, we emphasise that the specific risk associated with any individual hotel investment is determined by the characteristics of that investment, including location, property, ownership, management and so forth. Various hotel investors have different risk profiles, investment appetite and stimulants as well as perception of time. Once these are better understood, the hotel asset classes and risks can then be chosen!

Risk Assessment and Key Risk Areas

A risk assessment is an important step in protecting your workers and your business, as well as complying with the law. It helps you focus on the risks that really matter in your workplace – the ones with the potential to cause real harm. In many instances, straightforward measures can readily control risks, for example ensuring spillages are cleaned up promptly so people do not slip, or cupboard drawers are kept closed to ensure people do not trip. For most, that means simple, cheap and effective measures to ensure your most valuable asset-your workforce-is protected.

The law does not expect you to eliminate all risk, but you are required to protect people as far as 'reasonably practicable'. This 'five steps to risk assessment' guide tells you how to achieve that with a minimum of fuss.

Example Risk Assessment for Food Preparation and Service

Important Reminder

This example risk assessment shows the kind of approach a small business might take. It can be used as a guide to think through some of the hazards in your business and the steps you need to take to control the risks. Please note that it is not a generic risk assessment that you can just put your company name on and adopt wholesale without any thought. This would not satisfy the law-and would not be effective in protecting people.

Every business is different-you need to think through the hazards and controls required in your business for yourself.

This example risk assessment applies to food preparation and food service areas (restaurants, cafés, sandwich bars, pubs, takeaways or hotel kitchens).

Setting the Scene

The catering manager carried out the risk assessment in this café. The business employs five permanent staff working a variety of shifts to prepare, cook and serve food. A young person under 16 helps on a Saturday to serve food and load and unload the dishwasher. An employment permit for the young person has been obtained from the local authority. One staff member does not speak English well. The business, which is located on the high street, is open from 7.00 am to 5.30 pm.

How was the Risk Assessment Done?

The manager followed the guidance in *Five steps to risk assessment.*

1. To identify the hazards, the manager:
   - o looked at the guidance on HSE's web pages for catering and hospitality and the employment of young people;
   - o walked around the kitchen, the stockroom and all other areas, noting things that might pose a risk and taking HSE's guidance into consideration;
   - o talked to staff to learn from their knowledge and experience, and to listen to their concerns and opinions. He paid particular attention to the requirements for ensuring the young person's safety;
   - o looked at the accident book, to understand what particular risks previously resulted in incidents.
2. The manager wrote down who could be harmed and how.
3. The manager then wrote down what controls, if any, were in place to eliminate or reduce the likelihood of somebody being hurt. He compared these controls to the good practice in HSE's guidance. Where he did not consider the existing controls to be good enough, he wrote down what else needed to be done.
4. The manager put in place the actions the risk assessment identified as necessary. He discussed the findings with staff, pinned it up in a prominent place so that all staff could see it and made it part of the induction process for new staff. He told the young person's guardians about the

findings of the risk assessment and how risk to that young person will be controlled. And he made sure that the worker, who had difficulty understanding English, had the safety arrangements explained to her in a language she understood.

5. The manager decided to review the risk assessment every year, or straightaway if major changes in the workplace happened. To get a better understanding of the risks, the manager also asked staff to report any accident, however minor.

Example Risk Assessment for a Night Club

Important Reminder

This example risk assessment shows the kind of approach a small business might take. It can be used as a guide to think through some of the hazards in your business and the steps you need to take to control the risks. Please note that it is not a generic risk assessment that you can just put your company name on and adopt wholesale without any thought. This would not satisfy the law-and would not be effective in protecting people.

Every business is different-you need to think through the hazards and controls required in your business for yourself.

Setting the Scene

The manager did the risk assessment at this nightclub, which is located in a city centre. It has three bars, three dance floors and an additional 'quiet bar'. Live bands also perform there.

Thirty staff are employed at the club, which is open to the public from 8.00 pm to 3.00 am. Five staff members do not speak English as their first language, but are sufficiently fluent to be able to do their job, understand safety instructions, deal with difficult situations etc. There is a staff room, where drinks can be prepared and food heated, and separate toilet and washing facilities for staff.

The club is cleaned every morning by cleaners from a general office cleaning contractors. The cleaners store the cleaning materials in a locked cupboard. Maintenance work with the exception of the most straightforward activities which are done in-house, is done by contractors. These are chosen from a preferred list of suppliers. Work is undertaken following procedures set out in the club's permit to work system for contractors.

The premises were built before 2000. The building has been surveyed for the presence of asbestos. Asbestos-containing materials (ACMs) were found but as the ACMs were in good condition and in places were they were unlikely to be damaged, worked on or disturbed, it was decided to leave them in place.

How was the Risk Assessment Done?

The manager followed the guidance in *Five steps to risk assessment*.

1. To identify the hazards, the manager:
   - o looked at HSE's web pages for small businesses, and for entertainment and leisure, to learn where hazards can occur.
   - o walked around the club noting, things that might pose a risk and taking HSE's guidance into consideration;
   - o talked to supervisors and staff to learn from their knowledge and experience of areas and activities, and to listen to their opinions about health and safety issues in the workplace;
   - o talked to the office cleaning contractors, and to his preferred suppliers of maintenance work, to ensure that their activities did not pose a risk to club staff, and vice-versa; and
   - o looked at the accident book, to gain an understanding of previous incidents.
2. The manager then wrote down who could be harmed by the hazards and how.
3. For each hazard, he wrote down what controls, if any, were in place to manage these hazards. He then compared these controls to the good practice guidance provided on the HSE website. Where existing controls were not considered good enough, the manager wrote down what else needed to be done to control the risk.

4. Putting the risk assessment into practice, the manager decided and recorded who was responsible for implementing the actions identified as necessary and when they should be done. When each action was done, he ticked it off and noted the date. He also made it part of the induction process for new staff.
5. At the staff meeting, the office manager discussed the findings of the risk assessment with staff and pinned up a copy in the staffroom. He decided to review and update the risk assessment every year, or straightaway if any major changes in the workplace happened.

Example Risk Assessment for a Pub

Important Reminder

This example risk assessment shows the kind of approach a small business might take. It can be used as a guide to think through some of the hazards in your business and the steps you need to take to control the risks. Please note that it is not a generic risk assessment that you can just put your company name on and adopt wholesale without any thought. This would not satisfy the law-and would not be effective in protecting people.

Every business is different-you need to think through the hazards and controls required in your business for yourself.

Setting the Scene

The manager carried out the risk assessment in this pub, which is located in a suburban, residential area.

This risk assessment only addresses liquid sales; a separate example covers the occupational health and safety aspects for food preparation.

The manager and his partner live on the premises, they also employ eight other bar staff, four full-time who work lunchtime and evening shifts, five-days every week and four part-time staff at weekends and providing absence cover for the full-time staff.

The pub has a function room with dance floor for live-music events and discos with a bar. It is cleaned every morning by a cleaner, the manager and his partner cover when the cleaner is on holiday. The manager buys cleaning products from the wholesaler or from a rep who visits once a month.

The premises were built before 2000; the pub building was surveyed for asbestos when it was acquired by the owner. Asbestos-containing materials found in the survey have been recorded, a copy of the survey is kept at the pub and the owner holds a duplicate copy. A further, more detailed survey can be arranged to send out to contractors when building works need to be done.

How was the Risk Assessment Done?

The manager followed the guidance in *Five steps to risk assessment.*

1. To identify the hazards, the manager:
   - looked at HSE's web pages for small businesses and for the hospitality and catering industry to learn where hazards can occur;
   - made clear who was responsible for what under the terms of the tenancy agreement. This was especially important for issues such as asbestos management, gas safety, pressurised equipment, replacement of carpets;
   - walked around the pub, noting things that might be dangerous and taking HSE's guidance into consideration;
   - talked to the staff (including the cleaner) about their work to learn from their knowledge and experience of areas and activities, and to listen to their opinions about health and safety issues in the workplace;
   - talked to his preferred suppliers of maintenance work, to ensure that their activities did not pose a risk to pub staff, and vice versa;
   - observed deliveries by his food and drink suppliers; and
   - looked at the accident book, to gain an understanding of previous incidents.
2. The manager then wrote down who could be harmed by the hazards and how.

3. For each hazard, the manager wrote down what controls, if any, were in place to manage these hazards. He then compared these controls to the good practice guidance provided on the HSE website. Where existing controls were not considered good enough, the manager wrote down what else needed to be done to control the risk.
4. Putting the risk assessment into practice, the manager decided and recorded who was responsible for implementing the actions identified as necessary and when they should be done. When each action was done, he ticked it off and noted the date. He also made it part of the induction process for new staff.
5. At the staff meeting, the manager discussed the findings of the risk assessment with staff and pinned up a copy in the staff room. He decided to review and update the risk assessment every year, or straight away if any major changes in the workplace happened.

Get Rid of the Risks With Hotel Insurance

Insurance is one of the most important investments a business can make. Having insurance protects not only you and your business but your clients as well. If something went wrong and you didn't have insurance, could you afford to cover the out of pocket expense? Odds are that your business couldn't handle that expense and it would end with the closure of your business, thus insurance is an absolute must!

If you are in the hospitality industry and your business is that of a night club, pub or hotel it is even more important for you to have insurance. Hospitality insurance can protect you from the losses you can't afford. Whether you worry your windows will be busted out during a vandal attack or that of a person being injured on your premises, hospitality insurance can help ease your worries.

Night Clubs are notorious for having issues of not being fully covered when it comes to insurance. When purchasing insurance for a night club it is important that you get the right coverage. Public and Employer liability, buildings and contents, all need to have coverage in your policy.

Public liability insurance will cover your business in the event that someone is injured on your property. Having public liability insurance will protect your business from the high settlement costs that your business could incur during the legalities of a claim. Employee liability insurance works the same way except it covers your employees.

Since night clubs are often a large investment it is absolutely essential that your hospitality insurance covers the building as well as your contents. Failing to get the proper coverage for these would be detrimental to your business. You should always check with your insurance provider to make sure that your policy covers you in the event that your license or rent is lost. Being fully covered is essential to the future of your business! The same is true for other businesses in the hospitality industry as well.

Pub and bar insurance coverage is similar to that of what a night club would use however hotel insurance requires a bit more than that. Since hotels often have a great deal of money invested in to their buildings as well as their contents inside the building making certain that your insurance policy covers the proper amount of contents is essential. It is also just as important to make certain that your policy covers any goods you may have in transit at times as well as coverage for any legal expenses your business may incur.

Regardless of what your business is in the hospitality insurance you must have the proper insurance in order to secure a beneficial and prosperous future for your business. Your goal should be to protect not only you and your business but your clients as well and having the proper insurance coverage is the absolute best way to make sure that you offer that protection. Investing in the appropriate insurance coverage will be an added expense however it will cut your expenses in the long run and is well worth it.

Insurance in Hospitality Industry

Every individual faces risk. Illness, accidents, the acts of others, and even death, are all potential hazards each of us faces in life. Your business will face possible calamities, also. Floods, fire, and the acts of guests, employees, and others can all put your business at risk. To guard against the financial loss these risks can bring, both individuals and businesses need to insure themselves. In its simplest form, insurance involves the spreading of risk from one person or business to a larger group.

Hospitality businesses seek insurance, or protection from risk, for two basic reasons. First, because doing so makes good financial sense. Second, some types of insurance coverage are required either by law (such as workers ' compensation) or by lenders to protect their collateral. Consider, for example, the restaurateur who owns a business that provides her with a salary of $ 100,000 per year. The restaurant is her sole source of income. If the restaurant were to burn down, she would lose this source of income.

To protect her business, and her income, she would want to buy a fire insurance policy that would pay to completely replace the restaurant in the event of a fire, provided that the cost of the insurance was reasonable. Not buying the insurance would put this restaurateur and her family at great financial risk. Buying the insurance would provide the restaurateur with both financial security, in the event of an accidental fire, and the peace of mind that such security brings.

To be protected from risk does not mean that hazardous events will not occur. Insurance does mean, however, that the person with insurance is provided some protection against the financial loss he or she may incur as a result of a hazardous event.

The insurance industry is built upon four fundamental premises:

1. The type of hazard the insurance company is underwriting must be faced by a large enough number of individuals or businesses so that statisticians can use actuarial (actuary) methods to predict the average frequency of loss involved in the risk.
2. The monetary value of the loss must be calculable against an accepted standard. For example, if a hotel seeks coverage for broken windows caused by vandals, it must be possible for the insurer to fairly determine the cost of replacing such a window.
3. The premiums (fees) for the insurance must be low enough to attract those who seek to be insured but high enough

to support the number of losses that will be incurred by the insurer.

4. The risk must not have the possibility of occurring so frequently during any given time period that the insurer cannot pay all legitimate claims. Insurance companies spend millions of dollars annually researching industries to determine the risk factor of providing insurance for a specific market, such as hospitality. Obviously, the fewer number of casualty losses, workers injured, lawsuits, and so on, the lower the risk that the insurance company may have to pay out money on a claim. Logically then, the safer the operation, and the safer the industry as a whole, the lower the cost of insurance.

The insurance contract between an insurer and an insured is called a policy.

There are a variety of policy types, but they can be conveniently grouped into three categories:

Life Insurance

Health Insurance

Property-casualty (often referred to as " property-liability ").

Life insurance policies generally are written to pay a certain amount of money at the time of the insured ' s death, or to pay the insured an annuity upon the insured ' s reaching a specified age. Health insurance is generally created to pay for hospital and doctor bills, as well as annuity payments for those who are disabled. In the hospitality industry, it would be common for you, as a manager, to receive some level of both life and health insurance as part of your compensation package.

Property-liability insurance provides financial protection (indemnification) in the event of occurrences such as floods, fires, lawsuits, and automobile accidents. As a manager, it is important to know the types of insurance policies that make sense for your operation and how to evaluate the quality of the companies that offer insurance, as well as the merits of the actual policies.

It is also important to remember that insurance companies, like hospitality companies, are in business to make a profit. Profits in the insurance industry are the result of increasing premium amounts, increased return from the investment of premiums, and the reduction of costs, including the payment of insurance claims.

Because this is true, insurers are very careful to pay only those claims that are proven to be legitimate and within the terms of the insurance policy.

Because insurance protects against risk at an agreed-upon price, it is critical that you as a hospitality manager know:

- The risks you are insuring against.
- The amount of coverage you will receive.
- Any exceptions to your coverage that are written into your policy.
- How much the insurance will cost.
- The likelihood that the insurance company is financially sound enough to pay, if it becomes necessary.

To purchase insurance, a potential buyer must demonstrate that he or she has an insurable interest in the premises to be insured. That is, he or she must demonstrate that a loss would, in fact, affect him or her in a material way. This insurance concept is fundamental and helps protect against possible intentional acts of destruction or fraud. In addition, an insured must honestly divulge information needed by the insurer to enable the insurer to establish appropriate premium rates.

Security Threats – the Hospitality Industry is on the Front Line

Terrorist attacks and threats against the hospitality industry, whether large international chains or individual properties, have grown alarmingly since 9/11. It is my conviction that this trend will continue to grow in terms of numbers and level of sophistication.

Modern day terrorism, which until the second half of the 20th century was mainly focused on targeted attacks, has since been increasingly directed against soft targets (targets that are not major public or government centers or sites). By attacking soft targets because of their relative ease of access, terrorists have improved their chances to achieve their objectives which include inflicting higher numbers of causalities, causing extensive property damage, and undermining the well-being and public morale of local, as well as national populations.

The hospitality and tourism industries, which in this case refer to hotels, malls (including large complexes such as gaming/ mall/hotel complexes etc.), mega-events and transportation services, are certainly natural targets: the effects of attacks on such sites are obvious and far-reaching. Even with this new awareness, it appears that only the airline industry has adopted strong measures in light of the 9/11 attacks. One has just to look around and compare the investment in security measures between airports and hotels. Are hotels that different from airplanes? A well-placed bomb in a hotel lobby could cause much more damage and casualties than an airborne bomb. Obviously, not enough is being done.

During my tenure as Israel's National Police Commissioner, security plans and programs were implemented for Israel's hospitality and related tourism industry. As the problem was extensively studied, a series of approaches and practices were developed and implemented.

The success of this process was also reflected by the fact that freedom of movement in public spaces was maintained with minimal restrictions by the security measures. The anti-terror police activity helped to formulate policies that have evolved into security standards within the industry. As a result, the state of Israel has established a set of methods and security procedures specifically designed to foil and mitigate attacks and protect soft targets.

Up until the time I was appointed as Commissioner, my prior positions focused on security and intelligence issues. Most of my work included developing comprehensive security concepts and programs based on progressive levels of security, intensified intelligence gathering capabilities and modes of cooperation between the various security organizations both in times of crisis and during normal operations.

It was during this period that I was also responsible for establishing Israel's elite counter terror unit, The YAMAM, recognized today as the most effective counter terror force in the country and used as a model for anti-terror paramilitary forces around the globe.

The continuous daily threat against soft targets in Israel and the policies developed in response are based on a learning curve that has evolved over a long period of time. An added-value benefit of these programs has actually been the reduction in crime in environs surrounding the protected targets.

The Israeli model shows the real needs of the global hospitality industry which must be immediately addressed. The industry must better prepare itself by adopting improved security measures such as those successfully applied in Israel. The negative consequences of a successful attack on even a single hotel can have far-reaching ripple effects on the industry as a whole. An attack on a hotel in Boston can have an immediate costly impact on the industry across the country, therefore not only "visible" targets must prepare, but every single site must take steps to protect itself from terror attacks, and just as important, steps to mitigate the economic effect of an attack anywhere in the USA.

A professional security assessment should be conducted at each individual site by a qualified company. The company should have experience and expertise in the hospitality industry. Plans should be cost effective, prioritized, and implemented in stages to cover all aspects of an overall security program.

With growing rates of increased terrorist activity reported in the media, I am firmly convinced that the hospitality and related industries are faced with an increased potential threat of international and homegrown terrorism. Although most attacks so far have occurred outside of the US, operators and officials must not assume that "it will not happen to us." Frequent arrests of terrorism planners as well as foiled attempts reported periodically throughout the US and abroad should be cause for alarm as to the severity of the threat of future attacks. Denying this reality and doing nothing can potentially lead to future disaster if appropriate action is not taken now.

Evidence seems to indicate that hospitality and related industries are still not prepared to take appropriate action. Management's reluctance to invest accordingly is dangerous, especially for high-risk situations. Establishing a secure environment is not an easy task, particularly during peak seasons. The accumulated experience in Israel dictates that utilizing state-of-the-art technologies in conjunction with improved, modern securities measures and approaches does in fact improve overall security in addition to addressing terrorism concerns.

TIX expertise is based on years of successfully proven Israeli experience that demonstrates how improved security systems and programs can be implemented cost-effectively utilizing existing budgets without major investments.

The Shadow of 9/11: Terrorism and Premises Liability for Hotels

Introduction

Recent terrorist attacks on hotels in the Middle East, in Islamabad, Mumbai, Peshawar and Jakarta, and flying major international flags including Marriott, Taj Mahal, Oberoi and Pearl, resulted in many hotel guest deaths and injuries, and substantial property damage. One of these attacks was carried out by guest suicide bombers detonating bombs manufactured in their hotel rooms.

Those attacks and this article should be seen as a wake-up call to hotel operators, not only in that region but also in the West since Western hotel brands and Western tourists were targets in some locations. Also, new terrorist methodologies used in these attacks are affecting and changing legal standards for premises liability to guests, invitees, patrons, customers, etc. ("guests") who might be killed or injured with attendant property damage in any similar attack in the United States or its territories.

The tragedies of September 11, 2001 generated numerous Congressional initiatives designed to prevent the recurrence of such devastating terrorist activity. However, most of these new laws and their attendant regulations have been directed toward better airport and aircraft security through the federalization of airport passenger and baggage screeners and increased aircraft security measures, but there are no new specific federal requirements for hotels.

Congress has also created laws to provide terrorism insurance subsidies for airlines which were in economic jeopardy as a result of these events, and extended government terrorism underwriting to other industries in order to provide the foundation for writing of terrorism insurance for businesses which might otherwise be in economic jeopardy.

As part of this legislative effort the Transportation Security Administration and the Homeland Security Department were established to address the United State Government's primary duty and responsibility to protect its citizens. But if the government fails to protect as in 9/11, hotels may bear greater responsibilities to their guests.

However, perhaps the most significant development from the events of 9/11 is the awareness of need for greater vigilance and implementation of some forms of protection for hotels which invite guests and others into their facilities. Prior to 9/11, there were few security requirements except those based on protection from potential criminal activity wherein some civil liability for damage to guests and property might surface *only after some prior criminal act had occurred*. In other words, like the basis of liability for a first time a dog bit a mailman or an invitee to a home, a prior bite by the dog was necessary to show foreseeabilty; so *"the dog got the first bite!"*

Many cases dealing with liability for hotels included a similar theory that required a prior bad or criminal act on the hotel premises before any liability attached because the act was not "foreseeable." It was hornbook law that in order for an owner or operator of a facility to be liable to a guest or invitee, there must be a form of harm that is "foreseeable" and damage to the person or property.

In lawsuits filed as a result of the 9/11 attacks against airlines, aircraft manufacturers and others, Judge Halerstein of the Supreme Court of New York held that the attacks were foreseeable in view of the prior history of attacks.

The prior standard for hotels required the Innkeeper to "create a reasonably safe environment" for guests, but the events of 9/11 and similar attacks, when considered collectively, suggest that such attacks are now foreseeable, which requires the attention and appropriate action on the part of owners and operators in the hospitality industry.

The question that must be asked is whether hotels should institute some additional security measures similar to those now mandated for airlines and airports, and whether the economic trade-off of cost savings of inaction and/or providing minimal security, is worth the risk and cost of liability in the event of a terrorist attack.

Furthermore, such questions should consider whether more stringent anti-terrorism security concepts should be applicable only in "high risk" areas such as New York, Washington, Los Angeles, San Francisco and Chicago, and whether the foreseeable risks are the same in remote, "lower profile" locations.

The new legal concept for assessing such risk is the "Totality of the Circumstances," an analysis that includes the idea that terrorists might perceive that a target hotel might have lax security. If so, resulting publicity and political value of damage may be significant in the absence of owner or government antiterrorist and anticrime security procedures, thereby providing an invitation for an attack. Whether such decisions by terrorists or criminals are random or strategic, these acts are now foreseeable within the meaning of the law of premises liability using the "totality of circumstances" test.

Security Regulations and Case Analysis Confirms Foreseeability

The passage of the Aviation and Transportation Security Act ("Security Act") establishing the Transportation Security Administration ("TSA") within the Department of Transportation to perform pre-employment background checks, hiring, training and supervising of all security personnel, purchasing of essential security equipment, and addressing an extensive array of actual or perceived deficiencies that existed in transportation safety protocols, indicates that, as Judge Halerstein opined, attacks were considered to be foreseeable.

Thus, the rules for aviation, including the processing of checked baggage through use of magnetometers, other electronic devices for luggage screening for explosives and strict control of access to secured areas all suggest that review of some of these procedures might be useful for the hospitality industry even though similar government security support may not yet be available.

The Patriot Act for the first time adds domestic as well as international terrorism to criminal statutes, therefore authorizing additional enforcement power for the Department of Justice ("DOJ"). Moreover, provisions of the act further emphasize that government believes further terrorist attacks are possible and therefore foreseeable, not only in the aviation context, but also in criminal and terrorist acts in the United States involving hotels and other public facilities.

If Terrorist Threats are Probable and Foreseeable, then what Action is Suggested for Hotels?

Prior to 9/11, aircraft hijackers would use the threat of explosives in a baggage compartment, or use firearms, grenades and other conventional weapons in the passenger cabin, to coerce the aircraft crew into landing at a neutral site, and thereafter extract ransom money or the release of other terrorists in Western custody. Flight crews were instructed to comply with the demands of these "traditional" terrorists and to land as instructed in order to avoid personal injury or death to passengers or crew.

Indeed, commentators have noted that even if the checked baggage of every passenger on the four flights involved in the September 11 attacks had been processed through explosive detection machines, and even if the carry-on baggage screeners had seen box cutters in the terrorists' carry-on bags, existing security measures would not have prevented the terrorists from boarding the aircraft with the box cutters, because box cutters did not appear on the list of prohibited items.

The September 11 scenario was a model of creative thinking by the terrorists, using a mock hijacking which appeared similar to past hijackings and then using the aircraft as a missile to crash into buildings, and thus was a new and unanticipated strategy. Other examples include explosives in baggage checked in remote third world countries reach connecting flights, checked guns and hand grenades,entry to protected areas through unsecured back doors, and bombs concealed as a pizza in a briefcase.

The installation and apparent success of better security procedures by the aviation industry to address these types of patterns for terrorist attacks may suggest a greater current risk for other less secure facilities as noted in recent hotel attacks in the Far East and subways in London and Madrid.

Indeed, hospitality industry risk managers must consider such possible alternative terrorism tactics and scenarios. If there are no magnetometers or explosive detection devices at entry ways of a hotel, how could management prevent entry to the hotel of a terrorist carrying a bomb or plastic components in a large suitcase, or worse, one containing a small nuclear device or dirty bomb?

Similarly, could a terrorist driving a car or small delivery truck with a large cargo of explosives be detected before reaching the hotel entrance, lobby or service areas? Could a terrorist who checks in as a guest carrying materials to construct bombs in his room be detected and prevented from duplicating in the United States the scenario preceding the attack which occurred in Jakarta? And could a terrorist gain admittance to a hotel through one of the merchant stores backing up to the lobby or other exits if entry security is not required in the store lease?

Risk managers should consider additional security in addressing these kinds of issues and the balancing of possible negative guest reaction to heightened security in comparison to liability, damage to the hotel's reputation and future loss of business. A review of existing General Third Party liability insurance coverage, terrorism riders if any, and war risk policies would also be a constructive exercise to determine coverage and whether new security protections might result in lower insurance premiums. If additional security procedures are not adopted, the owner or operator might have difficulty in defending lawsuits initiated by business invitees injured in a terrorist attack.

The argument that "the attack was not foreseeable" or that "the government should be responsible for failing to discover the terrorist plot" may no longer be a viable argument. Indeed, that is what Judge Halerstein determined in the 9/11 litigation. New security approaches might be needed to avoid higher exposure to damages, and even possible punitive damage and harmful publicity affecting future guests.

Congress initially enacted legislation providing for underwriting of terrorism insurance reimbursement for existing insurers, and insurance indemnity has been extended to other businesses in the form of the now extended Terrorism Risk Insurance Program Reauthorization Act. But "bail-out" funds for future terrorist attacks might not be available if heightened security procedures are absent. In assessing their risks, corporate managers and their experts need to evaluate the impact of developing premises liability law in various jurisdictions.

Premises Liability was Expanded by September 11 Events

New Definitions of Terrorism

Terrorist targets both inside and outside the United States have not been limited to airlines and airports, the Oklahoma City bombing, the 1992 World Trade Center bombing, the 1996 Atlanta Olympics incident, and many less publicized bombing and arson cases which were not designated as "terrorist" incidents, because there were no domestic terrorism statutes. Although the 1992 WTC attack was labeled terrorism, the perpetrators were prosecuted under criminal statue. Indeed most of the other terrorist-like incidents prior to 9/11 were considered criminal acts and were prosecuted under general criminal statutes such as murder, arson, espionage, kidnapping and aircraft piracy. Title 18 of the United States Code as it existed prior to September 11 only contained a definition of "international terrorism."

The Britannica defines terrorism as "(1) the act of terrorizing, (2) a system of government that seeks to rule by intimidation, and (3) unlawful acts of violence committed in an organized attempt to overthrow a government." This definition suggests a required "intent" to achieve some political gain or to intimidate political adversaries is a necessary element of an act of terrorism. This concept is part of the definition of a terrorist act that would trigger the proposed United States government terrorism insurance program. The definition in the extended insurance provisions now defines an act of terrorism as any act that is certified by the Secretary of the Treasury, in concurrence with the Attorney General of the United States, to: (i) be an act of terrorism; (ii) to be a violent act or act that is dangerous to human life, property or infrastructure; (iii) to have resulted in damage within the United states, or outside the United States in the case of (1) an air carrier or vessel, or (2) the premises of a United State mission; and (iv) to have been committed by an individual or individuals as part of an effort to coerce the civilian population of the United States or to influence the policy of the United States, or to affect the conduct of the United States Government by coercion or to affect government policy.

This definition creates a distinction between a previously defined criminal act such as murder requiring mens rea to kill, and the terrorist type of murder requiring the additional intent for political effect. The Patriot Act amended the prior statutes making domestic terrorism a crime when related to arson, fire, derailment, use of biological or other dangerous weapons, and interference with or conspiracy to attack. Therefore, many of these criminal acts which are not within the terrorism definition will not be covered by the government's terrorism insurance, since there would not be the required designation of the event as terrorism by the Secretary of the Treasury or the Attorney General. As to those non-terrorism criminal events, general liability insurance ("all risk") would be the source of coverage.

Obviously in that instance there would by no government terrorism indemnity. If a review of security provided by the hotel was considered inadequate, the insurer might reserve its rights or withhold coverage. In *Pan American World Airways, Inc. v. Aetna Casualty & Surety Co.* the court discussed the distinction between negligent/criminal activity and terrorism in determining the difference between the application of "war risk" and "all risk" insurance coverage for an accident caused by a terrorist bomb on a Pan American flight. The court concluded that unless "war" had been officially "declared" by a sovereign nation, terrorist activity was not covered by war risk insurance (the pre-curser for the U.S. government terrorism risk insurance). Only claims made under "all risk " (GCL) policies would probably be honored, and it would be prudent for a risk manager to carry a terrorism rider on those policies.

Effect on Premises Liability

The revised statutes criminalizing "domestic terrorist" activity will be extremely useful in prosecuting terrorists for non-aircraft-related domestic terrorist attacks and might help with discovery efforts in related civil damage cases. Although criminal statutes have some bearing on the exposure of transportation and commercial entities to liability for injury or death of passengers and guests, the questioned criminal activity might be foreseeable or anticipated based on the "totality of the circumstances" doctrine of premises liability. Commercial entity liability may differ significantly from airline liability where international treaties such as the Warsaw Convention provide for strict liability in airline disaster cases and case law makes the treaty-based claim exclusive.

The events of 9/11 now provide the necessary forseeability of potential harm. Previously, isolated criminal activity in buildings or on property would not generally establish liability unless the owner or operator of the property had a special relationship with the injured party.

Most business invitees including hotel guests, however, qualify under the special relationship test, and courts usually impose a duty of reasonable care on the property owner or operator, treating the resulting criminal activity as a "defect" if information was available and reasonable analysis suggests the need for protective action against possible threats. If a security review suggests possible defects in the process of responding to information about potential threats, liability typically will be established. The cases indicate a tendency toward foreseeability.

Based upon increased terrorist activity throughout the world, major security efforts brought to bear by Congress, and establishment of federal entities such as the Director of Homeland Security and the Transportation Security Administration, there is ample evidence that government officials believe that future attacks are foreseeable. Therefore, information regarding potential or anticipated criminal or terrorist activity, general risk in the particular area of concern, and a failure to exercise reasonable care under these circumstances will typically create liability under the "totality of circumstances" approach.

What Standard Will Apply to Premises Liability Issues?

In a claim brought by persons injured or killed by criminals or terrorists in a jurisdiction recognizing either the premises liability doctrine or some other breach of duty/negligence theory of recovery, a court would instruct the jury to determine what standard of care should apply under the relevant law and whether "totality of the circumstances" is the governing concept. As noted above, commercial entities including hotels and restaurants should be aware that they are potential targets, and they should recognize that the threat of criminal activity and terrorism not only exists, but that it might surface anywhere.

Hospitality owners and operators should review their security to evaluate possible use of some of the referenced procedures even though cost and a possible negative effect on hotel guest might be a problem. There is an argument that for a judge or jury to consider such benchmarks for hospitality entity security would be unfair because of the economic state of the industry, costs and the possible "fear effect" on hotel guests when they are subjected to heavier security.

However, recent studies in the hotel industry suggest that such fear reactions by some guest age groups have been ameliorated by their observation and toleration of travel security at airports, federal buildings and sports complexes which have educated many potential guests to the inevitability and possible security advantages.

Examples of selective use of aviation-related security procedures currently include: use of magnetometers to screen entrants; multiple security cameras in virtually all areas; screening of all employees; and stationing armed security personnel with or without uniforms in federal buildings, courthouses, some hotel properties in high risk areas, and in select U.S. railway stations. Depending on location and other circumstances hotels might implement many of these procedures and devices to supplement measures including better active coordination with police to cross reference guest check-in with photo ID cards against local law enforcement lists of possible offenders.

Other concepts would be useful such as the development and practice of an emergency plan which includes employee assignments in an emergency, observation of guest behavior with an established reporting process, and procedures for security of the air conditioning, heating and electrical back up systems. Consultation with independent security experts at a given location is probably a prudent step. Although protective countermeasures are undoubtedly expensive, their cost may pale in comparison to damages that can result from negligence litigation.

Conclusion

Negative publicity flowing from a terrorist attack or a criminal event and the consequent litigation could create serious damage to a defendant's "Reputation Equity" thereby affecting sales, and in the case of a public company, its stock value.

The existence of enhanced security to emphasizing the security measures taken by the property owner will be useful for future business, for constructing the defence to lawsuits, and for renewal of liability insurance. Many insurance policies contain coverage exclusions for "war" (declared or undeclared), invasion, rebellion, insurrection, war-like operations, civil commotion and criminal acts. In reviewing the existing policies a risk manager or operator should take steps to include riders to cover terrorism and war as well as criminal activity.

Arguments have been advanced that terrorist activities might fall within the exclusion clauses of commercial general liability insurance policies. Coverage for terrorism claims prior to September 11 was often initially excluded and subsequently provided in many policies through "buy-back" agreements, but until the government's insurance subsidy program, many insurance companies cancelled coverage for terrorist acts after the September 11 tragedies.

You Need to Reset Your Exit Strategy

Last year I posted a blog to remind hotel owners that they needed to have an exit strategy that embraces the circumstances and timetable under which they plan to exit their hotel investment. Since then, major and dramatic – some say seismic-changes have occurred in the domestic and international economy and in the hotel capital markets. It is advisable to revisit the exit strategy and revise it to reflect the current environment and foreseeable circumstances.

First the good news:

- The hotel industry is and remains cyclical and demand is closely correlated with GDP. So when the national economy becomes strong again—some are already calling an end to the recession—the demand for hotel rooms will improve.

- Supply growth has been sharply constrained by changes in the financial markets so little new product has entered most markets and not much is foreseeable for a while. So when demand strengthens, an existing hotel that has been well-maintained and well-operated through the down cycle will be likely to benefit.
- A property whose financial capital was put in place before the high-leverage, low cap rate era should, with aggressive asset management in place to tighten costs, be able to survive until the upturn.

Now the bad news:

- Average daily rates are going to take a while to come back. We saw this after the September 11th event and this time around it may take even longer for hotels to regain enough pricing power to achieve the rates that were in effect in mid-2008.
- Between tightened underwriting standards and increased interest rates, most five-year term loans that come due this year, or in 2010 or 2011, will not be able to be fully rolled over. The hotel's value is going to have to be reset and, in most cases, additional equity injected. The "experts" are forecasting "haircuts" ranging from 25-60% of 2005 – 2007 value. And a number of vulture capital funds are waiting patiently for weak owners who fall by the wayside.

Let us review and update some of the circumstances that indicate that it is time to leave a hotel investment:

- You are out of money ["the well is dry!"]

Either the hotel isn't doing well or financing to replace outstanding debt that is maturing isn't available. The hotel needs an infusion of equity and you don't have it, cannot get a return sufficient to warrant investing it or cannot raise it. This is what the bankers call a troubled asset and brokers refer to as "a distress sale." The selling price is going to be favorable only for the new owner.

- The picture isn't pretty ["it soon will be raining on my parade!"]

A new competitor is coming in – the brand is out of favour – the location is no longer prime – demand is declining—the property is older and needs much upgrading and refurbishment – a union agreement (or the threat of one) or a legislative mandate such as a "living wage" or retroactively applied building code change has changed the economics – and so on. For whatever reason or reasons, a large outflow and/or a small inflow of cash are foreseeable. Clearly, this hotel will not produce the desired return on investment in the near or medium-term future.

- My ship has come in ["here's my pot of gold!"]

There are at least two versions of this: One is the "Greater Fool Theory" where a prospective buyer wants the hotel so badly, for whatever reason, that he is willing to overpay for it, giving you a handsome profit.

The second is where the land the hotel occupies has become so valuable that it makes economic sense to buy the property, tear the building down, and replace it with a different, more profitable use –shopping center, mixed-use development, offices, condos and the like.

Believe it or not, these "ships" will be sailing again in the future. But presently they are far out at sea, or perhaps even in dry-dock. The challenge is to forecast how long it will take, and how much additional cash outlay will be required before they arrive at the pier.

- The time is right (again) ["timing is everything!"]

The bulk of the tax benefit has been realized – Opportunities considered more attractive (or safer) are available – cash is needed for other purposes — estate planning (or estate settlement) needs dictate a sale – the partners are arguing about objectives or future strategies. These are just a few examples.

If a potential or planned exit strategy is thought out, it can be modelled in a pro forma and the effects of various strategies considered and refined. The forecast and an asset management approach can then be utilized by the owner to increase his total return on the investment by:

- Managing the outflow of capital expenses (and maintenance costs) appropriately.
- Structuring financing and lease versus buy decisions for greatest benefit.

- Making short-term decisions on a host of other items, including service contracts, booking agreements, and sales and marketing activities.
- Creating an audit trail of exceptional expenses to make a case to a prospective buyer as to why the net operating income (NOI) should have been higher.

Several hotel owning companies periodically perform an exercise called a "re-buy analysis" on the hotels they already own. Considering present property and market conditions, availability of financing, new opportunities or potential threats that have arisen, capital needs, return on investment objectives and alternate opportunities available, would they buy that hotel asset today? Would they now revise their strategies from what was originally put in effect? This is a great asset management discipline that should be applied by any hotel owner on an individual asset basis.

If you model the likely income and realistically project the amount of debt that can be supported for at least the next five years, you will quickly pinpoint opportunities and roadblocks. If the hotel was highly-leveraged and its debt is maturing in the next few years, this would be a very good time to reset your exit strategy. Will it be on your terms or someone else's? If you plan to stay in the hotel, you will need to restructure your capital stack. If you can come up with strategies to add value, perhaps you can convince the lender to write down the loan by less than he would be facing if he put the property into foreclosure and sold it to a new owner at market rates. Even though the loan decision is likely to be made on the basis of trailing twelve-month's earnings, and not the proforma, if the future scenario is presented carefully and thoughtfully, it can enhance the prospects for a favorable outcome.

If the conclusion is to exit the investment, you need to become knowledgeable about today's cap rates and the amount of financing potentially available to a buyer. Couple that knowledge with a current cash flow forecast and you can easily determine how long you can hold out, and what a realistic value is for your equity.

A sound exit strategy, put in place and then reset to current conditions, will greatly increase the likelihood that when you exit your hotel investment it will be on the most favorable terms available, and that your return during the holding period will be optimum for the circumstances.

State of the Hospitality Industry – 2011

U.S. Economy/Introduction to Hospitality Market

Most economic forecasters believe that the past several quarters of economic growth were partly a result of fiscal stimulus. Based on that, the forecast for 2011 is for slower growth as the supports and stimuli are now dissipating. The recovery now depends more heavily on the private sector, which faces weakness in income based on high unemployment, reluctance of businesses to rehire aggressively and large overhangs of vacant homes and unused industrial capacity. Moreover, availability of credit is expected to be slow. Goldman Sachs is forecasting a reacceleration in growth to 3 percent in the fourth quarter of 2011 as the headwinds gradually dissipate.

This jobless recovery is creating an environment where expectations from several economists are for 10 percent unemployment again in 2011. Inflation is expected to remain well under control going forward based on the latest survey of Federal Reserve Board likely actions.

Will the recovery be strong enough to continue to boost lodging demand and pricing (ADR)? We've framed our response to this question considering the factors that will impact travel demand in 2011. A review of business travel shows us that as companies anticipate lower demand, certain facets of business travel ceased (sales training, multiple person sales calls). In a recovery, companies anticipate a higher level of activity and business travel volume started to increase earlier this year, leading to recovery of transient occupancy levels in hotels.

According to PricewaterhouseCoopers (PwC), the three main factors affecting leisure travel are wealth, cash flow and jobs. As we assess each of these, we see a foundation for consumer spending growth.

- Wealth effects are important, and housing has been the key driver. From a peak in 2006 of 56 percent above the long-term trend, home prices have fallen 30 percent, to a level five percent below the trend. The consensus is that we've reached the bottom in national home. In terms of consumer spending, the key is stabilization. As consumers see stability in their own net worth, and memories of steep declines recede, households are expected to look ahead to lifetime earnings and have greater confidence to increase spending on travel.

- Consumer cash flow is resuming. Through a combination of debt pay down, reduced availability of credit, and falling tax payments, consumers have cut debt service obligations from 19 percent of disposable income in the third quarter of 2007 to 17 percent in the first quarter of 2010, which is closer to the long-term average.
- Job growth remains key. The unemployment rate will remain high, but job growth has resumed, and household expectations on job prospects will gradually recover as the unemployment rate moves in the right direction.

The overall U.S. economy has a significant impact on demand for hotel rooms. Employment and housing are still weak. With tax policy possibly impacted by this week's elections, and a jobs bill being discussed because unemployment is still approaching double digits, at least we are past the trough in this time of economic uncertainty. The excesses of the past three decades caused this recession that we just endured for almost two years.

A look at the key indicators of the economy shows that we are clearly in a recovery mode, albeit a recovery that is not yet robust and is in fact growing at a two percent per year rate.

Today's economy has had an enormous impact on the fortunes of the U.S. lodging industry. Fortunately, all indications are that the U.S. economy is improving. Some markets have been impacted more than others. According to Smith Travel Research, (STR) the U.S. hotel industry is projected to end 2010 with increases in two of the three key performance measurements, according to their most recent forecast.

We estimate that U.S. revenue per available room (RevPAR) growth during Q3 2010 was approximately 8 percent vs. 6 percent growth in Q2 2010. RevPAR growth strengthened throughout most of the quarter but stabilized around the high-single-digit and lower-double-digit areas. We view this leveling off of growth as the next step in the cycle as occupancy growth begins to slow and is replaced by rate growth. STR projects 2010 occupancy will increase 4.4 percent to 57.1 percent. Average daily rate (ADR) is expected to end the year virtually flat with a 0.1 percent decrease to US$97.74, and REVPAR will rise 4.3 percent.

STR expects that supply will grow 2.2 percent during 2010, and demand will increase 6.6 percent. They further project the industry will end 2011 with increases in all three key metrics. Occupancy is forecast to rise 1.4 percent to 57.9 percent; ADR is expected to be up 3.9 percent to US$101.55, and REVPAR is projected to rise 5.3 percent.

U.S. Lodging Market

Favorable supply and demand dynamics are clearly setting the stage for a strong industry recovery. Q2 2010 was a turning point for the U.S. Lodging Industry with REVPAR and average rate turning positive for the first time since Q2 2008. The combination of limited supply growth and cost savings that have been put in place during this past recession bodes well for net income going forward for many years to come. There is indeed a benefit to a slow recovery which is being forecasted by many pundits. Supply growth will continue to be moderate, lenders will likely continue tight lending practices and as a result, the up cycle should last longer.

The Consulting and Valuation division of HVS International has issued revised forecasts for the U.S. lodging industry. The outlook for 2010 is for greater strength than previously anticipated, although average rate is forecasted to fall below the level recorded in 2009. The industry is now expected to recover more quickly than previously anticipated, and to regain stabilized levels of operation by 2014. Hotel values are also expected to rebound more rapidly, fueled by both stronger fundamentals and improving investment market conditions.

The following chart summarizes the forecast of occupancy, average rate, and RevPAR for the U.S. lodging industry through 2015:

> *Demand growth resumed in 2010, led by select markets that had recorded positive growth trends in the fourth quarter of 2009. The pace of demand growth has*

> *accelerated through the year, and HVS now forecasts that lodging demand in the U.S. will increase by 7.5% in calendar year 2010. A return of business travel and some group activity have contributed to these positive trends. However, we believe the resurgence in demand is being fueled in part by the significant price discounts that are now widely available. These discounting policies have resulted in further decreases in average rate through the first three quarters of 2010. The magnitude of the average rate decline is forecast to diminish over the balance of the year, as demand continues to strengthen.*

The HVS forecast for 2011 anticipates that demand growth will decrease from the accelerated pace achieved in 2010, as the economic recovery is expected to continue at a moderate pace. As employment levels improve through 2012 and 2013, demand growth is forecast to increase, but will remain below the levels recorded in 2010. The commercial and meeting and group sectors are expected to continue to strengthen throughout this period. These trends, combined with the low levels of supply growth anticipated through 2012, should boost occupancy to above the 60 percent mark by 2012, according to HVS. Strengthening demand and occupancy should permit hotels to reduce and eventually eliminate the deep discounts implemented in 2009 and 2010.(The current HVS forecast anticipates the U.S. lodging industry will stabilize by 2014, with occupancy of 62.7 percent and average rates of $117.54; this equates to roundly $98.00 in constant dollars, which is on par with the average rate level achieved in 2006. RevPAR in 2014 is forecast at $73.71, or roundly $62.00 in constant dollars.

The increased demand from the slowly growing economy is led by a combination of leisure travelers, gradually returning corporate profits, and finally the meetings sector. According to the U.S. Travel Association, business travel will be up 2.5 percent in 2010 with leisure travel up 1.9 percent. According to Rubicon, the group market is pacing strongly for 2011. Additionally, the latest travelhorizons survey indicates that travel intentions of U.S. travelers continues to improve, which is certainly good news for the lodging industry.

Moreover, the latest (October, 2010) YPartnership survey of travelers indicates that 27 percent of travelers make "last minute trips" and that those trips are planned, on average, 6 days in advance! This means to us that any uptick in the economy can be a quick reward for the lodging sector. One of the forces stimulating this last minute demand is the concept of "flash sales." This appears to be a trend toward more "impulse" travel according to Peter Yesawich, author of the study.

California Lodging Market

There are only a few markets in California that are currently thriving. These include San Francisco/San Mateo, with an occupancy rate through Q3 of 76 percent and average rates of $124, Santa Barbara with an occupancy rate of 66 percent and average rate of $141 and Santa Monica/Marina del Ray with a booming 78 percent at $203!

The chart that follows this report shows each city in California with occupancy and rate for 2010 through Q3. Note that average rates are not up in any markets except for the above because until occupancy grows to a certain level (usually about 66 percent) there is minimum opportunity to drive rate. In some cases, even strong markets like Santa Ana, Newport Beach, Anaheim and San Diego were unable to grow rate and are just starting to turn the "rate" corner so to speak.

San Diego Lodging Market

In San Diego, the leading economic indicators were up for 15 consecutive months according to the Burnham-Moores Center for Real Estate at the University of San Diego. However, the past few months have been flat. Will average rate growth finally return so that profits in the lodging sector will improve? In San Diego's hotel sector, the second quarter of 2010 began to move toward positive growth in revenue per available room (REVPAR) based on increases in demand (rooms consumed) of 7.7 percent and decreases in average rate of 6.1 percent for year to date 2010 through June.

REVPAR trends are be up for Q3 based on Smith Travel Research (STR) reports on San Diego. Hotel financial performance in San Diego will remain well below the peak of 2008 with a significant impact from both rate discounting caused in part by a reliance on the online travel agencies (OTAs) and a lack of group business.

While a return to early 2008 levels of business travel is not yet likely, a significant amount of deferred business travel is having an upward impact on room demand, according to a Tourism Economics report ordered by the San Diego Convention & Visitors Bureau (ConVis). Room demand has grown in each of the first 9 months of 2010. Group hotel bookings remain significantly weaker than transient room demand, but San Diego hotels have outperformed the state of California and the U.S. in terms of both demand and occupancy growth according to the report. For the first time in 2010, average room rates increased in San Diego albeit for a.4 percent increase in June.

Occupancy levels through September, 2010 are 69.1 percent at an average rate of $123.46, up from 65.2 percent occupancy year over year but down in ADR from $127.54. A return to 70 percent occupancy levels enjoyed by San Diego as recently as 2008 is not forecast to occur until 2013. At that time, there should be sufficient pressure to push rates up above the cost of inflation.

Most submarkets in San Diego have seen positive REVPAR growth this year, led by occupancy rates. No market has yet to fully recover in ADR. Occupancy in the Northeast submarket is up 12 percent year over year while La Jolla is up 9.7 percent and downtown is up 6.2 percent. Mission Valley moved up 4.7 percent, Carlsbad/Oceanside is up 3.8 percent (but negative REVPAR growth), San Diego South and East are up 3.6 percent and SeaWorld/Airport/Old Town is up just.6 percent, also with negative REVPAR growth. A full forecast appears at the end of this report.

The increased demand from the slowly growing economy is led by a combination of leisure travelers, corporate profits that are beginning to return and a desire to end a recession. Steve Swope, CEO of Rubicon says, "The average daily rate (ADR) shortfall is narrowing further." In a slide presented to R. A. Rauch & Associates, Inc. for this conference, Rubicon shows group business improving markedly in San Diego.

The bigger question is whether average rate growth will return so that profits in the lodging sector will improve. Our analyst,

Jeffrey Carlow, took a look at the public companies in both the lodging and cruise sector. He found the growth rates were much higher for the resort(sector than the other hotel categories based on the severity of the hit they took in the recession and the consumer base that they attract.

According to Carlow, "they are seeing a substantial rebound in occupancy as well as rates. This is a huge improvement from the dire situation they were in during late 2008 and 2009. The 5 year growth rate as well as the low P/E multiple shows how cheap the stock is and how impressive the future of the companies are. The cruise lines are also set up for very strong growth at relatively cheap P/E multiples due to the low fixed costs they incur and the fact that their occupancy can only be headed up from here since it has been at historic lows for the past 2 years." Mr. Carlow's analyses are located at the end of this report.

Lodging stocks began to recover before revenues hit bottom. This is an indication that some of the trading was done in anticipation of the recovery. However, the strong fundamentals should provide room for additional upside. Given the extended period of limited supply growth, long term investment returns should be available throughout this upcycle.

Hotel Values

Assuming the above scenario, what will be the impact on net income and hotel values? PKF Consulting reported that 9 of 10 hotels saw a drop in profits in 2009. Naturally, this was based on reduced occupancy and ADRs. In San Diego, HVS International reported a $48,000 per room drop in hotel values in San Diego. This is only bad news if one needs to sell or refinance. The good news is that values will begin to increase once REVPAR increases enough to compensate for increases in operational costs.

The improved outlook for the lodging industry fundamentals extends to hotel values, which are now forecast to rebound by 16.1% in 2010. This recovery is also being fueled by lower equity return requirements, driven by the large amount of equity capital entering the hospitality sector and the scarcity of quality assets for sale. Similarly, the mortgage component of the investment equation is returning to more normal levels. Debt is increasingly available for high-quality assets, as lenders have recognized that the lodging sector is recovering. Although spreads for hotel debt continue to be at the upper end of the range for commercial properties, the prevailing low cost of capital is keeping hotel interest rates at low levels. Loan-to-value ratios remain conservative, reflecting the lingering effects of the credit crisis. With lowered debt and equity return requirements, hotel values have begun to rise from their lowest point in 2009.

Improving fundamentals are expected to combine with a broadening of investment activity to drive values higher over the period 2011 to 2014. Accelerated average rate growth is expected to result in exponential increases in net income levels as compared to those recorded at the low point in the cycle, which in turn will support significant value increases.

Individual time horizons will be driven by knowledge of the market and operating skills as well as the current loan status of individual assets. Value creation is made by buying at the right time. Moreover, operating fundamentals are critical. In other words, manage your hotel first and foremost. An explosion of transactions is fast approaching due to the maturity of loans. Meanwhile, values are not quite predictable in the industry due to volatility of financial performance, risks of inflation, terrorism, and the rate of growth of economic fundamentals.

The advice that comes from all of this is simple. Do not sell if you are able to hang on for a few years when occupancy and ADR levels return to 2007 levels. This may take several years but it will happen sometime between 2013 and 2015. We are certainly happy to assist lenders, owners, asset managers and managers with any analysis they need to make on their San Diego hotels.

Sure, the recovery will be muted for many reasons. Corporate expense accounts are clearly loosening but there still remains a bit of the "AIG effect" that put a damper on group business in 2009 and early 2010. This pushes hoteliers to rely on leisure business, which is now being dominated by the Online Travel Agents (OTAs), and this may somewhat mute the otherwise positive effects of a corporate travel recovery in the near term. The U.S. budget deficit is real at $1.35T (yes "T" for trillion) and thankfully, a commercial real estate meltdown has not come to fruition in the lodging sector. Unemployment is still at unacceptable levels, but has certainly hit near the bottom. There is certainly good news.

The recession has ended, and we are truly seeing signs of a recovery. Interest rates remain low, and the federal government seldom moves rates in an election year. Moreover, vacations are still a high priority for U.S. residents, who will be spending more freely when the recovery proves to be real to them. All indicators point up. Airport arrivals are moving in the right direction; hotel demand is up; ADR is finally up and supply is leveling off. It is the right time to be an owner...the beginning of the recovery.

New supply in San Diego is expected to be less than 1 percent in 2010 and 2011. If demand grows by the average of the last 30 years, occupancy will move up in 2011 again. Following a two-year recession, there is unusually high "pent-up demand."

If you are asking if we will see an increase in profits, the answer is finally yes! Costs have continued to increase, and average rates are just starting to catch up with our modest inflation. Hotel values will remain somewhat depressed this year but as indicated on the HVS chart, are headed back up. Debt markets remain elusive so hang on if you can – there is light at the end of the tunnel. The tunnel only appears to be dark and endless, which is not a pretty picture if your interest payments put knots in your stomach.

The 10 Steps Of Crisis Communications

Crisis: Any situation that is threatening or could threaten to harm people or property, seriously interrupt business, damage reputation or negatively impact share value.

Every organization is vulnerable to crises. The days of playing ostrich are gone. You can play, but your stakeholders will not be understanding or forgiving because they've watched what happened with Bridgestone-Firestone, Bill Clinton, Arthur Andersen, Enron, Worldcom, 9-11, The Asian Tsunami Disaster, Hurricane Katrina and Virginia Tech.

If you don't prepare, you WILL take more damage. And when I look at existing "crisis management" plans while conducting a "crisis document audit," what I often find is a failure to address the many communications issues related to crisis/disaster response. Organizations do not understand that, without adequate communications:

- Operational response will break down.
- Stakeholders (internal and external) will not know what is happening and quickly be confused, angry, and negatively reactive.
- The organization will be perceived as inept, at best, and criminally negligent, at worst.

The basic steps of effective crisis communications are not difficult, but they require advance work in order to minimize damage. The slower the response, the more damage is incurred. So if you're serious about crisis preparedness and response, read and implement these 10 steps of crisis communications, the first seven of which can and should be undertaken before any crisis occurs.

5

Steps of Crisis Communications

Identify Your Crisis Communications Team

A small team of senior executives should be identified to serve as your organization's Crisis Communications Team. Ideally, the team will be led by the organization's CEO, with the firm's top public relations executive and legal counsel as his or her chief advisers.

If your in-house PR executive does not have sufficient crisis communications expertise, he or she may choose to retain an agency or independent consultant with that specialty. Other team members should be the heads of major organization divisions, to include finance, personnel and operations.

Let me say a word about legal counsel. Sometimes, during a crisis, a natural conflict arises between the recommendations of the organization's legal counsel on the one hand, and those of the public relations counsel on the other. While it may be legally prudent not to say anything, this kind of reaction can land the organization in public relations "hot water" that is potentially, as damaging, or even more damaging, than any financial or legal ramification.

Fortunately, more and more legal advisors are becoming aware of this fact and are working in close cooperation with public relations counsel. The importance of this understanding cannot be underestimated. Arthur Anderson lost its case and went out of business due to the judgment rendered by the court of public opinion, not the judgment of a court of law.

Identify Spokespersons

Within each team, there should be individuals who are the only ones authorized to speak for the organization in times of crisis. The CEO should be one of those spokespersons, but not necessarily the primary spokesperson. The fact is that some chief executives are brilliant business people but not very effective in-person communicators. The decision about who should speak is made after a crisis breaks—but the pool of potential spokespersons should be identified and trained in advance.

Not only are spokespersons needed for media communications, but for all types and forms of communications, internal and external, including on-camera, at a public meeting, at employee meetings, etc. You really don't want to be making decisions about so many different types of spokespersons while "under fire."

Spokesperson Training

Two typical quotes from well-intentioned organization executives summarize the reason why your spokespersons should receive professional training in how to speak to the media:

> *"I talked to that nice reporter for over an hour and he didn't use the most important news about my organization."*

"I've done a lot of public speaking. I won't have any trouble at that public hearing."

Regarding the first example, there are a good number of people interviewed by CBS' "60 Minutes" or ABC's "20/20" who thought they knew how to talk to the press. In the second case, most executives who have attended a hostile public hearing have gone home wishing they had been wearing a pair of Depends.

All stakeholders—internal and external—are just as capable of misunderstanding or misinterpreting information about your organization as the media, and it's your responsibility to minimize the chance of that happening. Spokesperson training teaches you to be prepared, to be ready to respond in a way that optimizes the response of all stakeholders.

Establish Notification Systems

Remember when the only way to reach someone quickly was by a single phone or fax number, assuming they were there to receive either?

Today, we have to have—immediately at hand—the means to reach our internal and external stakeholders using multiple modalities. Many of us have several phone numbers, more than one email address, and can receive SMS (text) messages or faxes. Instant Messenger programs, either public or proprietary, are also very popular for business and personal use. We can even send audio and video messages via email. Depending on how "techie" we choose to be, all of this type of communication—and more—may be received on or sent by a single device!

It is absolutely essential, pre-crisis, to establish notification systems that will allow you to rapidly reach your stakeholders using multiple modalities. The Virginia Tech catastrophe, where email was the sole means of alerting students initially, proves that using any single modality can make a crisis worse. Some of us may be on email constantly, others not so. Some of us receive our cellphone calls or messages quickly, some not. If you use more than one modality to reach your stakeholders, the chances are much greater that the message will go through.

For a long time, those of us in crisis management relied on the old-fashioned "phone tree" and teams of callers to track people down. But today there is technology — offered by multiple vendors and also available for purchase — that can be set up to automatically start contacting all stakeholders in your pre-established database and keep trying to reach them until they confirm (e.g., by pressing a certain number on a phone keypad) that the message has been received. Technology that you can trigger with a single call or email.

Identify and Know Your Stakeholders

Who are the internal and external stakeholders that matter to your organization? I consider employees to be your most important audience, because every employee is a PR representative and crisis manager for your organization whether you want them to be or not! But, ultimately, all stakeholders will be talking about you to others not on your contact list, so it's up to you to ensure that they receive the messages you would like them to repeat elsewhere.

Anticipate Crises

If you're being proactive and preparing for crises, gather your Crisis Communications Team for long brainstorming sessions on all the potential crises which can occur at your organization. There are at least two immediate benefits to this exercise:

- You may realize that some of the situations are preventable by simply modifying existing methods of operation.
- You can begin to think about possible responses, about best case/worst case scenarios, etc. Better now than when under the pressure of an actual crisis.

In some cases, of course, you know that a crisis will occur because you're planning to create it—e.g., to lay off employees, or to make a major acquisition. Then, you can proceed with steps 8-10 below, even before the crisis occurs.

There is a more formal method of gathering this information that I call a "vulnerability audit," about which information is available here.

Develop Holding Statements

While full message development must await the outbreak of an actual crisis, "holding statements"—messages designed for use immediately after a crisis breaks—can be developed in advance to be used for a wide variety of scenarios to which the organization is perceived to be vulnerable, based on the assessment you conducted in Step 6 of this process. An example of holding statements by a hotel chain with properties hit by a natural disaster—before the organization headquarters has any hard factual information—might be:

> *"We have implemented our crisis response plan, which places the highest priority on the health and safety of our guests and staff."*
>
> *"Our hearts and minds are with those who are in harm's way, and we hope that they are well."*
>
> *"We will be supplying additional information when it is available and posting it on our website."*

The organization's Crisis Communications Team should regularly review holding statements to determine if they require revision and/or whether statements for othe scenarios should be developed.

Assess the Crisis Situation

Reacting without adequate information is a classic "shoot first and ask questions afterwards" situation in which you could be the primary victim. But if you've done all of the above first, it's a "simple" matter of having the Crisis Communications Team on the receiving end of information coming in from your communications "tree," ensuring that the right type of information is being provided so that you can proceed with determining the appropriate response.

Assessing the crisis situation is, therefore, the first crisis communications step you can't take in advance. But if you haven't prepared in advance, your reaction will be delayed by the time it takes your in-house staff or quickly-hired consultants to run through steps 1 to 7. Furthermore, a hastily created crisis communications strategy and team are never as efficient as those planned and rehearsed in advance.

Identify Key Messages

With holding statements available as a starting point, the Crisis Communications Team must continue developing the crisis-specific messages required for any given situation. The team already knows, categorically, what type of information its stakeholders are looking for. What should those stakeholders know about this crisis? Keep it simple — have no more than three main messages for all stakeholders and, as necessary, some audience-specific messages for individual groups of stakeholders.

Riding Out the Storm

No matter what the nature of a crisis...no matter whether it's good news or bad...no matter how carefully you've prepared and responded...some of your stakeholders are not going to react the way you want them to. This can be immensely frustrating. What do you do?

- Take a deep breath.
- Take an objective look at the reaction(s) in question. Is it your fault, or their unique interpretation?
- Decide if another communication to those stakeholders is likely to change their impression for the better.

- Decide if another communication to those stakeholders could make the situation worse.
- If, after considering these factors, you think it's still worth more communication, then take your best shot!

"It Can't Happen To Me"

When a healthy organization's CEO or CFO looks at the cost of preparing a crisis communications plan, either a heavy investment of in-house time or retention of an outside professional for a substantial fee, it is tempting for them to fantasize "it can't happen to me" or "if it happens to me, we can handle it relatively easily."

Hopefully, that type of ostrich-playing is rapidly becoming a thing of the past. Yet I know that thousands of organizations hit by Hurricane Katrina will have, when all is said and done, suffered far more damage than would have occurred with a fully developed crisis communications plan in place. This has also been painfully true for scores of clients I have served over the past 25 years. Even the best crisis management professional is playing catch up — with more damage occurring all the time — when the organization has no crisis communications infrastructure already in place.

The Last Word — For Now

I would like to believe that organizations worldwide are finally "getting it" about crisis preparedness, whether we're talking about crisis communications, disaster response or business continuity. Certainly client demand for advance preparation has increased dramatically in the past half-decade, at least for my consultancy. But I fear that there is, in fact, little change in what I have said in the past, that 95 percent of American organizations remain either completely unprepared or significantly under-prepared for crises. And my colleagues overseas report little better, and sometimes worse statistics.

The Four P'S of Good Crisis Management

Every single day you work, something could go wrong; this is true no matter what type of organization with which you are associated-a manufacturing facility, a service provider, a health care organization, a financial institution, a not-for-profit agency or a small or large business.

You read about it in the newspapers or on-line and see it on TV. Accidents happen where people get hurt or even killed. The environment could be damaged because of your operations or a transportation incident. One of your products could harm someone (or someone could allege it harmed them). A disgruntled former employee could return with a gun. A competitor or an unhappy customer could conduct a smear campaign that spreads like wildfire on the Internet.

There is a cartoon of an ostrich with its head in the sand while a big lightning bolt aims for its backside. The caption reads, "When you insist on burying your head in the sand, a lot of your anatomy is left exposed!" It is those businesses and organizations which say, "Nothing bad will happen to me" that are really pressing their luck. Certainly they are endangering their organization's good reputation, which can significantly affect their ability to attract and retain customers and employees. In the worst of circumstances, they may be gambling with their very existence.

A better approach is to sit down for a few hours with your senior staff-whether that is one business partner or an executive team of people-and put some serious thought into "The Four P's of Good Crisis Management." They are summarized here. A more in-depth article is available by contacting me.

Prevent

Obviously, the best way to deal with a crisis is to avoid it, but this does not happen just by wishing.

The best organizations spend some time brainstorming on the question "What could go wrong?" They think through all of the crisis possibilities such as those mentioned above. If you put your mind to this task, you can fill up a number of flip chart pages! Move first to address those that are the most likely to occur or that would be most devastating to your company.

For each one, assign an individual to investigate what must be done to try to prevent the crisis, or at least minimize the impact if it should occur. Is there a new procedure which should be instituted, equipment that should be purchased, or training which should be undertaken? Yes, it may take time and/or money to do this, but spending a little now will prove to be a tremendous investment if it results in avoiding a crisis.

Plan

You must have a written plan for crisis response. Don't be discouraged about undertaking this project. A simple plan is not that hard to do. On a sheet of paper make five columns entitled (1) Crisis (2) Those to be Notified (3) Contact Numbers (4) Action Items and (5) Responsible Party. While that form is still blank, make a lot of copies of it. (If you want a copy of the template for this plan and some more details on it, please contact me.)

In the first column, jot down the top-ranked crisis you identified in your brainstorming. In the second column, note those individuals (both internal and external) who would need to be notified if this should occur. Think of everyone who could be of assistance and those who would feel they needed to know what was happening (e.g., town officials, neighbors). You may need to talk to some folks ahead of time.

The next column should contain every office phone/cell phone/fax/pager/beeper number or e-mail address where you could reach those individuals, whether it is day, night, weekend, or on vacation.

Under "Action Items," list those things you should remember to do if you want to be perceived as a responsible and caring organization post-incident. For example, if you had to institute a product recall, do you have plans in place that would allow you to utilize an 800 number immediately—and would you have people on call who have been trained to manage those phone calls competently and compassionately?

In the column "Responsible Party," assign an individual from your organization whose job it will be to prepare your organization to deal with this particular type of crisis and who must keep the information on the chart current so that it is useful when you need to put it into action. Pre-planning is necessary for all of this. The media and the public will notice if you are able to implement a plan quickly and competently or if you seem to be stumbling around. And they will remember that impression long after they've forgotten the specifics of the problem itself.

Prepare

Some organization leaders think that-just by virtue of having achieved a high-level position in a larger organization-they are prepared to take charge, make the right decisions and communicate properly during a crisis.

This isn't necessarily so! Good crisis managers recognize that it takes a specialized skill set to communicate effectively in a crisis-especially when the media becomes involved. The best ones are willing to call in a crisis communications expert ahead of time to help them refine their skills so that they will be able to perform at the highest level when the time comes.

In a full-or half-day workshop, the senior management team can work together on basic techniques like (1) identifying who their initial spokesperson should be; (2) following the "10 C's of Good Crisis Communications;" (3) recognizing the "Five Big Nevers" in dealing with the media; (4) identifying the most likely questions; (5) developing their key messages and learning to "bridge" to them; and (6) creating memorable "sound bites" that capture their messages in ways the media may repeat and the public can remember. Those involved in the training learn a great deal about how to act well as a Crisis Management Team.

Practice

Olympic athletes and astronauts have to practice in order to be excellent.

Those who are called upon as crisis leaders should do no less. Even if business owners and managers are usually good at thinking clearly under extreme pressure, they may not be prepared for how intimidating it can be when the TV camera lights go on. Then, every once in a while, you should-without warning—simulate one of your brainstormed crisis scenarios. Does everyone know his/her role? Is the needed equipment available? Are procedures in place? Do people have the necessary skills to carry out their responsibilities? Do the various groups coordinate as a team? Do communications break down? Theories of how to operate can be tested in active role-playing exercises which will challenge assumptions and clarify points that need to be strengthened.

Do whatever you can to prevent a crisis. Brainstorm what could go wrong. Put in place a simple, basic plan that will allow you to be organized so you can respond properly. Take the time to provide crisis management and media training to your management team.

Finally, put your plans to the test so you can identify your weaknesses in a low stress environment, instead of when you are in the midst of the real thing. When it is your organization in the glare of the media spotlight and you are on the "hot seat," you'll be glad you did!

How to Handle the Media During a Customer Service Crisis

There are times when being a manager can make you a media target:

> *The larger your organization, the greater the odds of something embarrassing happening that ends up for the world to see on YouTube. Over and over.*

It could be a spill that causes environmental damage, a defective product that needs recalling, or an employee videotaped sleeping-on-the-job. If you are that manager being asked by a reporter to comment, here are a few tips to ensure that your company's brand and your personal reputation withstand the barrage.

Silence may be the Best Option

Decide if you are the right person or the right company to make any comment at all. If you are not a senior manager in your organization, or a designated corporate spokesperson, you should refer media inquiries further up the chain of command. There may also be confidentiality issues that prevent you from commenting.

If the issue in under legal investigation, if you are working on behalf of a client, or if it concerns your employee's private life, then chances are, you are not the person or company who should be making a comment.

Don't Say "No Comment"

You'll sound like a mafia bookkeeper. And you'll appear to be guilty in the court of public opinion. Instead, if there are indeed reasons why you shouldn't comment, then explain, "It's inappropriate for me to comment on this because. (give the reason)."

Reporters can be relentless, so chances are they'll ask another question in another way. When that happens, use their name and give them the broken record response. "David, as I just explained, it would be inappropriate for me to comment. I wish I could help you more." Then sign off.

Don't Hide

In my customer service seminars I encourage all employees to identify themselves as a matter of course every time they answer the phone. Otherwise, customers-especially dissatisfied customers-perceive them to be hiding. Similarly, when disaster strikes, senior managers shouldn't hide behind subordinates.

There is a time for Presidents, CEOs, and Board Chairs to be front and center. You need to be perceived by everyone-including your own employees-as being visible and available when the heat is on. Go to the disaster site, talk to the accused employee personally. Get the facts first-hand. And speak using 'I' language.

Buy Yourself Time

You'll need it to gather the facts. Explain to the reporter that you are looking into this, and that you'll have a comment for them at such and such a time. Notice the positive wording. rather than saying, "I won't comment until.", instead state, "I'll have a comment for you as early as...." You'll be perceived to be upfront and cooperative rather than aloof and defensive.

Admit Errors and Apologize

This is perhaps the biggest mistake executives make when problems happen. They are afraid they'll be sued if they admit a mistake. The fact is, the mistake has already been made whether they admit it or not, and they may get sued anyway. Learn a wonderful lesson from Johnson & Johnson when they had the tainted Tylenol disaster.

They were so up-front about the problem and what they were going to do to fix it, that their brand ended-up even stronger than before the problems.

Avoid Rationalizing or Excuses

Think of a spouse trying to explain to their husband or wife why they were unfaithful. No matter what the reasons, stating them will only make it look like you're trying to justify your actions. It makes things worse. Don't go there.

Protect the Underdog

If one of your employees messed-up don't mention the individual by name. Everyone knows that person's reputation has been ruined. Instead you can refer to 'the individual concerned'. It shows that you are trying to protect them from more public humiliation. That doesn't mean they won't be held accountable.

It just means you won't kick a person when they're down or embarrass their innocent family any more than they already are.

Refocus on the Big Picture

Explain that you are committed to doing better as an organization. Remind everyone how long you've been in operation and your organization's mission to bring value and improve the lives of the people in your world. Explain how you want to re-earn their trust. Then describe what you'll do immediately to help the people who were adversely affected. Finally, outline the steps you'll take to prevent it from recurring.

Bottom line-in every organization there are human beings who will make mistakes and bad choices. No organization is immune. Those brands and individuals who earn the greatest respect are not those who avoid embarrassment: it's those who learn the skills to best-handle these unfortunate events.

Seasonal Safety and Security Reminders

Because hospitality establishments have a certain amount of cash on hand, agents and cashiers face the danger of robberies.

While it may seem simple to advise these staff associates to remain calm, the abundance of mixed messages from the mass media (movies, television and even video games) relating to how to best address this situation can be confusing.

There is never enough time to do everything, but there is always enough time to do the most important thing, *Brian Tracy.*

I am neither an attorney nor a law enforcement officer, but I have learned a number of reasonable care practices in my career. I also have had the good fortune to know one of the industry's leading professionals on security and loss prevention, Ray Ellis.

Ray finally retired in the spring of 2009 from the Hospitality Program at the Hilton School of Hotel Management at the University of Houston the age of 90, following an award-winning career. His career included service with AH&LA and his specialization in Facilities Management and Loss Prevention Management assisted him obtaining underwriting for both his position at the University of Houston and his monthly Loss Prevention Bulletin which is distributed regularly to thousands of hotels and all of the major brands.

Unemployment is at high levels in many locations globally, and the coming holiday seasons should be a reminder to observe common sense when dealing with this sensitive issue of preparedness. In my career, I have noted an increase in robbery attempts at a number of different types of hospitality operations in the period from late November through the end of the year.

The following ideas are among those championed by Ray in his writings and books, including Security and Loss Prevention Management, published by the Educational Institute of AH&LA and used in many hospitality programs.

1. Cashiers should comply with a robber's demands and make no sudden movements that the robber might interpret as an attempt to prevent the robbery.
2. Cashiers should not do anything to endanger their own or other lives.
3. Cashiers and desk agents should be aware that amateur criminals are often edgy and nervous, so cooperation is important.
4. Management and ownership might consider silent alarms in the cash drawer that automatically activates when a certain item or pack of bills is removed. Care should be taken to not draw attention to an alarm.
5. Cashiers should not attempt lengthy conversations or make unsolicited comments with a robber.

If your hotel is branded, there is likely a solid bank of training material available from your franchisor's training services.

Your hospitality association is another valuable source of information, as is your insurance carrier. Your local law enforcement agencies are also highly motivated to be of assistance.

The following is a representative form that contains the vital information needed in the event of an armed robbery. There are many variations available.

A Bakers' Dozen of Reminders for Crime Prevention for Armed Robbery!

1. Have you maintained visibility into your business?
2. Are your shop or outlet displays free from posters and signs?
3. Are your counters and cases law enough for line of sight?
4. Are all sections of business are visible from central cashier area?
5. Do you call authorities if you suspect someone?
6. Have you secured your desk or cashier operation if there is a reason for concern?
7. Have you installed a holdup alarm system and instructed staff in its use?
8. Do you keep minimal cash?
9. Is your routine for bank deposits varied?
10. Is your safe locked at all times?
11. Have you taught robbery prevention to employees?
12. Are references checked before hiring new employees?
13. Do two or more people open and close your business?

Examining the Jakarta Attacks: Trends and Challenges

On the morning of July 17, a guest at the JW Marriott hotel in Jakarta came down to the lobby and began walking toward the lounge with his roll-aboard suitcase in tow and a backpack slung across his chest.

Sensing something odd about the fellow, alert security officers approached him and asked him if he required assistance.

The guest responded that he needed to deliver the backpack to his boss and proceeded to the lounge, accompanied by one of the security guards.

Shortly after entering the lounge, the guest activated the improvised explosive device (IED) contained in the backpack, killing himself and five others. Minutes later, an accomplice detonated a second IED in a restaurant at the adjacent Ritz-Carlton hotel, killing himself and two other victims, bringing the death toll from the operation to nine—including six foreigners.

The twin bombings in Jakarta underscore two tactical trends that STRATFOR has been following for several years now, namely, the targeting of hotels in terrorist attacks and the use of smaller suicide devices to circumvent physical security measures. The Jakarta attacks also highlight the challenges associated with protecting soft targets such as hotels against such attacks.

Hotels as Targets

During the 1970s the iconic terrorist target became the international airliner. But as airline security increased in response to terrorist incidents, it became more difficult to hijack or bomb aircraft, and this difficulty resulted in a shift in targeting. By the mid-1980s, while there were still some incidents involving aircraft, the iconic terrorist target had become the embassy.

But attacks against embassies have also provoked a security response, resulting in embassy security programs that have produced things like the American "Inman buildings", which some have labeled "fortress America" buildings due to their foreboding presence and their robust construction designed to withstand rocket and large IED attacks.

Due to these changes, it became far more difficult to attack embassies, many of which have become, for the most part in our post-9/11 world, hard targets. (This is certainly not universal, and there are still vulnerable embassies in many places. In fact, some countries locate their embassies inside commercial office buildings or hotels.)

Overall, however, this trend of making embassies hard targets has caused yet another shift in the terrorist paradigm. As STRATFOR has noted since 2004, hotels have become the iconic terrorist target of the post-9/11 era. Indeed, by striking an international hotel in a capital city, militants can make the same type of statement against Western imperialism and decadence that they can make by striking an embassy. Hotels are often full of Western businessmen, diplomats and intelligence officers, providing militants with a target-rich environment where they can kill Westerners and gain international media attention without having to penetrate the extreme security of a modern embassy. Our 2004 observation about the trend toward attacking hotels has been borne out since that time by attacks against hotels in several parts of the world, including Pakistan, Afghanistan, Iraq, Jordan, India and Egypt. In addition to attacks against single hotels, in the attacks in Mumbai, Amman, Sharm el-Sheikh—and now Jakarta—militants staged coordinated attacks in which they hit more than one hotel.

Hotels have taken measures to improve security, and hotel security overall is better today than it was in 2004. In fact, security measures in place at several hotels, such as the Marriott in Islamabad, have saved lives on more than one occasion. However, due to the very nature of hotels, they remain vulnerable to attacks.

Unlike an embassy, a hotel is a commercial venture and is intended to make money. In order to make money, the hotel needs to maintain a steady flow of customers who stay in its rooms; visitors who eat at its restaurants, drink at its bars and rent its banquet and conference facilities; and merchants who rent out its shop space. On any given day a large five-star hotel can have hundreds of guests staying there, hundreds of other visitors attending conferences or dinner events and scores of other people eating in the restaurants, using the health club or shopping at the luxury stores commonly found inside such hotels.

Such amenities are often difficult to find outside of such hotels in cities like Peshawar or Kabul, and therefore these hotels also become gathering places for foreign businessmen, diplomats and journalists residing in the city, as well as for wealthy natives. It is fairly easy for a militant operative to conduct surveillance of the inside of a hotel by posing as a restaurant patron or by shopping in its stores.

Of course, the staff required to run such a huge facility can also number in the hundreds, with clerks, cooks, housekeepers, waiters, bellboys, busboys, valets, florists, gardeners, maintenance men, security personnel, etc. These hotels are like little cities with activities that run 24 hours a day, with people, luggage, food and goods coming and going at all hours. There are emerging reports that one of the suicide bombers in the Jakarta attack was a florist at one of the hotels and it is possible that he used his position to smuggle IED components into the facility among floral supplies. If true, the long-term placement of militant operatives within the hotel staff will pose daunting challenges to corporate security directors. Such an inside placement could also explain how the cell responsible for the attack was able to conduct the detailed surveillance required for the operation without being detected.

Quite simply, it is extremely expensive to provide a hotel with the same level of physical security afforded to an embassy. Land to provide standoff distance is very expensive in many capital cities and heavy reinforced-concrete construction to withstand attacks is far more expensive than regular commercial construction. Such costs must be weighed against the corporate bottom line.

Moreover, security procedures at an embassy such as screening 100 percent of the visitors and their belongings are deemed far too intrusive by many hotel managers, and there is a constant tension between hotel security managers and hotel guest-relations managers over how much security is required in a particular hotel in a specific city. In fact, this debate over security is very similar to the tension that exists between diplomats and security personnel at the U.S. Department of State.

And the longer the period between successful attacks (there had not been a successful terrorist attack in Jakarta since September 2004 and in Indonesia since October 2005), the harder it is to justify the added expense — and inconvenience — of security measures at hotels. (Of course, in very dangerous places such as Baghdad, Islamabad and Kabul heavy security is far easier to justify, and some hotels in such locations have been heavily fortified following attacks on other hotels in those cities.)

In many places, hotel guests are subjected to less security scrutiny than visitors to the hotel, as the hotel staff seeks to make them feel welcomed, and it is not surprising that militants in places like Mumbai (and perhaps Jakarta) have been able to smuggle weapons and IED components into a hotel concealed inside their luggage. We have received a report from a credible source indicating that one of the Jakarta attackers had indeed been checked into the JW Marriott hotel.

The source says the attacker, posing as a guest, was an Indonesian but was likely from a remote area because he did not appear to be familiar with how to use modern conveniences such as the room's Western-style toilet. That the attackers were Indonesians supports the theory the attack was conducted by the Southeast Asian group Jemaah Islamiyah (JI) or a JI splinter group. JI has conducted (or is a suspect in) every high-profile terror attack in Indonesia in recent years.

Sources advise that significant similarities exist between the unexploded device discovered in the attacker's hotel room in the JW Marriott and known JI explosive devices used in past attacks and recovered in police raids. This is another strong indication JI was involved.

One other important lesson that travelers should take from this string of hotel attacks is that, while they should pay attention to the level of security provided at hotels, and stay at hotels with better security, they should not rely exclusively on hotel security to keep them safe. There are some simple personal security measures that should also be taken to help mitigate the risk of staying at a hotel.

Size is Not Everything

As Stratfor has noted since 2005, the counterterrorism tactic of erecting barricades around particularly vulnerable targets — including government buildings such as embassies and softer targets such as hotels—has forced militants to rethink their attack strategies and adapt.

Instead of building bigger and bigger bombs that could possibly penetrate more secure areas, operational planners are instead thinking small—and mobile. In fact it was the October 2005 triple-bomb attacks against restaurants in Bali, Indonesia, by JI and the November 2005 triple suicide-bombing attacks against three Western hotels in Amman, Jordan, that really focused our attention on this trend.

Like the July 7, 2005, London bombings, these two attacks in Jakarta and Amman used smaller-scale explosive devices to bypass security and target areas where people congregate. Such attacks demonstrated an evolution in militant tactics away from large and bulky explosives and toward smaller, more portable devices that can be used in a wider variety of situations.

Flexibility provides many options, and in the case of the operative who attacked the JW Marriott on July 17, it appears that he was able to approach a meeting of foreign businessmen being held in the lobby lounge and attack them as a target of opportunity. A vehicle-borne IED (VBIED) detonated in front of the hotel would not likely have been able to target such a group so selectively on the fly.

Of course, this trend does not mean that large VBIEDs will never again be employed any more than the trend to attack hotels means aircraft and embassies will never be attacked. Rather, the intent here is to point out that as security has been increased around targets, militants have adapted to security measures designed to stop them and they have changed their tactics.

At first glance, it would seem logical that the shift from large VBIEDs would cause casualty counts to drop, but in the case of JI attacks in Indonesia, the shift to smaller devices has, in fact, caused higher casualty counts. The August 2003 attack against the JW Marriott in Jakarta used a VBIED and left 12 people dead. Likewise, the September 2004 attack against the Australian embassy in Jakarta used a VBIED and killed 10 people.

The use of three smaller IEDs in the 2005 Bali attacks killed 23, more than JI's 2003 and 2004 VBIED attacks combined. Additionally, the 2005 attacks killed five foreigners as opposed to only one in the 2003 attack and none in the 2004 attacks. The operatives behind the July 17 attacks surpassed the 2005 Bali attacks by managing to kill six foreigners.

The reason that smaller is proving to be more effective at killing foreigners is that the rule for explosives is much like real estate—the three most important factors are location, location and location. Though a larger quantity of explosives will create a larger explosion, the impact of an explosion is determined solely by placement. If a bomber can carry a smaller explosive into the center of a heavily packed crowd—such as a wedding reception or hotel lobby—it will cause more damage than a larger device detonated farther away from its intended target. These smaller devices can also be used to target a specific person, as seen in the December 2007 assassination of former Pakistani Prime Minister Benazir Bhutto.

A person carrying explosives in a bag or concealed under clothing is much more fluid and can thus maneuver into the best possible position before detonating. In essence, a suicide bomber is a very sophisticated form of "smart" munition that can work its way through gaps in security and successfully seek its target. This type of guidance appears to have worked very effectively in the July 17 Jakarta attacks. As noted above, of the seven victims in this attack (the nine total deaths included the bombers), six were foreigners. JI has received criticism from the Islamist community in Indonesia for killing innocent bystanders (and Muslims) and such targeted attacks will help mute such criticism.

In addition to being more efficient, smaller IEDs also are cheaper to make. In an environment where explosive material is difficult to obtain, it is far easier to assemble the material for two or three small devices than the hundreds of pounds required for a large VBIED. An attack like the July 17 Jakarta attack could have been conducted at a very low cost, probably not more than a few thousand dollars. The three devices employed in that attack (as noted above, there was a third device left in the hotel room that did not explode) likely did not require much more than 60 pounds of explosive material.

This economical approach to terrorism is a distinct advantage for a militant group like Noordin Mohammad Top's faction of JI, Tanzim Qaedat al-Jihad. Due to the Indonesian government's crackdown on JI and its factions, the Indonesian militants simply do not have the external funding and freedom of action they enjoyed prior to the October 2002 Bali attack. This means that, at the present time, it would be very difficult for JI to purchase or otherwise procure the hundreds of pounds of explosive material required for a large VBIED – coming up with 60 pounds is far easier.

Even though JI is fragmented and its abilities have been degraded since the 2002 Bali attack, a cell like the one headed by Top certainly maintains the ability and the expertise to conduct low-cost, carefully targeted attacks like the July 17 Jakarta bombings. Such attacks are easily sustainable, and the only real limiter on the group's ability to conduct similar attacks in the future is finding attackers willing to kill themselves in the process.

Perhaps a more significant limiter on their operational tempo will be the law enforcement response to the attack, which could force the cell to go underground until the heat is off. It might also be difficult to move operatives and IEDs from safe houses to targets when there is more scrutiny of potential JI militants.

Increased security at potential targets could also cause the cell to wait until complacency sets in before attacking a less wary—and softer—target. Of course, the group's operational ability will also be affected should the Indonesian government capture or kill key operatives like Top and his lieutenants.

From the standpoint of security, the challenges of balancing security with guest comfort and customer service at large hotels will continue to be a vexing problem, though certainly it would not be surprising to see an increase in the use of magnetometers and X-ray machines to screen guests and visitors at vulnerable facilities. This may also include such measures as random bomb-dog searches and sweeps in areas where dogs are not a cultural taboo.

Additionally, in light of the threat of suicide bombers using smaller devices or posing as guests, or even placing operatives on the hotel staff, much more effort will be made to implement proactive security measures such as protective intelligence and countersurveillance, which focus more on identifying potential attackers than on his or her weapons.

Hotel staff members also need to be taught that security is not just the role of the designated security department. Security officers are not omnipresent; they require other people on the hotel staff who have interactions with the guests and visitors to be their eyes and ears and to alert them to individuals who have made it through security and into the hotel and appear to be potential threats.

Of course, the traveling public also has a responsibility not only to look out for their own personal security but to maintain a heightened state of situational awareness and notify hotel security of any unusual activity.

Key Card Security: The Urban Myth Redux

That electronic key cards store proprietary credit card data of guests is a story that seems to have more legs than a millipede.

Despite being debunked over the years as an urban legend, the story surfaces yet again on a UK based security website with the weight of credit reporting agency (and guardian of identity theft) Equifax behind it.

The article notes forewarns holidaymakers who "do not realise that hotel key cards can contain their name, part of their address and their credit card number" confirmed Neil Munroe, External Affairs Director, Equifax. "And, in the wrong hands, that could provide some really useful information to get an ID fraud scam going. If consumers' hand the cards back in to the hotel reception, or throw them away when checking out, they could make themselves particularly vulnerable to this unseen crime".

It is unclear where Mr. Munroe of Equifax got his information about hotel electronic key cards but people in the industry know that hotels use only one of three electronic tracks to store information pertaining to guest arrival and departure details.

The secure aspect of these cards were once explained by the delightfully named Mr. Hacker, deputy director of government affairs for the Ohio Hotel and Lodging Association who noted that "key cards usually have three tracks for potential information of which banks and credit card companies use two tracks, but hotel key cards only use one track".

He goes on to explain that "the software product that has been given to the hotel community actually prevents the use of the first two tracks on the magnetic strip, So the guests are not in fear at all of having any personal information on those cards whatsoever."

There are others (including this detailed article in smartertravel.com) who have countered the inaccurate technical information on this issue to no avail. Perhaps, someone with a name other than Hacker can come forth to put the matter to rest?

Hotel (In) Security

Emergency management as a proactive security measure has been mentioned on this site recently.

Hotels need to continually evaluate and evolve new methods to combat terrorists, thieves and the unwelcome publicity that follows causing a potential loss in clientel. Terrorist attacks, dire economic news and a host of real and imagined malaises are just a few of the reasons that almost every publication discusses hotel security. The latest include the following:

The Financial Times (subscription required) takes a relatively balanced look at security needs in an article headlined "Executives seek five-star security". Focused on Mumbai, India, the article canvasses opinions from guests, operators and consultants. Among the reasoned quotes from security consultants was one who noted that a "hotel's security is only as good as the intelligence support it gets from the government and national security bodies". It is now fairly widely acknowledged that the Indian government performed abysmally in that regard.

Another interesting point raised in the FT that is relevant to hotels worldwide is that "hotel staff are as important as any security hardware a hotel provides. Security requires a real mindset from hotel staff". Even after 9/11, many urban hotels in the US remain susceptible to bombings similar to the one that demolished the Islamabad Marriott and, a very long time ago, the Vista hotel in New York.

USA Today has an article on how the terrorist attacks on Mumbai have dented business travel with occupancy rates dipping by a third. The article quotes the Association of Corporate Travel Executives as having surveyed 134 corporate travel managers after the Mumbai attacks.

ACTE found that "just 6% planned to curtail travel to the region, but 78% were reviewing their hotel contracts with a greater emphasis on security". Among some of the findings: Companies are placing the onus on hotels to prove "to corporations that their security is up to date. Companies are asking the hotels they deal with to coordinate better with police, fire and military authorities, train staff in evacuation techniques, install back-up communication systems in guest rooms, and improve surveillance".

On a similar vein, MSNBC's Mika Brzezinski was mugged in the area immediately outside her unnamed (presumably) luxury hotel entrance. Her co-anchor, Joe Scarborough, demanded on his eponymously named show that the hotel be called to account for its perceived lack of security.

So what are hotels to do in an environment that they, arguably, in limited control of? Beyond emergency management, in today's terrorism driven atmosphere it behooves properties to also consider sensitizing staff to extraneous threats. Measures could include:

- Making employees aware of world events and ongoing threats.
- Encouraging staff to be alert and immediately report any situation that may constitute a threat or suspicious activity via the hotel's emergency response system.
- Staff should be made to know the location of the closest police stations and hospitals.
- Ensuring staff take notice and report suspicious packages, devices, unattended briefcases, or other unusual materials. Most importantly, they should not attempt to handle or remove such objects.
- Take any threatening or malicious telephone call, facsimile, or bomb threat seriously and set up a standard reporting format for them that provides as much detail as possible for law enforcement authorities..
- Personnel must know emergency exits and stairwells (the Mumbai hotel staff apparently did a remarkable job of escorting many guests out of harm's way)
- Rearrange exterior vehicle barriers, traffic cones, and road blocks to alter traffic patterns near facilities.
- Rotate security staff schedules so as to avoid routine and repetition.
- Limit the number of employee access points and loading docks with thoroughly documented entry/exit procedures.
- Conduct periodic reviews of vendors and their delivery staff to minimize facility entry by unwanted personnel

Illegally parked vehicles in the hotel "loading zone" area should be challenged and moved expeditiously.

Ultimately, hotel security is best unseen when unneeded but highly visible and omnipresent when needed. With that underlying principle in any hotel's security program, guests are more likely to be at ease even in today's environment.

Black Friday Lessons for Hotels

It's that time of the year again-suddenly even politics and news as well as celebrities are on the backburner as that phenomenal holiday herald called Black Friday shook people out of their slumber starting 12 midnight on Thursday! Preliminary results indicated that the operative word in the phrase was black as results on the registers were more along the lines of hope than expectation.

Considering that BF deals were the most searched most-discussed, probably the most emailed term/subject, perhaps the hotel industry could have got into the act-by tapping the frenzy into more room-nights. New York's Macy's Thanksgiving Parade and myriad glittering shops for every kind of taste and budget and, as usual, made for an especially attractive for shopping package.

The weakening US dollar certainly stoked the shopping appetites for many tourists-high-profile American brands and designer names were suddenly accessible to the rest of the world.

Perhaps the hotel industry could tap the holiday shopping mania in other ways (taking cues from a Target ad that endlessly drilled the early-AM-get-to-the-store mantra last few days)

- Offer a special BF alarm to motivate guests to beat the rush!
- Special transportation to take them to and fro-from store to store to cover all the specials. A "TG shopping circuit shuttle! "-checkout times not included.
- Free high-speed Internet Cafe for guests who prefer to shop online (with a customized local webpage pointing to the best offers in the city)
- A specially fortified complimentary breakfast to get guests ready for the grueling challenges of bargain-hunting and deal-grabbing!

Shopping has become too ingrained in the American culture to dismiss as a weekend activity vacation! The travel industry must find ways to tap the flavor of the season and the huge hordes that frequent the all-enduring symbol of America-the retail mall! A travel equivalent of a BF blowout deal is yet to come by.

Crisis Management Requires More Speed than Ever Before

A decade isn't what it used to be- think of the big changes we've seen in those ten years in terms of how you should handle a crisis; and one thing stands out above all others, the impact of the Internet.

It's a Curse

When I was the Manager of Public Affairs and corporate spokesperson for a chemical manufacturing company—and when I started to teach my workshops back in the 90'—I could tell my company and my clients that they didn't have to rush into answering questions of reporters. They could accept what the reporters wanted to know and promise to get back to them in time for their deadline. Then they could huddle, spend whatever time they had gathering the facts, developing statements, running them past the decision makers (and lawyers), and responding to the reporters in time to make the 6 a.m., 3 p.m. or 10 p.m. deadline. They would still be thought to be responsive.

The Internet has a 24/7/365 kind of deadline. Breaking news goes up on the web almost instantaneously. Taking your time putting your story together and getting it out to the media is now a luxury we can not afford.

There are many different news channels competing to "scoop" everyone else. This ratchets up the pressure on the subjects of those stories. Many times it isn't easy to gather the facts quickly, especially if the situation is chaotic in terms of a sudden explosion or fire. You do need to be able to confirm facts before you give them to the news media or you run the risk of spreading false information or being inconsistent and having to retract things, thus damaging your credibility.

It's a Blessing

As much of a problem as the Internet presents, thankfully it is also part of the solution. For the past few years I have been advising my clients – almost all of whom have web sites for their businesses – that they need to establish a "dark page" on their web site. This is a section of the site that could be activated by any authorized management employee so that information relative to a breaking incident could be addressed quickly.

The media has come to expect that they will get answers to their questions by looking at the company's web site. They don't have time to wait until the company president can wake up the IT staff person and get him or her to physically come into the office to get things going.

In the past few months, I have become aware of a much more effective and helpful tool to aid organizations in communicating quickly and responsibly. It is called the Public Information and Emergency Response (PIER) system, run by a company called AudienceCentral whose business it is to enhance internal and external communications, especially during a crisis.

When Hurricane Dennis slammed the Gulf Coast earlier this month, it left an oil-drilling rig owned by BP and Exxon/Mobil broken and listing dangerously out at sea. BP was already a customer of AudienceCentral. Within 15 minutes of BP notifying AudienceCentral of the incident, the company's communications professionals had access to their PIER web site. They got busy investigating the situation and developing the content of press releases, got them approved, and had the information the media needed to know posted on their web site within four hours.

Unfortunately BP also had a previous occasion to use their PIER system. You may remember the March 23rd explosion and fire that killed 15 workers and injured another 100 at their refinery in Texas City, TX. At their site bpresponse.org, the media and the frightened residents in the area had access to the most recent news available. The site was updated periodically – first a few times a day, and then weekly – with the status reports of the investigation into the accident, letters from the CEO and Plant Manager, etc. The PIER system can also help you track and respond to inquiries from the media and the public.

The U.S. Coast Guard employs the PIER system as do a number of major chemical manufacturers and other industries. It is also useful for developers who are attempting to get approvals for big projects. Posting information on the site and having a way to counteract rumors being circulated by those who oppose their project has been instrumental in the support of Cabela's, a store that wants to build in a suburb of Denver.

If the News Media Expects to See You on the Web, You Had Better Be There!

Yes, the world has changed a lot in the last decade. In some ways, it makes it tougher on those of you who have to deal with fast-breaking situations. Luckily, some bright people are coming up with ways technology can meet those challenges. If you'd like to find out more about this organization please go to audiencecentral.com and take their virtual tour. Whether or not you decide to sign up for their services, you will learn a great deal about the types of things you should be prepared to do when the time comes that a crisis hits your organization.

If you want more details, call 360-756-8080 and ask for Jamie Imus. Tell him Judy sent you and he will give you a free virtual tour and demonstrate what PIER can do for you. Oh wait, he'd do that anyway...oh, well, tell him Judy sent you and it will make you and me both happy.

Special Note: By way of full disclosure, I want to tell you that I have a formal working arrangement with the folks from two different organizations—Community Alert Network (CAN) which I have told you about previously, and now AudienceCentral. I believe strongly in the value of the services that they can offer my clients and colleagues and business acquaintances, so I am willing to promote them in my workshops and writings.

In return, they have promised that – should someone I recommend them to become a client – they will provide me with a small remuneration. All of you who know me hopefully realize that I would never jeopardize my reputation by recommending an organization which was not of the highest quality.

Identity Theft at Hotels

Few other means of cyber crime get as much attention as identity theft

Yesterday's Wall Street Journal notes how-contrary to general impression-the identity thieves of today use the stolen information to rack up small charges that makes prosecutors unwilling to spend as much effort as when a large amount is stolen.

The article notes the various ways in which thieves steal data ranging from phishing scams to low-tech thefts to stealing post-office boxes (sic) to hotels. Among the modus operandi in hotels is that hoary old chestnut, the night auditor. Long a focus of internal controls in the hotel industry, it remains a defiant sieve with malignant employees finding new ways to punch holes in the audit regimen.

In the instance cited in the Journal article, a night auditor in a San Diego hotel merely used his access to stacks of receipts that included personal information of guests to create an identity theft nightmare that focussed on out of town visitors as, apparently, law enforcement officials are less inclined to pursue those.

But there are plenty of other holes in a hotel environment that remain open for exploitation. Among the absurdly simple ones are folios left in waste baskets in the lobby which are then picked up by thieves lurking in the background; empty meeting rooms (often found in convention hotels) where meeting participants leave for a break with computers and personal effects lying around and business centers with internet access where cached data are not purged as well as print outs in waste baskets that lie waiting for identity thieves to exploit.

Among the many implications for hotels is not only a potential law suit but also a loss of goodwill when guests are subject to monetary losses on account of the hotel's negligence. One way out is not only to educate employees but also guests on the need to safeguard personal information by not discarding material carelessly through discreet signage in areas and blurbs on printed matter.

Management's Guide to Communicating Change

When an organization embarks on any new project, or simply attempts to change established processes or procedures, inevitably it will encounter resistance from individuals as well as formal groups.

This opposition appears almost immediately, drawing on the individual or group's fear of doing something different. Resistance ignores the responsibility by the individual or group to take the time to understand the reasoning or need for the change. But when the reasoning for the project is not made available to individuals and groups, then a "knee jerk" reaction to protect agendas and self interests' takes place. Interestingly enough, resistance is a normal, not an abnormal reaction by human beings. Defensiveness is the counter productive idea.

What is important to recognize is "who" has the authority of control and who is suggesting change? The power of control drives strategies for change. These strategies are developed based on values, principles, economic need and a whole host of other ideas by those in authority. But make no mistake, new projects or change strategies are founded on the premise of having power and the desire to achieve.

The "Something You Have" component of the process means management has been entrusted with the power to manage, lead and implement. The "Something You Know" component relates to managements development or assigned strategy to initiate change or create change based on needs. Even greater than this is management's responsibility for implementation and success.

Creating new initiatives and effecting change can not be viewed only as the responsibility of management, namely, senior management. Mid-managers and individual department or unit supervisors also have that responsibility. Keep in mind that even at the lowest level of management resistance is encountered even for the smallest of changes.

So how does a manager assure that the strategies and plans have an opportunity for success? One important piece of the puzzle is in putting together a communication/marketing effort that will do the following five things.

- Present the right message
- Present it to the right people
- Present it at the right time
- Present it using the right media (method of delivery)
- Present it with the right person (who delivers the message).

Now this may sound simple, but it takes a commitment of time to create a communication strategy plus a plan of action to make the "change" initiative work. In short, the goal should be to get people who normally would resist change to join in the plan to assure success of the change initiative. This is frequently where mangers fail to see the benefits of a communication strategy and frequently experience failure.

Another way to look at this is from the viewpoint of the people affected by the change initiative. It is generally accepted that no one really likes to be told to do something.

It just rubs people the wrong way to have someone say "here, do this". That is why communication is so very important in any change endeavor.

Communication strategies and plans offer people most affected by the change the opportunity to hear, see, learn, question and provide in-put. In others words, they are involved and feel part of the process change and success, rather than just "being told" to do something.

Presenting the Right Message

Right from the start, a project has to be clearly defined and understood by the manager. If a manager is not sure of all aspects of the change, why would anyone expect employees to join in acceptance? Once a clear vision of the change has been established, then identification of the different items of detail must be documented and communicated. Again, although this may sound simple, identifying specifics is not an easy task and it will take time and effort.

The messages that will need to be delivered throughout the implementation of the project must be mapped to a project's timeline. The messages can be categorized as follows.

- Vision and Benefits-messages that explain the reasoning for the initiative and exactly what are the identified benefits for all of this effort by both management and employee.
- Education-identified key members who must be educated in the capabilities to support implementation.
- Changes to Process-addressing identified changes to existing organizational processes and procedures. This may require policy and procedure revisions.
- Milestones Achieved-Continuous announcements of project successes corresponding to implementation objectives.

- Training-Identification and scheduling of process task change details, new technical requirements and company expectations.
- Impacts to End-users-Management's identification and actions of correction to current processes and procedures. This includes key "impacts" to the organization as they become known. Not only must these impacts be identified, but clear action plans to mitigate the impacts must be identified, implemented and checked for compliance.

Presenting it to the Right People

Presenting the initiative to the right people, challenges management to identify the specific groups who will be directly or indirectly affected by the change. Defining these groups aids in the timing of when information will be communicated to each group in order that a logical sequence of implementation events can take place.

Key categories of "right "groups of people are:

- Board members
- Senior level management
- Directors
- Middle managers
- Supervisors
- Leads
- Union Representatives
- End-users (union and non union members)
- Outside Vendors
- Government officials
- General public.

Presenting Information at the Right Time

Critical to success is the identification of when identified messages should go out in conjunction with the scheduled deployment of the change or initiative. It does no one any good to speak of specific training times and dates in January when the initiative is not scheduled to be finalized until November. However,

A specific topic can be presented at a high level and supported with terms like " more precious detail on training dates and times will be communicated in September" to provide a timeline to the initiative.

Presenting Information Using the Right Media

Equally important is choosing the right way to communicate the messages to the employees. Here management must understand if the organization communicates better by e-mails, large group meetings, small group meetings, one-on-ones, newsletters, rallies etc.

In most cases it will take a combination of some or all of these to effectively communicate messages. In most organizations, these types of media can be ranked or prioritized fairly easily by management based on previous exposure to past successes and failures. Another resource for determining the most efficient means of communication can come from an organizations marketing department.

Present Messages using the Right Person

Credibility is the key. The source of the message or information plays a critical role in whether employees accept quickly the change initiative or procrastinate based on who is communicating the information.

Normally, major initiatives with sweeping or broad changes demands that senior management layout the reasons for and the benefits of the initiative. This needs to be followed by support from middle management.

Initiatives of a smaller scale and directly impacted small segments of employees, demand that the leader/manager closest to the end-user communicate information that directly to the affected end-users.

Summary

Managing Change is not an easy task and a strong communication effort is just one of many aspects of change management. However, putting together a communication strategy and plan is extremely important in providing the opportunity to be successful.

Change is a process and communications along with other change management plans are designed to achieve specific outcomes for any business. Success depends on management's ability to induce acceptance by communicating to employees the following desired outcomes.

ADKAR®

- Awareness of the need for change
- Desire to participate/support the change
- Knowledge on how to change
- Ability to implement required skills and behaviors
- Reinforcement to sustain the change.

Managers/Leaders have an obligation based on their position (Something you have); to inform and promote support from the people they lead. Communicating the need and the benefits of change (Something you know) is a responsibility that must not be avoided, but aggressively pursued.

Crisis Lessons Learned From Tragedy

Prior to September 11th, when was the last time you heard of a politician having an 85-90% approval rating? Probably never.

Former NYC Mayor Rudy Guliani achieved this because of his strong yet compassionate leadership in the aftermath of the terrorist attacks on his city.

Through my tears for the human tragedy that was unfolding just 50 miles from my home, I watched from the perspective of a crisis management consultant. I was interested to see how the Mayor would communicate during this period of monumental crisis. Now that it is some months after that horrific event, I'd like to share some thoughts on what I observed. Perhaps it will help you prepare yourself for less catastrophic but still distressing crises that could occur in your company.

- *Be Cooperative:* The Mayor knew from years of experience that he had to make himself personally available to the press immediately. Any attempt on his part to avoid or delay meeting with reporters who were under the gun to relate the latest news would have led to miscommunication, rumour, and possibly panic.

- *Maintain Control:* He and his staff quickly set up a room for the media where they could be assured he would come to report the latest news. You do not want the media wandering around, getting in the way of emergency responders or officials trying to do their jobs.
- *Demonstrate Caring and Concern:* Expressions of compassion for those who have been victimized by an incident are always in order. Don't let your lawyers talk you out of this because they are afraid it will be interpreted as an admission of legal liability. Work with your legal advisors to find the best ways to word your expressions of condolence and comfort, but be sure to show kindness. Judges tend to throw the book at organizations which appear callous and uncaring.
- *Display Competence:* Some executives and managers believe that, because they have achieved a position of authority, they somehow know instinctively what to do and say in a crisis. Many have learned that, sadly, this is not necessarily the case. Planning, preparation, and practice promote competence. When David Letterman asked the Mayor how he seemed to always know the right things to do and say, Rudy's answer was, "We DRILL on these things."
- *Be Credible:* There are two major components of credibility. The first is to never lie. Hiding or even shading the truth will come back to haunt you. Some days after September 11th, even when the families of the victims did not want to hear the truth, the Mayor had to tell them the chances of rescuing anyone alive were extremely remote. The other aspect of credibility has to do with not speculating. Even though the media pushed for definite answers to important questions, if the Mayor did not have certain knowledge, he refused to be stampeded into an answer just to satisfy them.
- *Be Consistent:* Speak with one voice. Be on the same page. Get your story straight. These are ways to express this

vital component of crisis communications. If a situation is long-term, where several spokespersons must be used, they must all coordinate their messages to prevent confusion or the impression that things are not quite as represented. Even slightly different versions can damage credibility. The Mayor and his deputies/department heads obviously briefed each other prior to appearing in front of the media.

- *Speak with Clarity:* Several things come into play here. Even when exhaustion is inevitable due to lack of sleep, try not to mumble. Do not use jargon or technical language. If a 5 cent word expresses your thought well, do not use a 50 cent word because you think it will impress people. Your goal is to communicate clearly.
- *Be Concise:* This is a skill that comes with practice. The public does not want long drawn-out detailed explanations in the first throes of a crisis. They want the basic facts-as many as you can provide. The media is looking for "sound bites"-concise, memorable descriptions that conjure up a mental picture and lead to understanding. If your major message is buried among unimportant details, it may all end up on the editor's cutting room floor. Rudy was excellent in his ability to respond with answers that were to the point.
- *Keep Current:* Reporters have to know for a fact that they will be kept up to date with the latest developments if they stay in the designated media center. If too much time passes between briefings, they will become impatient and wander off to talk to other sources-anyone who will grant an interview.
- *Act with Calm:* Note this does not say "BE calm." In a serious crisis, it would be a rare individual who would not be anxious. But a person who can demonstrate a steady confidence is highly regarded. If your company experiences a crisis of any kind, you would be well served to remember the example set by Mayor Guliani as he led New York City through some of the darkest days anyone could ever imagine.

Hotel and Hospitality Risk Management

The hotel and hospitality industry faces constant pressure from the evolving marketplace that impacts important issues in risk management and threatens profit margins. As issues that affect bottom line constantly change, so does the industry's need for proactive solutions for risk prevention and management. A comprehensive plan covering the broadest spectrum of potential issues will provide the most protection.

Industry properties often provide a variety of amenities for guests and clients, which in turn can generate different sources of risks. For example, the risk of physical injury can arise from almost any area, including accidents in pool areas, property grounds, sports and activity areas, guest rooms, bathrooms, or spa facilities. There are also risks associated with food preparation in restaurant or food vending facilities. Other potential risks exist, including property loss from transportation services and certain terrifying risks exist from fire or other catastrophic events.

As industry properties expand the number of guest services that are part of an active and robust hotel and hospitality business, there is the need for constant reevaluation of the risks associated with these services to maximize profit, as well as to provide protection from injury and property loss. Indeed, to a risk manager, these amenities represent vast potential exposure for injury or insurance-related loss. While injuries and losses cannot be avoided entirely, they can be minimized along with the number of financially damaging insurance-related claims affecting the hotel and hospitality industry.

Proper risk management in the hospitality industry starts with an industry specific insurance plan. Businesses must ensure they are working with a broker who understands the risks typically faced in the hospitality industry. Businesses must also understand where their broker or agent buys its insurance, and confirm their broker has other hotel and hospitality clients and experiences in handling industry-related claims.

Moreover, comprehensive risk management practices must be established and implemented. While proper insurance coverage can help shield a business from liability once a lawsuit arises, hotel and facility operators are also advised to mitigate the factors that can lead to injury or insurance-related loss. Discussed below are some recommended management solutions that were implemented by a successful and multifaceted resort facility, Woodloch Pines Inc., located in Hawley, Pennsylvania. During its peak summer season, Woodloch employs approximately 1,000 employees. The recommendations discussed below were implemented by Woodloch with good success in response to some common and potentially costly risks.

Keep Employees Healthy

One way in which hotel and hospitality facilities and their operators can protect their business from work related injuries and losses is by keeping their employees healthy. Health care and workers' compensation premiums/claims, and lengthy employee absences, often result from work related illness or injuries and are perhaps the most significant cost to any industry.

However, these issues can have a significant impact on hotel and hospitality businesses that depend on seasoned, well trained staff to provide quality guest services, which, in turn, ensures continued growth and vitality of the business. Hotel and hospitality businesses should, therefore, consider implementing wellness incentives and job safety programs. Woodloch increased the number of these programs, with good result both in terms of employee health, decreased sick time and lowered insurance premium expense.

For example, Woodloch has implemented a "Wellness Rewards Program," which provides all employees with three assessments per year (on a voluntary and confidential basis) measuring each employee's weight, body mass index, blood pressure and waist size. If an employee reaches certain wellness goals, then he or she is rewarded with "Woodloch dollars" that can be used at any Woodloch restaurant, gift shop or vehicle maintenance service center.

Additionally, Woodloch offers challenges to its employees, *i.e.*, "The Biggest Loser," which encourages groups of employees to compete against each other, to attain weight loss and wellness goals, and become healthier. Woodloch also has certified staff members who offer smoking cessation classes to employees. Woodloch has utilized these wellness programs with great success, resulting in happier and healthier employees, who, in turn, provide quality guest services and ensure continued growth and vitality of the business.

Furthermore, Woodloch distributes a monthly publication via email to all department managers with recent updates on wellness or safety programs. In turn, the department managers are expected to focus on the particular monthly topic and execute changes into the workplace, if necessary. Woodloch has also utilized consultant sessions during which qualified safety instructors demonstrate onsite proper safety technique to employees and educate the staff about the resort's safety policies and procedures. In addition, these safety consultants have assisted in the development of a comprehensive health and safety manual. Instruction from the most basic issues, *i.e.*, ergonomically correct posture while sitting for extended periods of time, proper use of tools, shoe gear, or other work equipment, to more complex safety procedures, can significantly limit the number of work related injuries or claims.

With the above mentioned recommendations, Woodloch has been able to successfully educate and empower their department managers, who are the onsite operational employees with the best ability to control risks and losses within their work areas on the property. This has translated into a tremendous cost savings in terms of limiting employee-related work place accidents, injuries and workers' compensation claims.

Bibliography

Broggi, M. : *Sanfter Tourismus: Schlagwort oder Chance Für Den Alpenraum?*, Vaduz, Commission Internationale pour la protection des Regions Alpines (CIPRA), 1985.

Carter, John: *Chandler's Travels: A Tour of the Life of Harry Chandler*, London, Quiller Press, 1985.

Chambers, Erve: *Native Tours: The Anthropology of Travel and Tourism*, Prospect Heights, Waveland Press, 2000.

Conlin, M. V. : *Proceedings of the Travel and Tourism Research Association twenty-second annual conference*, Hyatt Regency Hotel, Long Beach, California, 1991.

Conroy, B. : *Quality in Education and Training for Tourism*, London, Tourism Society, 1997.

Cooper, Chris: *Geography of Travel and Tourism*, The, London, Heinemann, 1987.

Cukier, J. : *Tourism Employment in Bali: Trends and Implications*, London: Thompson, 1996.

Donald, M.: *Customer Service in the Hospitality and Tourism Industry*, Englewood Cliffs, Prentice Hall, 1994.

Douglas C: *Practical Tourism Forecasting*, Oxford, Butterworth Heinemann, 1996.

Elio, C.: *The Hospitality Law Desk Reference*, Miami, Southern Beverage Journal, 1994.

Foster, Douglas: *Travel and Tourism Management*, London, Macmillan Educational, 1985.

Fowler, Peter: *Heritage and Tourism: In the Global Village*, London, Retailed, 1993.

Ghimire, Krishna: *The Native Tourist*: Mass Tourism within Developing Regions, London, Earthscan, 2001.

Hoffman, Edward: *Project Management Success Stories: Lessons of Project Leaders*, New York, John Wiley & Son, 2000.

Hoffman, Edward: *Project Management Success Stories: Lessons of Project Leaders*, New York, John Wiley & Son, 2000.

Holloway, J. C. : *Labour, Vocational Education and Training, in W. Pompl and P. Lavery,* Tourism in Europe - Structures and Developments, Oxford, CAB International, 1993.

Ireland, Lewis: *Quality Management for Projects and Programs*, Upper Darby, PMI, 1991.

Jakle, John: *Tourist, The: Travel in Twentieth Century North America*, University of North Nebraska, 1985.

Judy A: *Tourism: Management of Facilities*, London, Pitman: M & E, 1993.

Kotler, Philip: *Marketing for Hospitality and Tourism*: New Jersey, Prentice-Hall, 1998.

Larkham, P J: *Building a New Heritage: Tourism, Culture & Identity in the New Europe*, London, Routledge,1994.

Laws, Eric: *Tourist Destination Management: Issues, Analysis & Policies*, London, Routledge, 1995.

Lock, Dennis: *Project Management*, New York, Wiley, 1996.

Medlik, S: *Management of Tourism*, The, London, Heinemann, 1975.

Morrell, J. : *Employment in Tourism*, London: British Tourist Authority, 1985.

Nancy N.: *Choosing a Career in Hotels, Motels, and Resorts*, New York, Rosen Pub. Group, 1997.

Nightingale, M. : *Tourism Occupations, Career Profile and Knowledge*, Annals of Tourism Research, 1981.

Nijkamp, Peter: *Sustainable Tourism Development*, Aldershot, Avebury, 1995.

Peters, M: *International Tourism*, London, Hutchinson, 1969.

Phipps, A: *Tourism and Intercultural Exchange: Why Tourism Matters*, Clevedon, Channel View, 2005.

Prentice, R: *Conceptualising The Experiences of Heritage Tourists*, 1997.

Index

A

Accommodation Providers, 156.
Airport Arrivals, 204.
Asian Tsunami Disaster, 204.

B

Buildings and Contents, 176.
Buildings and Furniture, 152.
Business Activity, 2.
Business Strategies Proactively, 2.
Businesses and Communities, 1.

C

Capital Management, 37, 137.
Capital One Financial Corp, 161.
CERA Qualification, 135, 136.
Chartered Enterprise Risk Analyst, 134.
Chief Compliance Officer, 65.
Chief Executive, 137.
Chief Financial Officer, 109, 137.
Chief Operational Risk Officer, 70.
Chief Risk Officer, 65, 131, 137.
China Insurance Regulatory Commission, 43.
Commercial Properties, 31, 203.
Company Experiences, 241.
Consulting and Valuation, 198.
Consumer Fraud Act, 161.
Contractual Obligations, 1.
Crisis Communications, 160, 204, 205, 206, 208, 209, 210, 211, 214, 241, 249.
Critical Aspects, 141.

D

Daily Basis, 160.
Dangerous Condition, 155.
Department Managers, 244.
Development Risk, 162, 163, 168.

E

Economic Capital, 137.
Economic Fundamentals, 203.
Economic Growth, 196.
Economic Viability, 166.
Employment Risks, 157.
Epsilon Data Breach, 158, 161.

F

Financial Performance, 141, 200, 203.
Food and Beverage, 1, 141, 164.
Fundamentals Extends, 202.

G

Global Transportation Networks, 138, 139.
Guest Services, 242, 243, 244.

H

Health and Safety Manual, 244.
Health Care, 8, 124, 211, 243.
Heartland Financial, 160.
Hedging Strategies, 1.
Hilton Grand Vacations, 159.
Hospitality Management, 4, 5, 157.
Hotel Companies, 158.

Hotel Risk, 151, 160.

I

Important Aspects, 151.
Information Security, 11, 13, 62, 65, 72, 76, 77, 144, 160.

J

Job Safety Programs, 243.

K

Key Risk Areas, 170.

L

Laundry Facilities, 153.
Lodging Demand, 196, 199.
Lodging Industry, 141, 197, 198, 199, 202.

M

Macro Approach, 149, 151.
Management is Critical, 151.
Management Issue, 136.
Managing Stock, 126.
measuring Risk, 80, 137.
Ministry of Finance, 43.
Mitigate Risk, 2, 132.

N

National Defence Transportation Association, 138.
National Insurance, 26, 38, 43.
Natural Conditions, 154.
Night Clubs, 176, 177.
Numerous Risks, 1.

O

Occupational Health & Safety Advisory Services, 72.
Online Travel Agents, 203.
Organizational Partnerships, 2.

P

Payment Card Industry, 160.
Performance Reviews, 67, 157.
Physical Characteristics, 162.
Prevention and Management, 242.
Privacy Strategy, 2.
Procurement Services, 1, 2.

Q

Quality Management, 139, 140.

R

Risk Agenda, 2.
Risk Assessment Element, 133.
Risk Components, 162, 249.

S

Security Standards Council, 160.
Service and Budget, 166.
Service Interruptions, 2.
Supply Chain Logistics, 126.

T

Total Quality Management, 139.
Total Security Management, 137, 138.
Trading Performance, 164, 165.
TSM Methodology, 139.

U

Unforeseen Events, 140.

V

Valuation Division, 198.
Various Economic, 166.

W

Water Portion, 155.
Wellness Rewards Program, 243.
Woodloch Restaurant, 243.

□□□